The Buckeyes

A Story of Ohio State Football

The Buckeyes

A Story of Ohio State Football

by

Wilbur Snypp

THE STRODE PUBLISHERS
Huntsville, Alabama 35802

Photographs Courtesy of
The *Columbus Dispatch*, The House Of Portraits,
The Ohio State University Department of Photography,
Bill Foley, Malcolm Emmons, and Lester Nehamkin

"Then strip, lads, and be to it, tho sharp be the weather.

"And, if by mischance, you should happen to fall,

"There are worse things in life than a tumble on heather,

"For life, itself, is but a game of foot ball."

—Sir Walter Scott

To
Dr. James E. Pollard

Contents

Foreword

Wilbur Snypp is as much a part of Ohio State University football as any player or coach associated with the sport during its 84-year history at the university. Starting as a sports writer for the Ohio State University student newspaper, the *Lantern*, in the stadium era of the early twenties, he has seen Buckeye gridiron fortunes in good times and bad.

Prior to retiring in 1973 from his post as director of athletic publicity, he was a keen observer, loyal friend, and valued colleague of six head football coaches. His special perspective, his close association with players, sports writers and fans, as well as his ability to detail the big games and chronicle the seasons, make this book a treasury of information.

Each reader will add his own facts and feelings to this comprehensive account of Ohio State football. Indeed, avid fans are entitled to their own interpretation of football history. But all of us are glad to have this special book, drawn from years of experience. Here then is a picture of the broad sweep of a fascinating subject, taken from behind the scenes. Here is a backdrop which will enrich the future of football at Ohio State. I join the readers in thanking "Bill" Snypp for sharing this story.

Harold L. Enarson
President
The Ohio State University

Preface

A favorite topic of conversation among all of those who have ever been associated with the Ohio State University relates to the fortunes of the Buckeyes on the gridiron. I doubt if any major school in the country has more loyal, dedicated fans.

It all began in Columbus, Ohio, in 1890 when a few students started to "throw a ball around." It grew from year to year to its prominence as a member of the Intercollegiate (Big Ten) Conference which it joined April 6, 1912.

Though Ohio State is loosely referred to as the "graveyard of coaches," the Buckeyes nonetheless can point to the illustrious years under Dr. J. W. Wilce, sixteen in number. And an even more impressive record in time and victories is the current one of W. W. Hayes, who has concluded his twenty-third year.

It is a privilege for me to speak a word about the author. Few, if any, collegiate sports information directors across the country can match the respect that Wilbur E. (Bill) Snypp holds from members of the media. It has been my privilege to know Bill for some thirty years, and no one could be closer to the subject about which he writes.

He has lived with the football fortunes of this university for twenty-nine years, even more than that if you count his days here as a student and undergraduate sports writer. He has commanded the respect of the coaches with whom he has worked. He has been both efficient and fair in the dissemination of information about our "battling Buckeyes."

Anyone interested in collegiate football will find this story by Wilbur Snypp to be most revealing, interesting, exciting, and accurate.

It is good that this book can be written to go along with many other publications dealing with outstanding accomplishments related to the Ohio State University.

J. Edward Weaver
Director of Athletics
The Ohio State University

Introduction

No one is more qualified to write about Ohio State football than Wilbur Snypp. He has followed football in the "giant horseshoe" since the early '20s. He is a discerning student of the game and its many great players, but he goes beyond this in being able to depict the color and drama in the "Football Capital of the World."

Mr. Snypp has always been noted among newspapermen as a fair-minded and able administrator of the Ohio State press box. In June, 1973, at the annual convention of sports information directors in Denver, he received the Arch Ward Memorial Award "for bringing inspiring excellence and dignity to the profession, through association with the press, radio, television, and his colleagues." No one ever deserved this award more than "Bill."

As football coach at Ohio State, no one could ask for a better sports information director than "Bill" Snypp. His book will be a rare treat in the annals of football reporting.

Woody Hayes
Head Football Coach
The Ohio State University

The Beginning

During Ohio State's early years little was said about sports and even less about football, then a two-word game. The university opened its doors in 1873, and what sports fans there were spoke mainly of tennis and track and field. But seventeen years later, in 1890, Ohio State football began officially, and it was not long before the gridiron sport took over in Buckeye land. Then, as now, it provided most of the livelihood of the athletic program, small as it was.

When Professor William Lyon Phelps, the eminent Yale authority on English literature, was asked which he preferred, a perfect recitation in Chaucer or a victory over Harvard, he replied that he always appreciated a perfect recitation but it never made him throw his hat away. This typifies the interest and excitement identified with Ohio State football over the years.

Commencement time, 1890, found a petition signed by nearly 200 students requesting the board of trustees to enclose an athletic field which would contain, among other things, "foot ball grounds, or that a sum of $200 be set aside annually to be expended under the direction of the athletic association on baseball, foot ball, tennis and general athletics."

As Dr. James E. Pollard wrote in his book, *Ohio State*

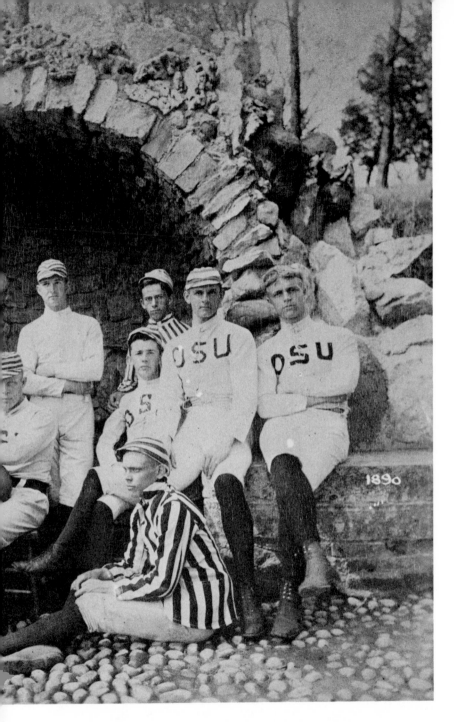

The first Ohio State football team, 1890, played with an oval ball resembling the present-day basketball. Holding it is captain Jesse Jones.

Athletics, the petition was referred to the president and the executive committee. Five months later a faculty committee recommended that "special pains should be taken to furnish facilities for field sports." A grandstand seating 300 was recommended also, with "special practice grounds for foot ball so that baseball could be played at the same time without interference."

It was estimated that 5½ acres would be required at a cost of $1,950, but after hearing the report the trustees voted $200 for the athletic association to be expended under its direction for the furtherance of its objects.

By 1890 athletics had gained enough prominence to warrant considerable mention in the annual report of President W. H. Scott, who said there was a "new and unprecedented interest in athletics with teams in baseball, foot ball and tennis."

President Scott let it be known that he was concerned about absence from class by the athletes. He cited that the baseball team had made a tour to play three games, causing "an absence of two and a half days from college exercises." There also was one match game of foot ball, he said, with a team of another college, unidentified. It is presumed that this was the spring game of 1890 with nearby Ohio Wesleyan University, carried in the records as a 20 to 14 victory for the neophyte Buckeyes.

President Scott had more to say on the subject, particularly about football:

"Most of the time, there is but little practice; then comes a tremendous overstrain. Lawn tennis is not subject to criticism, as practice is more regular and match games are less violent. To foot ball, on the other hand, the criticism is especially applicable, as in this game accidents are frequent. Another evil that attends the present system of athletics is its interference with university work. This is particularly true of intercollegiate games. An effort is made to restrict them to Saturdays and other holidays, but it is apparently impossible to play them without more or less neglect of regular studies, not only at the time when they are played but during the period of training for them."

"The faculty has adopted no plan for regulating these

games so as to abate the evils that already exist or to prevent those that seem likely to arise. We have great confidence in the loyalty and earnestness of our students. Some of our most loyal and earnest are members of the various teams and others are zealous friends and supporters of the association. Yet the history of athletics in eastern colleges and the manifest tendency of those of Ohio indicate that some limits should be prescribed."

In 1891 the football squad petitioned to be excused from military drill "in order that they might devote that hour to foot ball practice." This had the endorsement of athletic association managers and of the commandant, with the suggestion that football practice, if the petition was granted, "be made subject to the same rules as govern military drill." On this condition the request was granted by a 3 to 2 vote. At the same meeting the athletic association managers petitioned the trustees to fence the athletic grounds and erect a grandstand at an estimated cost of $1,150. This was refused "because of lack of funds."

Slowly, but effectively, football and other sports gained favor. In the spring of 1892 the trustees granted the athletic association permission to erect a fence and grandstand at a place to be designated by the chairman of the executive committee and the secretary of the board. In line with the previous action in excusing the football squad from military drill the trustees granted a request to have certain members of the baseball squad excused. The nine starters were in this group.

In 1893 the general faculty took an action on athletic eligibility which resulted in student disapproval. The discontent lay in an action to the effect that no student or preparatory pupil of the Ohio State University be allowed to take part in intercollegiate games "unless his record in the past has been above average. The president of the university is to decide what constitutes such record." Apparently the students thought the rule was too exacting, for they petitioned the faculty to reconsider the matter, which was done the following month.

The earlier rule was amended to read that "no student or preparatory pupil of the Ohio State University be allowed to take part in intercollegiate games, who has, within two preceding terms, incurred a failure in any subject or has incurred conditions in more than five hours' work. This regulation shall go into effect at the opening of the university year 1893-94." The amended rule was less stringent and was not to take effect until the start of the next school year.

The university's fourth president, James H. Canfield, moved ahead to take the lead in what nowadays would be termed a housecleaning of intercollegiate athletics. The regulations were the consummation of student and faculty efforts "to place Ohio State athletics on a basis of absolute purity." Of the seven regulations the two most important were:

1. No person shall represent Ohio State in any athletic games or other public events who is not a student doing full work in the regular course.

2. No student shall take part in any intercollegiate contest unless he has been in regular work for at least six months of the academic year in which said contest takes place.

While the first varsity football was not played on the campus until the autumn of 1890, dormitory grounds were the scene of impromptu activity as early as 1881. The *Columbus Dispatch* of October 8, 1887, reported that "a new foot-ball was obtained today at the dormitory and promises to furnish considerable amusement for the boys."

It was not long before talk began of meeting teams from other Ohio colleges. Thus the *Lantern*, Ohio State student daily, reported on April 21, 1887, that Marietta College students had sent word that they were "willing to play us a game of foot-ball."

Footballs were so rare they belonged to individuals of considerable means. Often the balls were home-made, and on other occasions a collection had to be taken from several boys to get a "store-bought" ball.

In 1893 the *Dispatch* recalled the beginnings of college football in Ohio, although the details were at variance. In its November 27, 1893, issue, the newspaper said..."figuratively speaking, the students of colleges of Ohio had never seen a foot ball until the fall of 1890 when several of them organized an intercollegiate association and Columbus was represented by the OSU eleven. The game did not receive a very enthusiastic reception, as it was, locally, a new one and consequently a very small number were acquainted with it." But interest, the story added, increased rapidly.

20

George N. Cole, of the Ohio State class of 1891, was credited with being one of those influential in introducing football to the campus. Cole had gone to school in Columbus with Alexander S. Lilley, who then attended Lawrenceville Prep. and Princeton. Lilley and K. L. Ames, an early Princeton all-American, were in Columbus later.

Cole said he helped Ohio State get started in two ways: by writing Spaulding's for a rule book and talking Lilley into coaching the team without salary. According to Cole's account, Lilley, who lived several miles from the campus, rode an Indian pony to practice while Ames, also working without pay, taught the squad how to kick the ball.

So, 21 years after the first college game was played between Rutgers and Princeton, the stage was set for a spring game May 3, 1890, involving Ohio State and Ohio Wesleyan at Delaware, 25 miles north of Columbus.

"Anything went except brass knuckles," Cole reported in an interview in 1938. There was no passing or razzle-dazzle, he said, but emphasis on power plays and wedge work. Cole said it was all right to step on a man's face as long as care was exercised in the performance.

These tactics were later confirmed by Campbell Graf, captain of the 1914 team, who played as a sophomore in the 1912 game against Penn State. Graf said the Penn State linemen were expert spitters of tobacco juice. "They were both powerful and accurate," Graf reported. "They blinded us most of the afternoon by using our eyes as targets."

Neither the *Columbus Dispatch* nor the *Ohio State Journal* made any immediate mention of the May 3 game, which also was ignored by the *Delaware Democratic Press,* a weekly. The student *Lantern,* however, carried an account of the game, which was called for 9:30 a.m.

With touchdowns counting four points and goals-after counting two, Ohio State led at the half 14 to 6. With 10 minutes to play in the second half, the *Lantern* said Ohio Wesleyan tied the score but that Ohio State formed a flying wedge and scored on the second attempt from four feet out. The kick was good, making the final score 20-14.

The *Delaware Gazette* reported: "The game was a spirited one, and from the interest aroused, it is safe to say that foot

Alexander S. Lilley was Ohio State University's first football coach in 1890. His team played a spring and fall schedule, winning one game and losing three.

ball has taken a firm hold upon both the students and citizens."

The *Gazette* also needled losers by stating: "Had our boys worked a little harder and displayed a little more head work in the first half of the game, there is reason to believe that the result would have been different."

A Challenge From Otterbein

In the beginning of college football in Ohio, an undergraduate team manager handled all details and arrangements for a game. The young man did everything from getting the team to bed to actual scheduling of the games. He had charge of finances, headed the ticket selling, and made all trip arrangements. He actually bought the equipment and was responsible for it, along with having other sundry jobs, now so highly departmentalized in athletic environment.

Thus it was on November 26, 1890, that the following letter arrived on the Ohio State campus from Westerville, Ohio, 12 miles away. It was signed by B. V. Leas, student manager of the Otterbein University football team.

> *"Manager, Football Team*
> *Ohio State University*
> *Columbus, Ohio*
>
> *Dear Sir:*
>
> *"Can we arrange a game of ball to be played on our grounds, Saturday, December 6? We will give you $10 and hotel expenses while here. You can get here at 1:00 p.m. and leave at 7:00. We are very anxious for our team to meet yours as we never have contested for any honors before.*
>
> *"If Saturday is taken, can you come Thursday or*

23

Friday of the same week? Hoping you will give this your careful consideration, we remain,

> *Respectively yours,*
> *(Signed) B. V. Leas, Manager Otterbein University Football Team"*

Apparently the Ohio State manager, later determined to be Charles B. Mowry, failed to reply in time for the game to be scheduled. A letter dated December 5, 1890, was written to Mowry by Otterbein manager Leas.

The letter said:

> *"We sent you a challenge on November 26 and expected an early reply. Just having one-half day to advertise the game, it will be necessary to cancel the date.*
> *"I had excused two of our men from town, thinking you would not answer at such a late date. We will accept a later date if you notify us at once. Hoping this will not put you to any inconvenience, reply soon.*
> *(Signed) Yours, B. V. Leas*

There is no record if Mowry or anyone else responded to Leas' second letter. The two schools did not meet on the gridiron until the opening game of the season for both teams in 1893.

Perhaps Otterbein gained some measure of satisfaction for being ignored, winning the game, 22 to 16.

When football was resumed in the fall of 1890, it was not so successful as the spring game.

Wooster was the opening opponent, the first team to play in Columbus. The *Columbus Dispatch,* in an announcement several days before the game, attempted to shed some optimism on the game by saying, "Our boys will use every endeavor to win and a splendid contest may be expected."

The sad result was 64 to 0 in favor of Wooster, and it was noted that "A number of ladies were present and attempted to cheer the OSU boys to victory, but to no avail, as there was not the remotest possibility of their winning."

The other two games of the 1890 schedule also were

losses—to Denison, 14 to 0, and Kenyon, 18 to 10.

When the first two games of the 1891 schedule resulted in losses to Adelbert (later Western Reserve) and Kenyon, the situation was pretty gloomy, particularly when the respective scores were 50 to 6 and 26 to 0. The Adelbert game was played at Recreation Park, then in the southern part of the city, while the Kenyon game was played at Gambier.

The student daily, the *Lantern,* said that the Adelbert game "has sadly confirmed the fact there must be an awakening in our interest in athletics if we wish to be recognized with any degree of respect among the colleges of Ohio." The *Dispatch* called the game "a match of boys on one side and men on the other."

In regard to the Kenyon loss, the *Lantern* reported that the game "was not as unequal as the score would indicate." It called the Kenyon field "very poor" and charged the umpire, furnished by Kenyon, with being "clearly and stubbornly unfair and prejudiced."

The five-game losing streak came to an end, appropriately enough, on Thanksgiving morning when Denison was defeated 8 to 4 at Recreation Park. On the following day the *Lantern* said that the team had worked out beforehand in "the drill house" and that this extra preparation had been instrumental in winning the game.

The following week the team went to Akron to play Buchtel (now Akron University) and won 6 to 0. Despite the *Lantern's* report that "both teams played like high school boys," the young Buckeyes were happy with a 2-2 season.

It appeared that the up-and-down team had turned the corner.

The season of 1892 proved to be a winner, 5-3, but Oberlin inflicted two of the defeats in convincing style, 40-0 and 50-0. The other loss was to Western Reserve, 40-18.

Thanksgiving Day proved to be a good omen for the Buckeyes, as arch rival Kenyon was defeated for the first time, 26 to 10. Since Kenyon fielded good teams consistently in the early days, this was a big home town victory. The *Columbus Dispatch* praised the team as one that could hold its own with any in Ohio and also patted coach Jack Ryder on the back. The "coacher," the paper said, was a "mighty man and a mighty

With officials wearing black suits and sporting derbies, Ohio State played Denison University at Recreation Park on November 26, 1891. Ohio State won, 8 to 4, much to the satisfaction of the Thanksgiving morning crowd.

player."

Dr. Pollard reported in his athletic history book that quarterback Homer Howard told him that Kenyon had its choice that day of taking a cash guarantee of $85 or 60 percent of the gate. Kenyon decided to take the cash, and the receipts were $1,134. It was a bad day for Kenyon all around.

This game boosted public interest considerably, and the *Dispatch* gave more space to the team, including listing of menus at the training table. The newspaper also pointed out that a new formation, known as the "Ryder wedge," was instrumental in winning the game. Inasmuch as a dismal financial picture had been painted in some quarters for the 1892 season, the $1,049 net from the Kenyon game gave everyone a big lift, including the worried administrators.

The team scored in all nine games in 1893, but this time lost twice to Kenyon, 42-6 and 10-8, the latter on Thanksgiving Day, ending the Turkey Day good-luck pattern. After losing

An Ohio State football practice session in 1892 resembled mob action. In the center of this skirmish in the dark jersey is coach Jack Ryder, Williams College alumnus, who later became a prominent Cincinnati sports writer.

Jack Ryder established a coaching record at Ohio State by serving three different "hitches." His 1890 team, the Buckeyes' first, failed to win in three starts. He then coached from 1892 through 1895, when his combined record was 19-17-1. After a two-year lay-off from coaching, Ryder returned for the 1898 season, winning three, losing four, and tying one. Tired of playing "catch up" in an effort to establish a winning record, Ryder quit with an overall six-year record of 22-24-2.

four of the first five games, the team righted itself and put on a three-game winning streak at the expense of Akron, Cincinnati, and Marietta, but the season-end loss to Kenyon chilled the fans more than usual during the winter months that followed. When Kenyon came from behind to win, the *Dispatch* reported that the crowd of 4,000 tore down portions of the fence and the game had to be stopped "until police cleared the grounds."

In 1894 Ohio State football games were made a part of State Fair Week, and contests were scheduled with Antioch, Wittenberg, and Buchtel. The *Dispatch* pointed out that these games should be classed as "exhibitions" and scores not counted in the regular season. However Ohio State records show 12 to 6 and 32-0 victories over Buchtel and Antioch respectively and a 6-0 loss to Wittenberg.

Popular Jack Ryder came back as coach in mid-season after M. C. Lilley, a Yale alumnus, had directed the team in early games. The team won four of its last five games and finished with a 6-5 record. As usual Kenyon was played on Thanksgiving, and it was a 20 to 4 victory, noteworthy, the *Dispatch* pointed out, for being "free from slugging and dirty work." No players were injured, but the 17th Regiment, stationed at Columbus Barracks, was present to keep "the field clear and maintain order on the outside."

The 1895 season was highlighted by a four-game schedule in eight days, although one—with Starling Medical—was not played. There were two precedents: back-to-back games on Friday and Saturday, and a tie game. The Buckeyes defeated Kentucky 8 to 6 at Lexington and then played and lost to Centre at Danville, 10 to 0, the next day.

The first tie game involving football occurred when an 8-8 deadlock was played with Ohio Wesleyan in mid-season. Oddly there were one or more tie games during each of the next seven seasons. Again Kenyon was defeated on Thanksgiving Day, 12 to 10, and the *Dispatch* said that the "crowd went wild and carried the winners off the field."

That long hair was common among players in 1895, as it is today, is evidenced in the *Dispatch's* observation that "The players will now seek the barber shops to be shorn of their lengthy locks."

As a tribute to William McKinley, the Ohio State-Otterbein game of 1896 was shifted to Canton, Ohio, the president's home. There is no indication he attended the game, won by Ohio State 12 to 0. The game started late in the afternoon and was called on account of darkness by mutual agreement. The season's record was 5-5-1, with the Buckeyes taking a 34-18 pasting from Kenyon in the finale. The 52 points represented the highest-scoring game up to that time and only the second time the Buckeyes had lost with an 18 point total. The team had two coaches, Sid Farrar, a former Princeton player, who was an Ohio State medical student, and Charles Hickey, captain of the 1895 Williams College team.

The roof fell in during the 1897 season, resulting in the most disastrous campaign on record. The new coach was David F. Edwards, a Princeton grad of '96, who had starred as a halfback for his alma mater. The team won one game, lost seven, and tied one. The only victory ended in a row, a 6-0 affair with Ohio Medical, with Ohio State claiming a forfeit.

The team failed to score in its seven losses, getting on the scoreboard only in a 12-12 tie with Otterbein. Meanwhile the opposition ran up 170 points. The highlight of the season was playing Michigan for the first time, a game at Ann Arbor, won by the Wolverines 34 to 0. Michigan had just played Ohio Wesleyan, and the Ann Arbor fans were still objecting to the fact that Fielding H. Yost had played, as well as coached, the Wesleyan eleven. As a result Ohio Wesleyan was dropped from the Michigan schedule, and managers of athletic teams were warned by the administration not to make any engagements with any team representing the Delaware school.

Ohio State wound up the season playing Yost's team on Thanksgiving, losing only 6 to 0. This must have been a good showing in an otherwise deplorable year, as the *Lantern* pointed out that "Despite trick plays by their crafty coach, Yost, only one touchdown was scored."

Having experienced a season they wanted to forget and also one they reviewed with bitterness, campus editors demanded some changes before another year rolled around. In language which was to have a familiar ring 40 to 50 years later, the *Lantern* not only advocated alumni coaching, but, as Dr. Pollard points out in his book, it said: "The experience the Ohio State University has had during the past two years with high-salaried eastern coaches who were supposed to know the game, but who did not, has taught a lesson not to be forgotten soon. If the Ohio State University could secure the services of several of its alumni to coach the team next year, as is done at the University of Michigan and eastern schools, it would undoubtedly put a winning team on the gridiron and would meet with hearty approval of the alumni faculty and student body."

31

Yost Applies For Coaching Job

It is almost unbelievable, but the same Fielding Yost applied for the head coaching job at Ohio State in February of 1897. He might have gotten it, too, but for his own exuberance. According to Fred E. Butcher, of the class of 1901, Yost, who had coached and also played at West Virginia University, wanted to demonstrate his physical prowess while on the campus. This he did, first on a student and then on a faculty member. The performance was so vigorous the professor called Butcher to "get rid of that wild man." It is an open secret that Yost's later successes at Michigan were painful to Ohio Staters.

Capable Jack Ryder came back as head coach for his sixth and final season in 1898, winning three, all by shutouts, losing four, and tying one. The team blanked Heidelberg, Denison, and Ohio Wesleyan, and tied Ohio Medical. Losses were to Ohio Medical in a return game, Case, Kenyon, and Western Reserve. Ryder's teams had always averted losing streaks, but in between the Denison and Ohio Wesleyan victories were the four losses. He was particularly discouraged by successive defeats at the hands of Kenyon, 29-0, and Western Reserve, 49-0.

The season of 1899 was as pleasantly shocking as the previous year had been disappointing.

John B. C. Eckstorm, a student of physical fitness and hard as a rock, took over as head coach. All he did in his first year was post an undefeated season of 9-0-1. It was the first in Ohio State history and was not to be repeated until 1916, when the Buckeyes won their first Big Ten championship.

The most successful football coach in the early days was Dr. John B. Eckstorm. His teams of 1899-1900-1901 won 22 games, lost only 4, and tied 3. The 1899 team was undefeated but tied Case 5 to 5. It was Ohio State's first undefeated season, and the next one did not occur until 1916.

A strong Case team held the Buckeyes to a 5-5 tie, but all other opponents not only were defeated but shut out. Only three games were close, 6-0 with both Oberlin and Western Reserve, and 5-0 with Kenyon. Meanwhile the Buckeyes piled up 185 points in an amazing showing of both offensive and defensive strength.

WA-HOO! WA-HOO! NEITHER SIDE SCORED
NINE HUNDRED OHIO ROOTERS
CHEER ON THEIR HUSKIE TEAM
Three Thousand People Witness the Great Game of Football

Those were Page One headlines of the *Ann Arbor Daily Argus* on Saturday evening, November 24, 1900, after a scoreless tie between Michigan and Ohio State that afternoon. It was another great day for Coach Eckstorm and his improving Buckeyes, who had to be quite an underdog, as they were to be for many years to come whenever Michigan was played. The story indicates that 25 minute halves were played, with officials being Fred Haynon of Lake Forest as referee and Bob Wrenn of Harvard as umpire. Ohio State was permitted to have one of the linesmen and the timer.

The "play-by-play" reads, as the score would indicate, that the game featured punting and defense. Michigan reached Ohio State's 30-yard line in the first half, but a field goal try failed. The Buckeyes came back to Michigan's 25, but a penalty stopped the drive. In the second half Michigan reached the Ohio State 37 but was stopped, after which Michigan blocked a Buckeye punt but the visitors were fortunate and recovered on their own 15. Michigan had another chance when Ohio State fumbled, the Wolverines recovering on the Ohio 22, but again the Buckeyes held at the 18. The game ended with Ohio State back on its own 10-yard line. It is indicated that several punts by halfback Westwater of Ohio State and fullback Sweeley of Michigan carried 40 to 50 yards.

Editorial comment at the end of the story reads:—"Ohio State takes it as virtually a victory, their band playing and the crowd gathering."

Judging from the pre-game excitement, the only difference between 1900 and recent years is the size of the crowd, yet the

Daily Argus says, "It was the biggest crowd that ever invaded Ann Arbor. The guests had the keys to the city and were welcomed here by the U of M band and 300 Michigan students. As the two sections of the train pulled into the Ann Arbor depot, the rival yells went up and the lung duel had commenced. Ohio State brought a band of 20 pieces and it marched down Main St., thence to the campus, where visiting students were given a glimpse of what Michigan thinks is the greatest state institution in the country."

The *Argus* goes on to relate early-day gambling on the outcome "...at the hotels, the Ohio boys wore an air of confidence, but when the question of backing up their opinion with money was brought up, they demanded odds."

Evidently coaches "scouted" games in those days, too. In the stands was Amos Alonzo Stagg, of Chicago, and one of his assistants. Chicago was scheduled to play Michigan at a later date.

Such was the high point of the 1900 schedule, which saw the Buckeyes win eight, lose one, and gain their "moral" victory over Michigan. The loss was to neighboring Ohio Medical, 11 to 6, one of three teams to score on Eckstorm's lads. The other teams to score were Case, beaten 24 to 10 and Kenyon, defeated in the season's finale, 23 to 5. In 20 games over a two-year span only 31 points were scored against the Buckeyes.

A Successful Turn

Ohio State University made the turn of the century with only four losing seasons out of eleven.

It was a good omen, despite the fact that Coach Eckstorm had his poorest year in 1901 of 5-3-1. All three losses came together against Michigan, Oberlin, and Indiana, the Hoosiers being played for the first time. An 11-6 victory over Kenyon in the usual Thanksgiving Day finale helped to ease the pain.

Perry Hale took over the head coaching duties in 1902-03 and received a rough initiation from Michigan to the tune of 86-0. However there were several bright spots, including ties with favored Illinois and Indiana and a 51-5 trouncing of arch rival, Kenyon. The 1903 schedule included 11 games, and the Buckeyes won 8 of them, losing, as predicted, to Michigan, Indiana, and Case, the Cleveland school that always gave Ohio State a hard time.

E. R. Sweetland became the head coach in 1904 for two seasons. His team broke even in 10 games during his first year, winning the first 4 games by shutouts for a fast start. Then Michigan inflicted the usual defeat, 31-6; Illinois made it worse, 46-0; Oberlin won an oddity, 4-2; and then the Carlisle Indians were played for the first time. The redskins scalped the Buckeyes, 23-0, and Indiana took an 8-0 decision back to Bloomington.

A 12-game schedule was played for the first and last time in 1905. It was a good season at 8-2-2, the two losses being to Michigan and Indiana. The ties were with Otterbein and Case.

Perry Hale was Ohio State's head coach in 1902-03, during which his teams won 14, lost 5, and tied 2. One of the 2 losses in 1902 was an 86-0 whomping by Michigan. The Wolverines did it again in 1903, but the outcome was a more respectable 36 to 0. Easing the pain over the two-year span were victories over West Virginia and tie games with Illinois and Indiana.

Fans came to early Ohio State games in Columbus in buggies, surreys, and tally-hos. Here they watch a game with Michigan in 1901, won by the Wolverines 21 to 0. Spectators later protested that they could not see the game because people stood on top of their horse-drawn vehicles. This resulted in their eventual removal from the field.

Wooster was back on the schedule for the first time since 1890, and the Buckeyes gained some measure of revenge for the early 64-0 spanking by winning, 15-0.

E. R. Sweetland, from the University of Chicago, was Ohio State's head coach in 1904-5. The 1904 team broke even in 10 games, but the 12-game season in 1905 resulted in 8 wins, 2 losses, and 2 ties.

Proudly displaying his "M" for Michigan, no less, Al Herrnstein was Ohio State's head coach from 1906-09. He had winning teams each year and had a three-year record of 28-10-1. He was not able to stop his Alma Mater, however, as Michigan won all four games by scores of 6-0, 22-0, 10-6, and 33-6. Two intersectional victories were scored over Vanderbilt, 17 to 6 and 5 to 0.

Al Herrnstein, a native of Chillicothe, Ohio, took over the coaching reins in 1906, and the former Michigan athlete and alumnus had four successful seasons. He had good information on his alma mater, but Michigan edged the Buckeyes, 6-0, for the only loss in 1906. Ohio Medical scored eight points, and the fourteen points comprised the season's total by the opposition.

Hall of Fame Coach Howard Jones tutored the Buckeyes in 1910. He came to Ohio State by way of Syracuse and Yale. He later coached at Iowa, Duke, and Southern California. His 1910 team won six, lost one, and tied three, one being a 3-3 deadlock with Michigan.

The 1907 season was 7-2-1, Michigan and Case inflicting the defeats while Wooster was tied, 6-6. Northeastern Ohio schools, Case, Reserve, and Wooster, joined Michigan in stopping the Buckeyes in 1908, but the Wolverines did not run away with this one, the score being 10-6. Herrnstein bowed out after 1909 when a 7-3 record was posted. Oberlin and Case joined Michigan in thumping the Buckeyes, but Wooster was trampled 74-0 and Vanderbilt was defeated for the second time, 5-0.

Howard Jones, who showed great promise as a coach at

Without previous coaching experience Harry Vaughn, a Yale law student, had charge of the 1911 Ohio State football team. He did an outstanding job, winning five games, losing three, and tying two.

Syracuse and Yale, assumed command in 1910 and continued his good work which was to become even more prominent at Iowa and Southern California. His one-year stint showed six wins, one loss, and three ties, a record for deadlocked games which stood until 1924. One of the ties was a 3-3 battle with Michigan, which pleased the Buckeye fans no end. The others were with Denison and Oberlin. The loss was 14-10 to Case, the old Ohio nemesis.

Harry Vaughn took over for the 1911 season which resulted in 5-3-2. Only four teams scored on the Buckeyes, but three of them won: Michigan, Case, and a new opponent, Syracuse. Cincinnati scored but was defeated 11-6. Old rival, Kenyon, which had been met on 20 previous occasions, was dropped from the schedule after the Buckeyes won 24 to 0. It was evident that the teams from Gambier could no longer compete with the up-and-coming Buckeyes.

Vaughn, who had no previous coaching experience, was lauded before he returned to Yale to resume his law studies. His supporters pointed out that he had inherited only three regulars from the previous season, yet had done a fine job. It was a good year, financially, too, as the athletic association paid off $3,500 in notes.

The conclusion of the 1911 season marked the end of an era. The year of 1912 was to see the Buckeyes move in with the "big boys."

A New Era — Important
Personalities Move In

The year of 1912 could be called the turning point on Ohio State's football highway. The Buckeyes were taken into the Western Conference.

The year of 1912 also brought in John R. Richards from Wisconsin to be athletic director and football coach. Although Richards had been successful at Wisconsin and elsewhere, his tenure at Ohio State was a one-year stand. His team started well, with one-sided victories over Otterbein and Denison. After losing to Michigan 14 to 0, refreshing triumphs were recorded over Case, the old nemesis, 31 to 6, and a good Oberlin team, 23-17.

Then a game was played in Columbus with Penn State which undoubtedly changed the future of Richards as well as Ohio State football.

The visitors came to town undefeated, numbering among their victims strong Cornell and Washington & Jefferson teams. With the score 37 to 0 in Penn State's favor and nine minutes to play in the fourth quarter, Richards ordered his team off the field. He said the visitors were guilty of unsportsmanlike conduct and that officials were lax in calling or enforcing penalties. Ohio State records show the score as standing 37-0, but others say the official result was a forfeit, 1 to 0.

The student *Lantern* said the officials should have banished the offenders in the third quarter, then the contest likely would have been completed in orderly fashion. Richards claimed it was a case of "sportsmanship vs muckerism" and issued statements defending his action.

It was an embarrassing day in other ways. President Edwin E. Sparks of Penn State, an alumnus of Ohio State, was in the stands after spending part of the day with his Chi Phi fraternity brothers. He was forced to watch the Penn State colors burned on the goalposts, for which a freshman took the blame. A committee of alumni and students apologized to Dr. Sparks before he left the city, and a student apology was sent to Penn State.

The season ended with a 36-6 victory over Ohio Wesleyan and a 35-20 loss to Michigan Aggies (now Michigan State). Although the Buckeyes had won the "Ohio championship" for the first time, the Penn State fuss lingered on, and Richards resigned both suddenly and voluntarily, effective January 1, 1913.

So, the youngest member of the Western Conference had a schedule for its first season in the league, but no coach. Neither was there a director of athletics.

The athletic directorship was decided first.

Lynn Wilbur St. John, who had earned a letter as a halfback in 1900, was already on the staff as football line coach and head basketball and baseball coach. He also served as business manager. In his book, *Ohio State Athletics,* Dr. Pollard points out that St. John was not consulted about his promotion but merely told about it after it occurred. For more than 10 years St. John had wanted a medical career, but this move ended all thoughts of becoming a doctor.

Another sudden turn of events authorized the employment of Carl Rothgeb of Colorado College as football coach, but Rothgeb declined, leaving the door open to John W. Wilce, a star Wisconsin football and basketball player, as well as a member of the Badger crew. Wilce, who had been teaching and coaching at LaCrosse, Wisconsin, High School, accepted the Buckeye challenge from his new post as freshman coach at Wisconsin.

Under the new regime, Wilce had general responsibility; St. John was to coach the line and Frank Castleman, who was brought from the University of Colorado as track coach, was to assist with the backs. When spring practice opened, George Little, a former Ohio Wesleyan star, assisted on a part-time

John R. (Jack) Richards was both director of athletics and head football coach in 1912, but he resigned suddenly after one season. Many thought his decision was based on an incident in the Penn State game of that year when he took the Buckeyes off the field for what he claimed was unsportsmanlike conduct.

Lynn W. St. John served as Ohio State's director of athletics from 1913 to 1947, during which he elevated the Buckeye athletic program and became a powerful personality in the Big Ten and NCAA.

basis.

Three opponents were scheduled in the first conference season: Indiana, Wisconsin, and Northwestern. It was an oddity that Michigan, considered a rival by this time, was not a member on the league in 1913. The Wolverines had withdrawn from the conference in 1908 over disputes involving training table issues. Many faculty members and students expressed a desire for Michigan to return to the conference, which it did after the 1917 season.

Schedules had been running as high as eleven and twelve games per season, but now that the Buckeyes were in the conference, schedules dropped to seven games. Wilce's first year was 4-2-1 with losses in the conference to Indiana, 7-6, and Wisconsin, 12-0. However Northwestern was beaten solidly, 58 to 0. Three of the four Ohio games were won with Ohio Wesleyan, Western Reserve, and Case, while Oberlin was tied, 0-0.

Another important factor in the transition to the conference was the improvement of academic standards. The registrar's office reported that only a handful of men from teams of previous years would have been eligible on the 1913 squad.

Dr. John W. Wilce, an alumnus of Wisconsin, was Ohio State's coach from 1913 through 1928, a 16 year regime which saw the Buckeyes win three conference championships and finish second in three other seasons.

49

The record continued to improve in 1914 when Indiana was defeated for the first time, 13 to 3. Northwestern again was beaten 27 to 0, but losses were to Wisconsin, 7-6, and Illinois, 37-0. The three state rivals, Ohio Wesleyan, Case, and Oberlin were defeated.

It was amazing, but true, that young Wilce, not yet 27, could improve upon his record for the third straight time.

The 1915 team won the first two games from Ohio Wesleyan and Case, 19-6 and 14-0, then tied a strong Illinois team, 3-3. After losing to Wisconsin for the third straight time, Indiana was shaded 10 to 9. It was the second straight win over the Hoosiers, who had spoiled the Buckeyes' inaugural in the conference, 7-6. Oberlin was blanked the following week, 25-0, and again Northwestern was easy, falling 34 to 0. It was the third straight whitewash for the Wildcats, who gave up 119 points in the process.

Not only was the offense improving, but the defense was tightening. The 1915 team gave up only 39 points to 55 the previous year. Ohio Wesleyan's lone touchdown was the only one scored by the three state rivals and Illinois had failed to cross the goal line.

Meanwhile a strong freshman team was waiting in the wings, headed by a slight, shy youngster from Columbus East High School who was destined to carry the Buckeyes right to the top, and thousands of fans with him. It is true that the "glory days" were just ahead.

"Chic" Harley — Legend
Of Success

It is doubtful if any college football player ever made a greater impact on his eventual alma mater than did Charles W. (Chic) Harley.

Harley came to Ohio State from Columbus East High School, where he had established an enviable record as an all-around athlete, a career he was destined to follow as a Buckeye.

Born in Chicago, Harley moved to Columbus when he was 12 years old along with three brothers and three sisters. After eight years the Harleys decided to return to Chicago, a decision which disturbed John D. Harlor, principal of East High School and John Vorys, captain of the 1913 team, on which Harley had played as a junior. They along with other friends persuaded Chic's mother to let him finish high school at East.

Many colleges sought the fleet-footed Harley, but members of the Phi Gamma Delta fraternity, with which he eventually became affiliated, influenced him to stay in Columbus, a choice which later was to be applauded by thousands of Buckeye followers.

After completion of his freshman year in 1915, Harley lost no time in making his presence felt in the varsity lineup a year later.

In his first conference game as a sophomore against Illinois, Ohio State had the ball on the Illinois 13-yard line with one minute and 10 seconds remaining. Harley faded back to pass, but, finding all receivers covered, faked a pass, cut around

Charles W. (Chic) Harley, 1916-17-19, was Ohio State's first all-American. More than just a triple threat, Harley was a dropkicker and place-kicker as well. On defense he was a vicious tackler, often giving away 30 or 40 pounds in stopping opposing runners. In 21 intercollegiate games, Harley scored 201 points made up of 23 touchdowns, 39 extra points and 8 field goals. Harley passed away April 21, 1974.

left end, evaded three tacklers, and scored standing up, tying the score at 6-6.

Then came one of the real dramatic moments in Ohio State history. Inasmuch as the field had been mud-laden with Illinois clay from an all-day rain, Illinois had missed the extra point. This was Harley's chance to put Ohio State ahead, and he did after changing his shoes for a dry pair. The 7 to 6 margin stood up, and Illinois had lost its first conference game at home in four years—all because of an upstart sophomore.

This was just the beginning.

Always-tough Wisconsin followed. Harley, playing safety, received a punt on his own 22-yard line. With one-man interference Harley brushed past the first would-be tackler, out-ran the next, and then dodged, feinted, and out-raced the remaining Badgers for a 76-yard touchdown run. Harley also scored the other Buckeye touchdown and kicked both extra points as Ohio State won another big game by one point, 14 to 13.

Elated over their success as neophytes in the Big Ten, the Buckeyes ran rough-shod over Indiana the following week, 46 to 7. Harley gained 107 yards in eight minutes of the first quarter and was removed from the game.

The homecoming game with Northwestern placed the championship "on the line" for the Buckeyes.

Again it was Harley who set the pace. He ran 63 and 15 yards for touchdowns, passed 40 yards to put the ball on the 2-yard line for an eventual score, kicked a field goal from the 40-yard line, and added 2 extra points. The score had been a 3-3 tie early in the fourth quarter until Harley broke the game wide open, 23-3.

Thus ended Ohio State's first title season in which Harley scored eight touchdowns, kicked seven extra points, and one field goal for fifty-eight points.

By the time the 1917 football season rolled around it was evident the Buckeyes had picked up hundreds of new followers and revived many old ones. People who previously had little or no interest in Ohio State football wanted to learn what it was all about.

When the first four opponents—Case, Ohio Wesleyan, Northwestern and Denison—failed to score while the Buckeyes

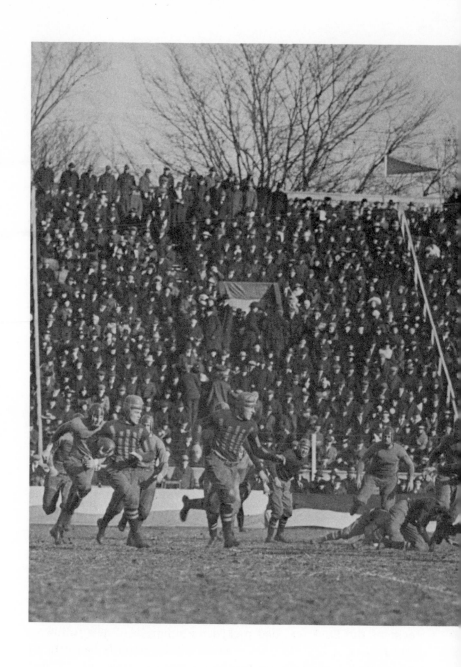

Dr. John W. Wilce, Ohio State football coach from 1913 to 1928, called this the "perfect offensive play." Made against Northwestern on Ohio Field in 1916, Chic Harley (at left with ball) went the distance for a touchdown, Ohio State winning 23 to 3 in a game that gave the Buckeyes their first Big Ten title.

ran up 209 points, interest continued to grow,

The next game, with Indiana, was played at Indianapolis instead of Bloomington or Columbus as both schools had men in the World War I camp at nearby Ft. Benjamin Harrison.

It did not make much difference to Harley where the game was being played. Withheld until late in the second quarter, "Chic" subsequently ran for the four touchdowns scored by his team on rambles of 40, 11, 33, and 8 yards. He also kicked two extra points, scoring all of the Buckeye points in a 26 to 3 victory.

An account of the game reads: "'Chic' was the only consistent ground gainer. His open field runs of 25 to 50 yards, his change of pace, dodging, squirming and diving, were nothing short of phenomenal."

Wisconsin's big, experienced team was a heavy favorite the following week, but, like Indiana, the Badgers were held to a field goal in a 16 to 3 triumph for Harley & Co. For the first time in more than a year the Buckeyes had to come from behind to win as the Badgers went ahead 3 to 0 on a 43-yard drop kick. With his running stopped by some sensational defensive play, Harley resorted to passing. With the ball on Wisconsin's 44-yard line, third down and 20, Harley dropped back as if to punt but instead wheeled and passed the distance to Charles (Shifty) Bolen in the end zone.

This put the Buckeyes on the way again, and Harley passed to Howard Courtney for a touchdown, then kicked an extra point and a 40-yard field goal to have a hand in all 16 points.

A 13 to 0 victory followed over Illinois in which Harley almost duplicated the routine employed against Wisconsin. He again passed to Courtney for a touchdown, then kicked an extra point and two field goals from the 14 and 29 yard lines.

For the benefit of service men two post-season games were played that year, a scoreless tie with Auburn at Montgomery, Alabama, and a 28 to 0 victory over Camp Sherman at home. The game at Montgomery was scheduled largely because numerous Ohioans were training there with the 37th Division (Ohio National Guard). Team members expressed over-confidence against Auburn and were annoyed considerably by having their winning streak stopped at 17.

Although his passing had replaced much of his running,

Charley Seddon, weighing only 147 pounds, was a regular guard on the Ohio State football teams of 1915, 1916, and 1917. Known as the "watch charm" guard, Seddon was the lightest player ever to play for the Buckeyes. The 1916 and 1917 teams were champions of the Big Ten.

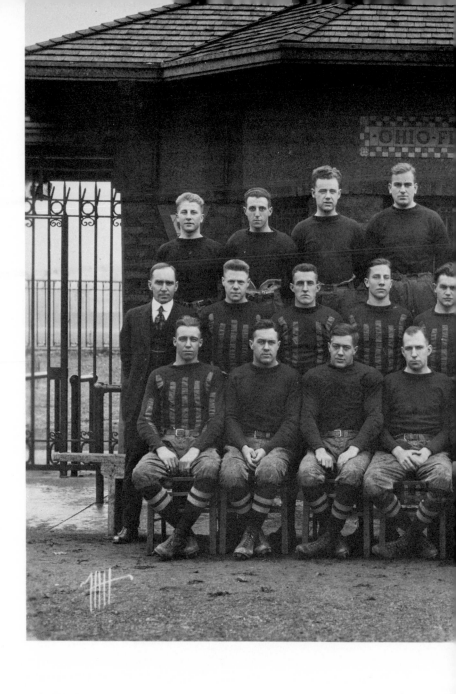

First Title Team—The Ohio State team of 1916 was the first to win a Big Ten championship. Conference victories were scored over Illinois, Wisconsin, Indiana, and Northwestern. A record Ohio State scoring mark was established of 128 points against Oberlin College. Charles W. (Chic) Harley, fourth player from left in second row, was named to Walter Camp's first all-American team, first Ohio State player so honored.

Harley still scored 72 points during the season, 14 more than his 58 as a sophomore. Included were 8 touchdowns, the same as in 1916, 15 points after touchdown, and 3 field goals.

With its goal line uncrossed, the team scored 292 points compared to 6 by the opposition: the field goals by Indiana and Wisconsin.

Shortly after the season Harley, along with most of his teammates, entered the service.

Harley's senior year of 1919 picked up where 1917 left off, despite a six game schedule in 1918 when most of the football talent was in service. The war shortened all schedules in the Big Ten, and Ohio State lingered through a 3-3 season, saddened by two war casualties, halfback Fred Norton and tackle Harold (Hap) Courtney.

With Harley as captain, playing one of the halfbacks, and another all-American to-be at the other spot in Gaylord (Pete) Stinchcomb, the Buckeyes rambled over Ohio Wesleyan 38 to 0, Cincinnati 46 to 0, and Kentucky 49 to 0. None of the three teams threatened to score, and Harley collected 52 points.

Then came one of those first-ever triumphs, a 13 to 3 victory over Michigan at Ann Arbor. With the exception of a scoreless tie in 1900 and a 3-3 deadlock in 1910, Michigan had inflicted 11 straight defeats on the Buckeyes, a source of annoyance that since has carried on for more than 50 years. As usual Harley sparked the Buckeye attack with a 42-yard touchdown, and tackle Iolas Huffman set up the other touchdown by blocking a punt.

After Purdue was blanked 20 to 0, in which Harley ran 30 yards for a score and passed to end Bill Slyker for another, Wisconsin was edged 3 to 0 on Harley's 22-yard drop kick.

Up to this point Ohio State's goal line was uncrossed. Only Michigan's field goal appeared in the opponents' scoring column.

Then came the heart-breaker, a game the old-timers wish they could forget, particularly for Harley's sake.

Illinois came to Columbus with a good team, but Ohio State held a 7-6 edge by reason of Harley's pass to Clarence McDonald which put the ball on the one-yard line. "Chic" ran it over and kicked the extra point. That is the way the score stood until only eight seconds remained.

60

Then it happened! Illinois coach Bob Zuppke, playing a "hunch," sent reserve Bob Fletcher into the game to try a place kick. Fletcher split the uprights from 30 yards out and with it went several items: an undefeated season, a championship which would have meant three in a row, and a three-year unbeaten career for Harley. Thus "Chic" suffered the same experience he had in high school, an undefeated career wiped out in the final game.

So the championship went to Illinois by the margin of eight seconds.

Harley scored 71 points during the season, one less than in his junior year. His three-year contributions showed 23 touchdowns, 39 extra points, and 8 field goals for a total of 201. This was a varsity scoring record until Howard (Hopalong) Cassady scored 222 points. However Cassady played four years, 1952-1955.

"Harley could do everything. He was the complete player."

Thus did Gaylord (Pete) Stinchcomb recently describe his former running mate, "Chic" Harley, Ohio State's first all-American.

"'Chic' was like a cat. you know how hard it is to catch a cat. It usually takes more than one person. It always took more than one player to catch Harley.

"He could dodge, feint, and run fast. In addition he used a straight-arm to ward off tacklers like nobody else could."

When Stinchcomb was a freshman in 1916, he watched Harley become an all-American, then played the opposite halfback in 1917 and 1919. After Harley finished in 1919, Pete went on to become an all-American himself in 1920.

"Harley's versatility showed in our game with Wisconsin at Madison in 1919," Stinchcomb added. "He missed three chances to place-kick a field goal, so we decided he should try a drop-kick. This he did, and we won the game, 3 to 0."

Stinchcomb's first Big Ten game was against Northwestern, and the defense was geared to stop Harley. "I scored three times, but 'Chic's' blocking was superb. Without it I would have been lost."

Pete's second Big Ten start was against Indiana in a game that was played at Indianapolis as a favor to men in service.

Gaylord R. (Pete) Stinchcomb was an all-American halfback in 1920 and recently elected to the Football Hall of Fame. He played opposite "Chic" Harley in the latter's all-American years of 1917 and 1919. Stinchcomb passed away in August of 1973 at the age of 78.

"For some strange reason we forgot to take our white jerseys, so both teams wore red. I was utterly confused. Harley told me to run interference for him, but I just saw too many red shirts. He told me to forget it and follow him. So we switched tactics and won easily 26 to 3.

"It was real fun beating Michigan for the first time,

The late Charles W. (Chic) Harley, left, and the late Gaylord (Pete) Stinchcomb, both 155 pound players, were Ohio State's first all-American halfbacks. Harley was named in 1916-17-19 and Stinchcomb in 1920. Here, they met on the campus in 1923 as youthful alumni.

particularly at Ann Arbor right after Michigan returned to the conference.

"Harley got away for 95 yards, and after that we stayed ahead to the end, 13-3.

"I had a peculiar experience in that game. Playing quarterback I passed against the wind, and when Sunday morning newspapers criticized Coach Wilce for my tactics he was upset. We had a squad meeting Sunday, and I thought he would be elated that we had won. Instead I was deflated and never played quarterback again.

"Harley had a way of staying out of trouble on the football field; in fact he was always helping some other player out," Stinchcomb said.

Harley never weighed more than 157 pounds, and Pete was usually five pounds lighter. "There is no substitute for speed. Both of us could run," said Pete.

Both were four-sport men. Both were outfielders on the baseball team; both played guard in basketball. Stinchcomb was a broad jumper in track and held the university record at 23 feet, 2 inches. Harley ran the dashes and held the school record for 50 yards.

Pete had to go without Harley in 1920 but led the team to the title. He helped pull two big ones out, 13 to 7, against Wisconsin and 7-0 with Illinois. In addition Purdue, Chicago, and Michigan were beaten.

"We knew the stadium campaign was coming up, so we dedicated the season in that direction.

"When we beat Winconsin in the last 50 seconds, I recall $100,000 was raised for the building fund," Stinchcomb said.

Rose Bowl Game —
January 1, 1921

Preparation for Ohio State's first Rose Bowl game in December of 1920 was vastly different from plans involving the several trips made since that time. Anticipating that an invitation might be received to play in Pasadena, the athletic board on November 24 authorized acceptance. Definite word did not come until after the conference meetings in December, however.

"We were on edge for a couple of weeks, wondering what the outcome would be," says "Pete" Stinchcomb, all-American halfback of the 1920 team.

The team practiced in the snow before leaving by train and also encountered snow in Iowa City, Denver, and even Sacramento, according to Pete. The last stop, for one night, was at Palo Alto.

"We did not start our Pasadena practices until four o'clock because of the heat, but it was still hot. We went from snow to seeing people faint from the humidity on the morning of the game. The temperature was 85, and moving the starting time up to 1:00 p.m. did not help, either," says Stinchcomb.

In explaining, in part, the 28 to 0 loss to the California Bears, Pete says, "Our reflexes were bad. We could not coordinate. We would call 'time out' and it would do no good. The heat really had us down. We did have a revival of sorts toward the end of the game when we moved from our own five yard line to the California five."

California, coached by Andy Smith, went into the game

65

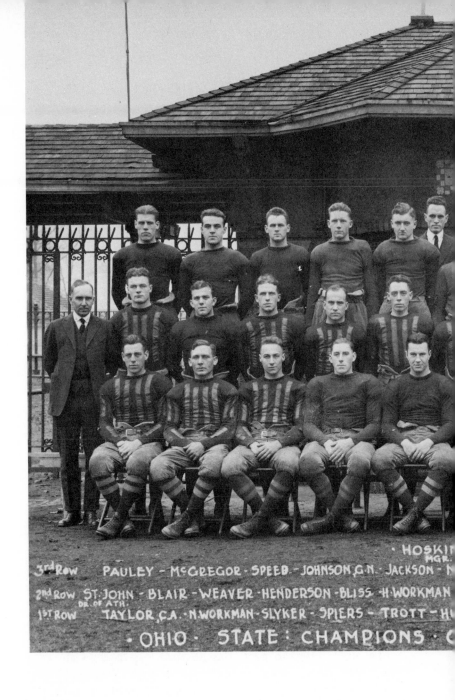

HOSKIN
MGR.

3RD ROW   PAULEY - McGREGOR - SPEED - JOHNSON, G.N. - JACKSON - N

2ND ROW ST. JOHN - BLAIR - WEAVER - HENDERSON - BLISS - H. WORKMAN
         DR. OF ATH.

1ST ROW   TAYLOR, C.A. - N. WORKMAN - SLYKER - SPIERS - TROTT - HI

· OHIO · STATE · CHAMPIONS · C

EY – WARD •
R   ASST. COACH
– MILLER – KAPLOW – PATCHELL – WEISS – LUSK
– COTT – WIPER – WILDER – ISABEL – JOHNSON , E.Y. – DR. WILCE.
                                                    COACH
– WEICHE – NEMECEK – TAYLOR , J.L.– MYERS – WILLAMAN –
• WESTERN • CONFERENCE • 1920 •

© F.H. HASKETT
  COLUMBUS. O.

*This 1920 team won Ohio State's third Big Ten title within a
five year period but lost to California in the Rose Bowl 28 to 0.
It was the first appearance of a Big Ten team at Pasadena since
the first Bowl game in 1902, involving Michigan and Stanford,
won by the Wolverines 49 to 0. Rose Bowl relationships with
the Big Ten were not renewed until 1946.*

67

with an 8-0 record, while the Buckeyes were undefeated in 7.

The passing combination of Harry (Hoge) Workman to Stinchcomb made the Buckeyes a slight favorite, but California fans were high on Harold (Brick) Muller, truly an all-around performer.

Writing in the *Pasadena Star-News*, Charley Paddock, the Olympic sprinter said, "Muller did everything a great end should do. He covered punts so swiftly he often beat the ball to the receiver. He caught every pass that was thrown to him. His passing, too, was phenomenal."

Writing in his book, *The Tournament of Roses*, Joe Hendrickson says that Paddock told of a play in which Muller

Pesky Sprott of the California Bears tackles all-American Pete Stinchcomb of Ohio State in this 1921 Rose Bowl action.

caught a trick flip behind the line from Pesky Sprott and then completed a long pass to Brodie Stephens in the end zone.

This resulted in a discussion of long duration involving the distance of the pass. Maxwell Stiles, a Los Angeles sportswriter, after considerable research stated that the figure was 53 yards. A *Spalding* record book originally said that it was 70.

Sprott later told George Davis of the *Los Angeles Herald Express* that it was his recollection that the play started on Ohio State's 38-yard line. "I handled the ball," Sprott said, "some 10 yards back of the line of scrimmage before flipping it to Muller, who dropped back another 15 yards before throwing it to Stephens on the goal line."

California won, 28 to 0, but the Buckeyes then won four straight in the Pasadena classic.

The play is said to have opened when fullback Archie Nesbet faked an injury. Then he suddenly jumped up, not as a fullback but as the center, and snapped the ball to Sprott. Actually the ball was handled by four players, with the scoring play being from Muller to Stephens.

California lost no time getting an early lead, recovering an Ohio State fumble and scoring in slightly over six minutes.

Howard (Red) Blair took the ball to the Bears' eight-yard line, but another fumble spoiled scoring chances. Early-game injuries to Workman and Stinchcomb lessened Buckeye opportunities, too. This passing combination had a fine record during the 1920 season, but against the Bears, Ohio State completed only eleven of twenty-five aerials.

The attendance was announced as 41,500, which prompted W. L. Leishman, tournament president, to say, "We can't go on much longer like this. Soon there won't be enough lumber in the city to seat them. We have to get started on our new stadium."

The Stadium Era

It was obvious that work should move fast toward a new stadium following three Big Ten championships and a second place finish in a five-year period. First plans were announced in the winter of 1919 and 1920. The original goal was $600,000, and plans called for a seating capacity of 50,000, with the first games to be played there in 1921.

A stadium edition of the *Alumni Monthly* in February of 1921 said that the stadium was to be horseshoe-shaped, with soccer fields, running track, and tennis courts. Inasmuch as the university was founded in 1870, it was decided that a 50-year mark, 1920, would be a good time to open the stadium campaign, and the week of October 18-23 was set. Not only Columbus but the entire state, as well as alumni centers all over the country, joined in the "kickoff."

All male students participating in athletics or engaged in physical education were asked to march downtown in athletic costume. Some 4,000 joined the parade, while artillery regiments and campus infantry marched in full equipment.

Historian Pollard notes that the downtown papers carried reams of publicity and that billboards were used and a huge horseshoe with electric lights denoting the progress of the campaign was suspended in front of the Deshler hotel, since razed.

By January 20, 1921, pledges stood at $1,001,071, with citizens of Columbus accounting for approximately one-half of the total. The contract was let on a bid of $1,341,017, some

Ohio Stadium has been one of America's leading attendance magnets. Here, the giant horseshoe, dedicated in 1922, holds one of its capacity crowds. Twenty-one gatherings in excess of 85,000 have watched the Buckeyes in the last four seasons. Standing room has been permitted only since 1969. Ohio State has led the nation in college football attendance in 21 of the last 23 years.

$300,000 more than could be accounted for. It was stipulated that the university itself was to incur no financial obligation in connection with the stadium and that the cost of the structure was not to exceed $930,000. In the final analysis it was to cost twice that much.

Meanwhile the 1921 season was another successful one, although clouded by two thoroughly unexpected defeats. A small but talented Oberlin college team defeated the Buckeyes 7 to 6, and Illinois inflicted a 7 to 0 loss in the final game of the season and also the last game to be played on old Ohio field.

Coach Wilce was both angry and depressed after the loss to Oberlin and ordered the squad to a practice session after the game. It is believed that this was the first and only time a workout was called for after a varsity game.

Illinois had not won a conference game and the Buckeyes were undefeated when the old rivals clashed, but wily Bob Zuppke was up to date on Ohio's tricks and the home team failed to threaten. The Illinois touchdown resulted in considerable discussion, many fans believing that the receiver of the scoring pass had allowed the ball to first touch the ground.

Prof. Thomas E. French, chairman of the engineering drawing department, is credited with being the father of Ohio Stadium plans. He served as faculty representative from Ohio State's entry in the conference in 1912 until his death in 1944, longer than any other man in Big Ten history.

The loss was hard to take as it allowed Iowa to win the title and relegated the Buckeyes to a second-place tie with Chicago.

Prior to the loss the Buckeyes had defeated Michigan 14-0, Minnesota 27-0, Chicago 7-0, and Purdue 28-0. The touchdowns scored by Oberlin and Illinois not only inflicted two defeats but were the only points scored by seven opponents.

One of the big features of the Ohio State University football program is the 150 piece Marching Band which plays before each home game and between halves. One road trip is made each year and sometimes two, depending upon finances available. Until recently the band had only 120 pieces, but now the student total is actually 187, with 150 of these appearing on the field and 37 remaining on the sidelines to handle props and act as alternates. Competition is keen, with all spots being open. Normally at least 250 appear for fall tryouts.

An all-male organization throughout its recorded history, the present band grew from a drum corps and a military band to

The crowd stands in Ohio Stadium as the Marching Band plays the National Anthem. The band has become an integral part of the football season.

its present size. Since Ohio State began playing football, only seven men have directed the Marching Band. Paul Droste, the current director, is the first former member of the band to be selected as its director. In 1973, coeds could try out.

Ohio State has had an all-brass and percussion marching band since 1934. It is the largest band of this type in the United States—perhaps in the world. All music performed by the band is specially arranged to suit the instrumention and style of the band. All music played on the field is memorized.

The Marching Band has pioneered many techniques that have been copied by other bands. Such innovations as floating formations, animated movement of formations, scriptwriting, measured step marching, and the fast cadence and the high step were first tried and proven at Ohio State.

Unlike most marching bands the Ohio State band plays at least one concert per season and has released many commercial recordings.

The band stepped off toward its present place as an all-American football accessory when it first used formations in 1921. The first maneuvers were rather simple compared to present standards. The band just walked into an "OHIO" to the beat of drums. But soon the craze for band formations was sweeping the country.

Drum majors soon discovered that the position they occupied was more dramatic than anyone had noticed. The first Ohio State major to exploit the potentialities of the job was Edwin (Tubby) Essington. His high-stepping, spirited strut in his $500 (1920 prices) gold-belted regalia is still a vivid memory among old-timers in Columbus.

In 1947 Professor Manley Whitcomb put the basses and drums in the middle, making it the only reversible marching band in the country. Music sounds the same on both sides of the stadium and the band can reverse direction without interfering with the quality of the music. He also introduced the pictorial technique with appropriate song script and the impressive ribbon outline.

The band has marched in presidential inaugural parades in Washington, D.C., and in seven Rose Bowl parades. In the Pasadena marches, which are five miles long, the band members carry an extra pair of socks. This precaution permits more

C. Edwin (Tubby) Essington was Ohio State's first drum major, serving in the 1920, 1921, and 1922 football seasons. In his first appearance on the football field at the head of the Marching Band, he wore regulation dress with a pillow stuffed under his coat. His high stepping was an immediate hit, which led to friends producing a gala Scarlet and Gray uniform for him. He wore this for the first time at Illinois in 1920 and continued to wear it every game for the next two years.

comfortable footing for the hours ahead in the Rose Bowl.

In the early days of Ohio Stadium, buckets were passed through the crowd at half time to solicit funds to send the band on an out-of-town game trip. Later students were assessed 50 cents on their season tickets. This plan soon was abandoned, and now the athletic department underwrites traveling expenses from football receipts.

Holstein Cow Wins Election

Election of a Homecoming Queen always has been a serious business. But one of the greatest college stunts of all time was perpetrated on the Ohio State campus in the fall of 1926 when a pure-bred Holstein cow, Maudine Ormsby by name, was elected Homecoming Queen.

In this case fraternities and sororites had their own candidates and students who did not belong to either felt they had been shunned. It was this independent group that decided to do something about it.

They came up with "Miss Ormsby," who really was Ohio Maudine Ormsby, a prize-winning cow. She had the instant support of the College of Agriculture, where students were fully aware of the identity of Maudine.

The university enrollment was only 9,000 then, but more than 13,000 ballots were cast, counterfeit fee cards resulting in a stuffed ballot box. Maudine won going away, which is what university officials wished—far away.

Chaperones of Maudine (after all, she was only three years old) would not permit her to appear in all of the homecoming festivities. This really was too bad, the "Ag" students protested, because Maudine really was No. 1 at the milk bucket. At the age of one year, nine months, and fifteen days she had produced 22,049 pounds of milk, containing 782 pounds of butterfat, an all-time record for any cow her age. Later, in a seven day test, she produced 743 pounds of milk and 28 pounds of fat, another world record.

Maudine Ormsby, a pure-bred Holstein cow, rode majestically in the 1926 Ohio State homecoming parade, having been elected queen when students stuffed the ballot box. The hoax, regarded one of the best college pranks of all time, eliminated the legitimate contenders for the honor.

There was nothing phoney about Maudine, but a more crooked election never has been held. Perhaps this had something to do with Ohio State losing to Michigan the next day—an "udder" disappointment.

First Years In Stadium

The first game played in the stadium, October 7, 1922, with Ohio Wesleyan University, was a rain-drenched affair won by the Buckeyes 5 to 0. After Oberlin was defeated 14 to 0, the official dedication game followed with Michigan on October 21, a courtesy move as the Buckeyes had helped dedicate the enlarged Ferry Field the year before.

Three Columbus newspapers, the *Dispatch, Citizen,* and *Ohio State Journal,* published stadium editions of considerable size, with each advertisement linked with the stadium or university. The two campus publications, the *Lantern,* and *Alumni Monthly,* also printed all of the historical and current facts they could research in behalf of the occasion.

Policies established at the dedication game have prevailed over the years, such as pennants of all Big Ten schools flying from "C," or top deck. Another is having the Buckeye gridders emerge from a southeast tunnel in full view of their supporters on the west side of the horseshoe. The question was raised concerning what air currents would do with the ball. More than 50 years later this is still a subject discussed by coaches in post-game interviews.

Several Ohio State player-pictures were used in advertisements, a practice no longer permitted by the NCAA. Such a policy today could result in the player's ineligibility.

Thirty former football captains had the privilege of sitting on the sidelines during the dedication game, but they were disappointed in what they saw as Michigan won, 19 to 0. The story listing the names of the captains pointed out that "All of those old leaders would have given up a year of their life to beat Michigan." The story went on to say that when the 1900 team held the Wolverines to a scoreless tie "the university declared a semi-holiday."

Two predictions cited in 1922 have proven true. M. A. Carter, architectural draftsman of the stadium, said that the seating capacity of 62,110 would not be sufficient to accommodate the crowds. He predicted that a miniature stadium, seating 15,000, would be erected adjoining the stadium within 10 years. He missed his guess about a second stadium, but he was right about greater crowds soon wanting to get into the horseshoe. The other prediction said that there would be an increased interest in co-ed sports as a result of the stadium. This definitely became true.

The Michigan game was a case of too much Harry Kipke, whose "coffin corner" punting kept the Buckeyes on their heels all afternoon. The Wolverines scored in every quarter with field goals in the first and final quarters and touchdowns in the second and third. Ohio State had eleven first downs to six for Michigan and once moved to the Wolverines' four-yard line but failed to score. So, for the first time in four years, the Buckeyes had lost to their rivals.

After such success wrapped around World War I seasons, it was ironical that fortunes should swing downward, particularly with the stadium, still to be paid for, as a drawing feature.

During the next 4 years the teams won 12 games, lost 14, and tied 5. By contrast the record from 1916-1921 was 33-4-1. Despite a 7-1 season in 1926, the only loss being to Michigan 17-16, the natives became restless and the alumni critical.

Marty Karow, 1926 fullback and captain, and currently Buckeye baseball coach, says that the score with Michigan might have been tied but for a disagreement over how one of the extra points was to be attempted—the one that failed.

Unfortunately for Dr. Wilce (he had gotten his medical degree while coaching), he was unjustly criticized for the downward trend of the team. Part of the difficulty stemmed from sharp differences between the head coach and members of his staff, particularly Grant P. Ward who was assistant line coach and intramural director.

The upshot resulted in Ward's resignation and a resolution of confidence in behalf of Dr. Wilce, which read, as follows: "The athletic board expresses its full confidence in Dr. Wilce, both as to his professional qualifications as a coach, his ethical standards, and his leadership. He has the entire support of this board and merits the loyalty of all those who have the best interests of Ohio State football at heart."

Despite a break-even season in 1927 and an exceptionally good year in 1928, Wilce turned in his resignation on June 2, 1928, which was to become effective June 1, 1929. He said that he wanted to enter the active practice of medicine and teaching. At the end of the 1928 season, which had included a 19-7 victory over Michigan and a 5-2-1 record, the athletic board granted him a leave of absence for the rest of the academic year, including the summer quarter.

The athletic board then turned its attention to obtaining a new head coach. Historian Pollard reported that director St. John was anxious to obtain Knute Rockne from Notre Dame and that at one time it was felt he was available.

Early in 1929, when it was evident that Rockne could not be obtained, St. John told the athletic board that in his opinion the choice should be Sam Willaman, former Ohio State fullback and later coach at Iowa State. George Hauser, Minnesota line coach, was hired also, along with Don Miller, one of Notre Dame's "Four Horsemen."

It was rather difficult to quarrel with Sam Willaman's five-year coaching record of 26-10-6. Nonetheless two items seemed to have brought on complaints against him—the manner in which he handled the squad and his style of play, which could not be termed glamorous.

He started well, winning from Iowa and Michigan in the first two conference games in 1929, then Indiana was tied 0-0. The Buckeyes then lost to Pittsburgh, Northwestern, and Illinois. In four games Ohio State had scored but eight points.

The 1930 season was better, five victories being credited against two losses and another scoreless tie, this time with Wisconsin. The losses were to Northwestern and Michigan. The score was evened with Pittsburgh, and Illinois was defeated for the first time in four years, 12-9. The first of a home-and-home series with Navy was played, the Buckeyes winning, 27 to 0.

81

Sam Willaman, former Ohio State player, was coach of the Buckeyes from 1929 through 1933. He followed Dr. J. W. Wilce and was succeeded by Francis Schmidt.

After finishing in a tie for fifth in the conference standing in 1929 and a tie for fourth in 1930, the Buckeyes held fourth place undisputedly in 1931. Three losses, to Vanderbilt, Northwestern, and Minnesota, were offset with six victories, including conference wins over Michigan, Indiana, Wisconsin, and Illinois.

It can be said that Willaman's teams were consistent, as another fourth place finish occurred in 1932. They also managed to be involved in many tie games, six to be exact, in five years. Three of them happened in 1932, Indiana and Wisconsin, 7-7, and Pittsburgh, 0-0. The only loss was to Michigan, 14-0, but that, as usual, was the big one.

By this time the coaching staff had been reorganized. George Hauser returned to Minnesota, leaving the line job open, and Don Miller, backfield coach, returned to Cleveland to devote more time to his law practice. Ernie Godfrey, former football coach at nearby Wittenberg College, had charge of the freshmen and was to assist with the line. Floyd Stahl, Illinois alumnus and a highly successful high school coach in Ohio, had the reserve squad and assisted with the backs. Wesley Fesler, an all-American under Willaman in 1929 and 1930, who later was to become head coach, assisted Godfrey. Dick Larkins, later to become director of athletics, was to have charge of the freshmen, under Godfrey's direction.

Willaman's fifth and final season was his best, with seven victories and only one loss—to Michigan again. The team finished third in the final standings.

Meanwhile there was pressure from within as well as from the outside. There is evidence that director St. John wanted a change, along with several members of the athletic board, because, on January 24, 1934, Willaman was asked to announce his plans by February 4. In other words he was being pressured to resign, which he did in a letter of January 31.

Temperament was said to be the chief cause of unrest, but there were other obvious factors, too. Ohio State had not won a Big Ten championship since 1920, and Michigan had won nine of the last twelve games. It was to prove amazing how much the Michigan game affected the lives of Ohio State coaches. In later years at least two others felt the bite of the Wolverine.

Willaman went to Western Reserve University as athletic director and head coach. He asked that Ohio State be placed on the Reserve schedule the following year, which was arranged. The Buckeyes won, 76 to 0, and it was the last time Ohio State played another team from within state boundaries.

Francis Schmidt Arrives

It is doubtful if any college football coach had more loyal, enthusiastic players—and friends for life, than Francis Aloysius Schmidt. Athletic Director St. John could not have made a more popular choice if he had spent a lifetime of picking and choosing, when he recommended the tall Texan to take over Buckeye football fortunes in the spring of 1934.

Not a "name" coach to Ohio State fans, Schmidt came from Texas Christian University, where, oddly enough, he spent the same years, 1929 through 1933, that his predecessor Sam Willaman had served at Ohio State.

Small wonder that St. John looked in Schmidt's direction. His five-year record at TCU defied the odds-makers. It showed forty-six victories, only six losses, and five ties. In each of the five years his teams won nine or more games and twice were undefeated. On two occasions he had undefeated strings of nineteen and then sixteen games. He coached at TCU for nearly two years before losing to Texas 7 to 0. That ended the non-losing streak of 19. TCU schedules ranged from ten to twelve games each year.

Schmidt had an undefeated record against some of the leading rivals, Texas A&M, North Texas State, Rice, Southern Methodist, and Hardin-Simmons. He lost to Arkansas once. Only Texas and Baylor could beat him twice. The sixth loss was to Tulsa, where he had coached, 1919-1921.

In 34 of Schmidt's 57 games at TCU the opponents failed to score. This prompted Ohio State halfback Dick Heekin to say

Francis Schmidt, the popular razzle-dazzle coach, headed Buckeye grid fortunes from 1934 through 1940. The gold football pants on his watch chain indicate victories over Michigan in 1934, 1935, 1936, and 1937.

in later years. "Schmidt knew something about defense, too."

When Schmidt arrived on the Buckeye scene, he seemed to

turn things completely around. Always wearing a bow tie, he resembled a successful businessman rather than a college football coach.

When someone asked him, "What about Michigan?" he replied, "Well they put their pants on one leg at a time, the same as the rest of us."

From this remark came formation of the Michigan Pants Club, which was made up of alumni and downtown businessmen. After each victory over Michigan, a dinner was held, attended by coaches and players as well as club members. Miniature gold pants were presented honored guests.

Schmidt was eccentric and, with it, amusing. He was constantly drawing plays and formations, whether in notebooks or on tablecloths. He also was absentminded on these occasions and once, while sitting in his hoisted car as it was being serviced, almost stepped out. Gas station attendants prevented him from falling to the concrete floor. He also was secretive with his new plays, often hiding them from his assistants while he went to lunch. Other times he would lock them securely in his desk. He also insisted that quarterbacks paste or draw plays inside their helmets to help them remember the offense.

Although he rated high in the profanity league, to which many of the faculty objected strenuously, Schmidt also had a soft approach. Many times during practice he would say, "Now, lookie." It became one of his favorite expressions.

Schmidt picked up at Ohio State where he had left off at TCU, a winner. His first Buckeye game was a 33-0 victory over Indiana, and after a 1 point loss to Illinois, 14-13, his team won all others, including Michigan, which was defeated, 34 to 0. It was a 7-1 season, the same that Willaman had had the year before, but there was much glamour and fanfare this time.

Schmidt's background would not have indicated that he some day would be a football coach. He held a law degree from the University of Nebraska, and his military career would have suggested that he had graduated from West Point. He was bayonet instructor with the 87th division and commander of Headquarters Company, 347th Infantry, AEF. Later he was captain of the 50th Infantry of the regular army. He was a Presbyterian and a Mason, being a member of Knight Templar, Scottish Rite, and Shrine.

Despite a heart-breaking loss to Notre Dame, which had no bearing on the Big Ten race, the Buckeyes won a share of the title in 1935, first since 1920, so Schmidt's record after 2 years was 14-2. He was a hero, not only on the campus but with the downtown followers and alumni as well.

Three losses were suffered in 1936 by a total of 12 points, 14-13 with Northwestern, 7-2 Notre Dame, and 6-0 Pittsburgh. Michigan was defeated for the third time 21 to 0, and it came on the heels of 2 other shutouts, 44-0 over Chicago and 13 to 0 with Illinois.

Indiana, which had failed to beat Schmidt's teams thus far, turned the tables in 1937 for a 10-0 victory, and Southern California edged the Buckeyes 13-12 for 2 defeats against 6 victories.

The 1938 season was Schmidt's poorest to date, a 4-3-1 year, with Michigan winning for the first time in 5 years. Southern California and Purdue joined the victorious Wolverines. Northwestern was tied 0-0.

Despite a season's ending loss to Michigan, 21-14, the Buckeyes won the Big Ten title outright in 1939 with victories over Northwestern, Minnesota, Indiana, Chicago, and Illinois. Cornell, being played for the first time, inflicted the other loss, 23 to 14.

Schmidt's final year was 1940 when he broke even in 8 games, his poorest season. The 40 to 0 loss to Michigan was the big blow, but losses also were inflicted by Northwestern, Minnesota, and Cornell again.

Schmidt's 7-year record added up to 39 victories, 16 losses and 1 tie, along with 2 titles, 1 outright and 1 shared.

The Notre Dame Game Of 1935

It has been nearly 39 years, but people are still talking about it. Meaning the Ohio State-Notre Dame game of 1935 in jam-packed Ohio Stadium. The attendance was announced as 81,018.

It was the first meeting of the two football giants, both undefeated at the time. The Irish had rolled over Kansas, Carnegie Tech, (then a football power), Wisconsin, Pittsburgh, and Navy. The Buckeyes had stopped Kentucky, Drake (85-7), Northwestern, and Indiana.

The Buckeyes were favored. Perhaps enthusiasm stemmed from the manner in which the team had finished the 1934 season as Francis Schmidt's first campaign showed only a one-point loss to Illinois, 14-13, and six straight victories to close the season. Included was a rollicking 34-0 triumph over Michigan and a season-ending 40 to 7 spanking of a good Iowa team.

A feeling prevailed through Buckeye-land: "We just cannot lose this one."

Many football games have been played in Ohio stadium since November 2, 1935, but none will leave a greater impression.

Fr. John Cavanaugh, president of Notre Dame University at the time, has said: "The game defied description." He has plenty of believers.

Sportswriters said it was fantastic (a word not used as much then, as now). Others said it was unbelievable.

The Buckeyes scored early in the first quarter after Frank Antenucci intercepted a pass on the Ohio State 24-yard line. He then lateralled to Frank Boucher, who, behind fine blocking, raced 76 yards down the west sidelines for a touchdown. With Stan Pincura holding the ball, Dick Beltz place-kicked the extra point.

The Irish came back to the Ohio 25 but failed to gain in 3 tries and a short punt was returned to the Buckeye 29 to get out of the hole. When the period ended, the Buckeyes were on the Irish 16, "Jumping Joe" Williams having been knocked out-of-bounds after a 1-yard gain.

As the second quarter opened, Boucher on a power drive went to the Notre Dame ten-yard line. Charley Hamrick then opened a hole for Boucher, who went to the four and a first down. After Pincura gained one on a sneak, Williams went over the Irish left tackle for a touchdown. This time Sam Busick missed the extra point.

The Buckeyes continued to play good defensive football, and the closest the Irish could get during the remainder of the half was the 29. Ohio State moved to Notre Dame's 31, but three successive passes failed, forcing John Kabealo to punt to Andy Pilney on the Irish eight-yard line. During this episode Coach Schmidt called for one of his famous triple laterals, and it gained five yards. It went from quarterback "Tippy" Dye to halfback John Bettridge to fullback Kabealo, and back to Dye again.

With the half ending 13 to 0, and the Irish really never threatening, it looked almost a cinch for the Buckeyes.

The Irish made their best penetration of the game toward the end of the third period when they marched to the Ohio 10, but there they lost the ball on downs.

Then came the big play of the day and one that swung the momentum toward Notre Dame. Kabealo got off another of his good punts, but this time Pilney took it on Ohio's 35 and zig-zagged 53 yards to the Ohio 12 before Boucher brought him down as the quarter ended, with Ohio still in front, 13 to 0.

Pilney later was carried off the field with a twisted knee and replaced by William Shakespeare, who was to have a big hand in the Irish comeback.

As the fourth period opened, two plays were stopped, but

89

Ohio State's pint-sized quarterback, William (Tippy) Dye, No. 50, carries the ball against Notre Dame in 1935. Notre Dame jerseys were numbered only on the back. Dye now is athletic director at Northwestern University.

on third down Pilney passed to Francis Gaul for a first down on the Ohio two, and from there Steve Miller, a substitute back, hit center for a touchdown. When the extra point was missed, Buckeye fans breathed easier.

This only served to make the Irish line battle furiously, and 2 plays lost 15 yards. When Notre Dame next got the ball in midfield, it put on a dedicated march that ended with a pass from Pilney to Mike Layden, good to the 1-yard line. Here, Miller hit the center of the line but fumbled, and Ohio State recovered back of the goal line for a touchback. It was a temporary reprieve.

The Buckeye offense failed again, which gave the Irish a new spark, and a pass from Pilney to Wally Fromhart put the ball on Ohio's 33. Two more passes took the ball to the 15, from where Pilney pitched to Layden for a touchdown. When Fromhart's placement try was low, the Buckeyes were still hanging on, 13 to 12.

Less than 2 minutes remained to be played, and Notre Dame attempted an onside kick. It failed to work, and Ohio State came up with the ball on its own 47-yard line.

At this point there was an opportunity to freeze the ball and run out the clock. However Pincura called for a direct pass from center to halfback Beltz, who fumbled after an eight-yard gain, being hit hard by a savage tackle. The ball was close to the sidelines, and Henry Pojman, a substitute Notre Dame center, touched it with his fingertips just before it went out-of-bounds. Present-day rules give out-of-bounds fumbles to the last team in possession. However, in 1935, fumbles out-of-bounds went to the team which last touched the ball.

The Irish knew this was their last opportunity, and they made the best of it. Pilney dropped back as if to pass, but finding no receiver open made a magnificent run to the Ohio 19. It was on this play that Pilney, who played his greatest game, suffered a wrenched knee. Shakespeare rushed in as his replacement and threw a long pass which Beltz partially intercepted, but could not hold on to.

This gave the Irish another opportunity, and this time Shakespeare passed high to end Wayne Millner who leaped between two defenders. When he came down he was in the end zone. It mattered little that the extra point was missed again.

There was just enough time left to take the kickoff and run one play, good for 3 yards. The Irish won, 18-13, all points coming in the final quarter.

It was a strange game, one that helped make Notre Dame football history and one that stunned Buckeye fans to the point many have not recovered yet. Certain it is the first half

From graduate manager to "father of athletics" to president of the university. This was the rapid step-up of George W. Rightmire who served as graduate manager in 1893, Ohio State's first. He became so active in sports administration that he was affectionately known as "father" and then became president of the university in 1926, serving until 1938.

93

belonged to Ohio State and the second to Notre Dame. Figures show that Ohio's pass defense, which paved the way for two scores through first-half interceptions, collapsed completely after intermission.

Notre Dame completed only 2 of 7 passes in the first half for a gain of only 12 yards and had 3 intercepted, including 1 which resulted in Ohio's first touchdown. In the second half the Irish aerials succeeded 8 times in 12 attempts and produced 128 yards, scored two touchdowns and set up the third. All told, Notre Dame advanced the ball 477 yards to Ohio State's 134, a convincing margin.

The game drained both teams, physically and mentally.

Notre Dame lost the following week to Northwestern 14 to 7, and Ohio State was hard-pressed to beat an inept Chicago team 20-13. The Irish also were tied by Army, 6-6, but did defeat USC in the final game, 20-13.

Ohio State fared somewhat better, defeating Illinois 6 to 0 and Michigan 38 to 0. The Buckeyes tied Minnesota for the championship, first since 1920. It was the second season for both Elmer Layden, Irish coach, and Schmidt. Notre Dame was still recovering from the shock of Knute Rockne's tragic death. Now a great victory had reduced the gloom.

The return game at South Bend the following year was a flat anti-climax. Notre Dame again won by 5 points, 7-2, in a game played in rain and mud.

The two schools have not met on the gridiron since. Unfortunately the games revealed religious overtones and differences among the faculty. President George W. Rightmire is said to have remarked that no football game was worth dividing the university. He did not elaborate, but athletic administrators got the message.

Schmidt was invited to speak at a Notre Dame football banquet at which he said, "I keep running and re-running the films of the second half of the 1935 game. Some day Millner is going to drop that ball."

He never did.

The Sarkkinen Brothers

One of the amusing stories to stem from military service during World War II involved the Sarkkinen brothers, Esco, an Ohio State all-American end in 1939 and his younger brother, Eino, a third string halfback on the 1940 and 1941 squads.

Esco was stationed at New London, Connecticut, with the US Coast Guard Academy while Eino was in the Air Force at Midland, Texas, along with Don Scott, a former Buckeye halfback teammate of Esco's.

One day a call came from the PR office, stating that Scott and Eino had been selected for the Army all-star team that was slated to work out at Yale University under the direction of Major Robert Neyland, former Tennessee coach. Another all-star squad was to train at Denver under Wallace Wade of Duke University.

Major Neyland said to Scott and Eino; "Go ahead. There will be no problems."

On the side, however, Eino said to Scott; "They think I am Esco. I think I ought to tell them."

At the urging of Scott, Eino decided he could have some fun.

The first conflict arose when Scott was sent to Denver, breaking up whatever collusion they might have had in mind.

This setback was overcome at Yale, however when Eino found Esco's college roommate, Frank Clair, on the squad.

"We had a ball for two weeks," Eino relates, "as we did nothing except go through calisthenics. And with Esco at

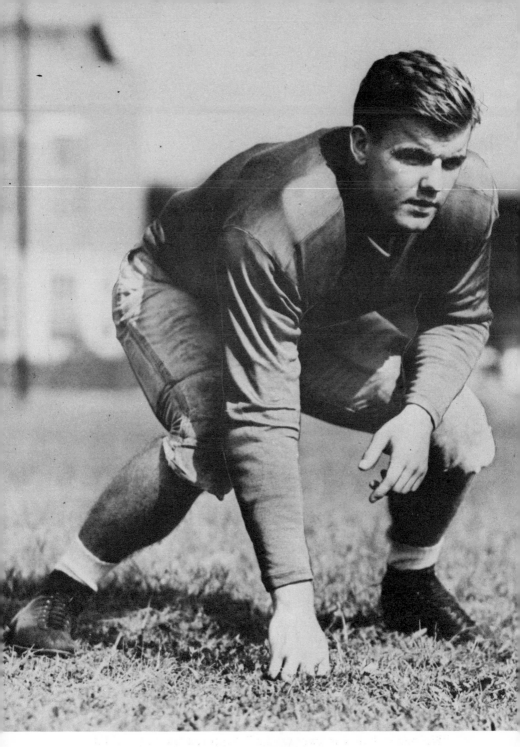

Esco Sarkkinen

Eino Sarkkinen

nearby New London we could get together often.''

It was not long before Major Neyland decided to step up the program with pass patterns. But, with Clair on the opposite team giving signals and clues, Eino was able to cope with his faster company.

Soon the pinnacle of success was to be achieved, temporarily.

George Cafego, all-American quarterback from Tennessee, one of Neyland's own proteges, was directing the squad on which Eino was playing. With Cafego pumping the ball prior to a pass, Eino found himself on the receiving end of a button hook, but only after a defensive back had over-committed himself. The result was that Eino ran 80 yards for a touchdown following a nifty catch and dazzling sprint.

"THAT," yelled Major Neyland "is the way an all-American end performs." Assistant coaches applauded and shouted encouragement.

Needless to say, Eino, Clair and Esco, who was a visitor that day, were soon rolling on the ground with laughter.

Adding to the luster of the day was the presence of a Pathe News photographer who filmed part of the scrimmage, including Eino's triumphant appearance in the end zone.

Then the truth had to come out.

Neyland decided to switch Eino to defensive end, a position he knew nothing about. Unfortunately Clair was on the same team, putting an end to their trickery.

"I went to the major," Eino relates "and told him I had never played end in my life.

"He took our little joke in stride, merely sending me back to Midland to fly bombers again."

This move prompted Joe Williams, sports editor of the New York *Herald-American*, to write, "Major Neyland must have quite a team at New Haven. He has just cut an all-American from the squad."

An amusing aftermath developed, however when Esco, scouting for the Coast Guard eleven, met Herman Hickman after an Army game.

"You don't look like the Sarkkinen I saw at New Haven," said the jovial Herman.

"You are right," replied Esco. "That was my brother."

"I have not been sure during these two months," said Hickman, "because the name is unusual. But I will tell you one thing. He never did line up like an end."

Yes, it was a sad day when Major Neyland decided to have Eino, otherwise known as "Shorty," try to play defensive end.

Paul Brown Succeeds Schmidt

Even if it was good, (and the *Alumni Monthly* of December, 1940, says it could not be), Ohio State partisans would never like a 40-0 shellacking at the hands of Michigan, but even the most rabid Michigan-haters were willing to admit that Tom Harmon and his associates on November 23, 1940, were one of the greatest aggregations that ever played in Ohio Stadium.

The answer seemed to be that Michigan players were keyed up as never before. They were playing their last game for Fielding H. Yost, who was retiring in the spring of 1941 as athletic director. They also were inspired by the great Tom Harmon who seemed to be at his best for his last game. This was a tough combination to face.

There was no dampening of enthusiasm at the football banquet, however. President Howard Bevis said, "We are not going to quit playing football here. There will be another season next year, and our team will be out there battling with chins up. As long as we observe the tenets of good sportsmanship, we can tell the rest of the world go hang."

Vice-president Lew Morrill said, "Winning the game is not the most important consideration in football. While we would rather win than lose, the experience of being a good loser is worth a hundred victories won unworthily."

L. W. St. John, director of athletics, said, "We will go right on playing football here. The fact that 73,000 fans came out to see us last Saturday after the team lost three previous games

Paul E. Brown, former coach of the Cleveland Browns and now coach of the Cincinnati Bengals, was Ohio State's head coach for the three seasons of 1941, 1942, and 1943. Brown was an instant success, winning the Big Ten and national titles in 1942 after a 6-1-1 record in 1941. After a 3-6 season in 1943, Brown enlisted in the Navy and did not return to Ohio State.

proves that fans are more interested in seeing a good game than the winning of it."

Captain Jim Langhurst of the 1940 team pulled the surprise of the banquet evening when he presented Coach Schmidt with a gold trophy from the seniors "In Appreciation of Your Efforts."

Schmidt, always highly emotional, broke down in tears and was only able to say, "This gets my goat. It means a lot to me."

Despite all of the fanfare that 1940 was not such a bad season after all, Schmidt and all five assistants were asked to resign December 16. This followed an "investigation of the football situation" by a special committee of the athletic board.

The No. 1 choice, by the proverbial country mile, to succeed Schmidt was Paul E. Brown, known as the "miracle man" of Massillon High School. Brown's teams won 81 games, lost 8, and tied 1 during his 9-year regime there. While numerous names of the coaching fraternity wanted the Ohio State job, it soon became "Brown against the field." The press was in his corner, as well as 500 members of the Ohio High School Coaches' Association, who were asked by the officers of the association to write a good word about Brown—which they did.

Brown seemed to make a hit with certain members of the athletic board when he said there would be no winter practice, as Schmidt had held.

"I do not believe in it," Brown said. "The boys are fed up with football when they get too much of it."

Impressed with the new coach, one board member said, "Mr. Brown may be the find of the country, or he may explode into a thousand pieces."

Answering a question on the difference between high school and college football, Brown said, "Football is football, wherever it is played. They still block and tackle and run with the ball, whatever the league. College players are high school players just one or two years older. I am not the least bit fearful of the difference."

Speaking of Brown's Massillon teams, St. John said, "Their success came from soundness in the fundamentals of blocking and tackling and better execution of the ABC's of football than their competitors. Out of it came a splendid spirit of loyalty to the coach and to each other, calculated to make them go on the field and give everything they had at all times. In short, the secret of Brown's success has been his genius of organization, his capacity for hard work and thoroughness, and a fine understanding and liking for boys."

It was apparent from the start that Brown was not going to require that players be 6 feet tall and weigh 200 pounds. He had entered Ohio State as a freshman in 1926 weighing 136 pounds after some experience as a high school quarterback. Realizing that he was too small for the Buckeyes, Brown went to Miami University at Oxford, Ohio. He had planned to be a lawyer but decided to switch to coaching and then earned a master's degree at Ohio State during summer periods. Meanwhile he played quarterback at Miami in the 1927 and 1928 seasons.

So at 32 Brown became the youngest coach in the Big Ten and one of the youngest in the nation.

President Bevis was quite impressed. He said, "I have talked with Mr. Brown and I am delighted. His qualities as an athletic coach have been explored thoroughly by the athletic board. My conversations with him have convinced me that his

Ohio State's first national championship team was the 1942 eleven coached by Paul E. Brown, later head coach of the Cleveland Browns and now with the Cincinnati Bengals. The

WESTERN CONFERENCE AND
BROWN-McGRANAHAN-BIXLER-SOUDERS-COLEMAN-REES-TAYLOR-WILLIS-
DYE-MACKEY-WIDDOES-DEAN-ANTENNUCI-SLUSSER-CLEARY-SELBY-VICKROY
DURTSCHI-FRYE-HORVATH-JAMES-HOUSTON-SCHNEIDER-PALMER-HACKETT

other qualities will make him a welcome and respected member of the university staff; one who will exert a wholesome influence upon the entire student body as well as upon the members of his own squad."

Brown was given a one-year contract, plus a gentleman's agreement of three.

He stayed three noteworthy years, 1941, 1942, 1943.

Football at Ohio State in 1942 was the realization of long-standing dreams of students, alumni, and fans. Each Saturday proved to be a big thrill as Paul Brown's precision-like Buckeyes won the Big Ten championship and was acclaimed the nation's No. 1 team by the Associated Press, representing 156 writers. Talent was both plentiful and individually outstanding, headed by timely strategy of quarterback George Lynn, regarded by many as one of Ohio State's all-time fine quarterbacks.

team lost to Wisconsin but won nine of ten games. The team produced three all-Americans in end Bob Shaw, tackle Charles Csuri, and guard Lindell Houston.

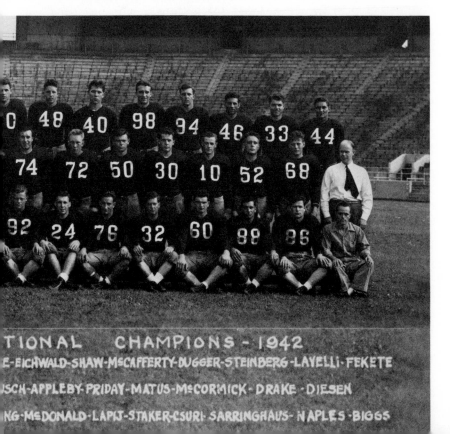

TIONAL   CHAMPIONS - 1942
E-EICHWALD-SHAW-McCAFFERTY-DUGGER-STEINBERG-LAVELLI-FEKETE
JSCH-APPLEBY-PRIDAY-MATUS-McCORMICK-DRAKE-DIESEN
NG-McDONALD-LAPIJ-STAKER-CSURI-SARRINGHAUS-NAPLES-BIGGS

Brown, selected that year as one of the 10 most outstanding young men in the country, had his team in excellent condition from the start. The team rolled up 337 points, blanked Purdue and Fort Knox, and finished with a 9-1 record.

A football team seldom figures in one "overtime" game, much less two. This rarity came to the Buckeyes within a five-year period, both resulting in victories in 1943 and 1947.

With the score tied 26-26 and the game to all intents and purposes ending in a tie, the head linesman threw a flag at the close of the Illinois-Ohio State game in 1943. Dr. Walter E. Duffee, Buckeye team physician, now deceased, saw the flag go down from the west side of the field, while the late Paul Walker, a *Dispatch* reporter, heard a horn on the east side. The flag, for an Illinois offside on the final play, was thrown as the crowd was starting to file out of the stadium and players of both teams were going to their dressing rooms.

Assistant coach Paul Bixler, later head coach, says that the officials had forgotten just where the ball had been but placed it in the vicinity of the 18-yard line.

Coach Paul Brown ordered John Stungis, who never had attempted a field goal before, to try for three points. He succeeded, and the Buckeyes won, 29-26, with some of the players standing around in street clothes.

Coach Ray Eliot of Illinois was in a daze, as were hundreds of spectators, who had left with the score tied. Most of them did not know until Sunday morning that Ohio State had won. Among them were President Howard L. Bevis, Lieutenant Governor Paul Herbert, and Lieutenant Colonel James H. Leusley, head of the university ASTP program.

While newspaper photographers had approximately 12 minutes to get set for the place-kick "added attraction," only one caught it, and he got it on a film he had exposed previously. His newspaper, the *Columbus Dispatch,* used it in four columns anyway, with the caption, "Excited? Who's Excited?"

The other half of the story occurred November 8, 1947, also in Ohio stadium.

Northwestern was leading 6 to 0 with 13 seconds to play. The Wildcats intercepted a pass by Pandel Savic, but Northwestern was penalized back to the seven for having 12

John Stungis, who never attempted a place-kick before, booted one successfully in an "overtime" game to beat Illinois 29 to 26 in 1943.

men on the field.

One second remained on the clock. Rodney Swinehart made three yards, but Northwestern was offside and penalized to the three. Savic then passed to Don Clark in the end zone for a touchdown.

Emil Moldea's try from placement was blocked, but again the Wildcats were penalized for offside, giving the kicker another try. This time, with no seconds left on the clock, Moldea made good, and the Buckeyes walked off with the charitable 7 to 6 decision.

Widdoes Takes Command

With Paul Brown in the Navy, Carroll Widdoes, his assistant at both Massillon High School and Ohio State, took command in 1944. His 2-year stint was one of the brightest since the early days of Dr. J. W. Wilce. The 1944 team won the Big Ten title in an undefeated season; it was acclaimed "national civilian champion," and Widdoes himself was named "College Coach of the Year." The 1945 team lost only to Purdue and Michigan, the latter 7 to 3 when an offside penalty put the Wolverines in scoring position.

Born in Philippines of missionary parents, Widdoes was a reserved, religious man. When he was six years of age, his parents received leave to return to Dayton, Ohio, for one year where he entered school, but he then returned to Manilla and remained there until he was thirteen. He then came back to Ohio and entered the United Brethren Home at Lebanaon, Ohio. With no football team there Widdoes participated in baseball, basketball, and track. He later became an all-around athlete at Otterbein College in Westerville, Ohio.

Widdoes' parents were captured by the Japanese during the war but eventually were released unharmed in 1946. Thus he was able to have a reunion with them while he was a member of the coaching staff.

While many thought Widdoes' selection as successor to Brown was a surprise, he soon made his presence felt as a fundamentalist and good organizer. He liked to teach blocking techniques, and in this department the Buckeyes stood out.

Soft-spoken Carroll Widdoes was Ohio State's head coach in 1944 and 1945 when his two-year record was 16-2. He was named College Coach of the Year in 1944 when the undefeated Buckeyes won the Big Ten title. The team also was acclaimed "national civilian champions."

There was some fine talent on the 1944 team, headed by Les Horvath, a 23-year-old "coach on the field." He worked with 4 outstanding freshmen, all under 18 years of age. The group consisted of Bob Brugge, Ollie Cline, Dick Flanagan, and Tom Keane. In addition Widdoes inherited tackles Bill Willis and Russ Thomas, end Jack Dugger, and guards Bill Hackett and Warren Amling. All made all-American except Thomas.

The team opened the 1944 season by swamping Missouri 54 to 0 and followed with a 34-0 triumph over Iowa—88 points in 2 games and the opposition had not scored. People were beginning to whisper. When a good Wisconsin team was defeated at Madison 20 to 7, they were talking out loud.

It was no problem to get the fans excited about the fourth

Ohio State's war-time team of 1944 produced a Big Ten champion and the unofficial title of "national civilian champions." While nearly all other major college teams had Army, Navy, Marine, or Air Corps assistance, the Buckeyes were

game of the season, for Paul Brown was bringing the Great Lakes Naval team to Columbus. It was a case of teacher vs student, and Ohio State won the decision, 26 to 6. More than 73,000 people were in the stands as a tribute to Brown's homecoming. The game was tied 6 to 6 going into the last period, but Horvath led the Buckeyes in a strong rally. Horvath played under 3 coaches at Ohio State, but it was the first time he had a hand in defeating 1 of them.

Minnesota, Indiana, Pittsburgh, Illinois, and Michigan fell in order. Illinois was played at Cleveland before 83,627, the largest crowd to witness an athletic event during the war. Defense against the speedy "Buddy" Young paid off in this one. He was held to 61 yards in 9 carries, his lightest output of the season. The Michigan game was an Ohio State epic, a 52-yard march late in the final quarter, culminating in a touchdown, naturally, by Horvath, for an 18-14 victory.

For the first time since 1920 there was talk of a Rose Bowl

made up of freshmen and military—deferred students. The team produced four all-Americans and a Heisman award winner in Leslie Horvath, who was one of the all-Americans. The others were end Jack Dugger, tackle Bill Willis, and guard Bill Hackett.

bid. That was the last time any Big Ten team had been invited and it was Ohio State, which had lost to California, 28 to 0. A special meeting of faculty representatives was held in Chicago on Sunday following the Michigan game, but the answer was "No." It was reported that the vote was 7 to 3 against sending a representative to Pasadena. Tennessee went instead, playing Southern California. Director St. John was pretty bitter but said he would abide by the wishes of the majority.

Widdoes' second season was approached with optimism, but even the most ardent fans could not expect a duplicate of 1944. Horvath had graduated along with Willis and Dugger. Brugge was in the Navy while Hackett had been injured in an auto accident during the winter. He suffered a head injury and was advised not to play football again. There were two valuable additions, however. Dick Fisher, who played halfback for Brown in 1941, returned along with Paul Sarringhaus who had played the same position in 1942.

William (Bill) Willis, all-American tackle in 1944 and an all-pro lineman with the Cleveland Browns, had the unusual distinction of playing on two national champions while a member of the Buckeyes. The 1942 team was so acclaimed, as was the war-time eleven of 1944. Willis, an outstanding student and campus leader, has been a member of the Ohio Youth Commission since retiring from professional football. He was elected to the National Professional Football Foundation Hall of Fame in 1972.

The first 3 games were on the right side of the ledger against Missouri, Iowa, and Wisconsin. The good offense and defense which had marked the beginning of 1944 again were in evidence, 101 points being scored against 6. The winning streak stopped at 12 in a row when Purdue rocked the Buckeyes 35 to 13. Bob DeMoss, recent Purdue head coach, threw 2 touchdown passes, and Ed Cody rambled for 3 more.

The Buckeyes went right back to their winning streak, however, waltzing over Minnesota, Northwestern, Pittsburgh, and Illinois. Only the 16-14 game with the Wildcats was close.

Both Michigan and Ohio State were in the title chase as they had been the year before. The Buckeyes led in this tight struggle at Ann Arbor until late in the fourth quarter, 3 to 0, by means of a 17-yard field goal by Max Schnittker. A 5-yard off side penalty against Ohio State, when the ball was on the 6, moved the Wolverines up to the 1, and on the second effort Henry Fonde scored on a reverse. The extra point was good, so, as Ohio State had won by 4 points in 1944, Michigan took this one by the same margin, 7 to 3.

Leslie Horvath:
An All-Time Favorite

The 1944 football team of Ohio State University not only proved to be the No. 1 civilian 11 in the nation but produced the No. 1 player in Leslie Horvath. A senior in the College of Dentistry, 167-pound Horvath was the inspiration which helped carry his younger teammates through the Buckeyes' first undefeated and untied season since 1916.

Deprived of varsity participation in 1943 because of the army specialized training program on the campus, Horvath reported for practice September 1, after his dental unit had been discharged from military obligations in August. Flattering offers to play professional football came to the Buckeye ace, but he voluntarily elected to remain with the Scarlet and Gray. Despite a heavy schedule of studies, Horvath never missed a practice and often was the first man on the field.

The 24-year-old star not only directed the team's play but participated in more actual combat than any other member of the squad. Though playing only 8 minutes against Pittsburgh that season, Horvath played 402 minutes of football, a full quarter more than any of his teammates. The lightest regular on the team and one of the slightest-built players in the Big Ten, Horvath carried the ball 163 times and gained 924 yards, an average of nearly 6 yards per try. He led the team in scoring with 72 points, 30 more than Bob Brugge, the runner-up. In forward passing Horvath completed 14 aerials in 32 attempts, thereby adding 344 more yards to Ohio State's offense. Despite lack of ruggedness Horvath was one of the team's big defensive

Leslie Horvath

113

cogs and often prevented touchdowns when he was the lone defender between the ball carrier and the goal line.

It is doubtful if any player in Big Ten history, before or since, has received as many individual honors as Horvath. Recipient of the John Heisman award, first Ohio State player to be so honored, Horvath likewise was voted the most valuable man to his team, a step which led to his selection as the outstanding player in the conference for 1944. Newspapers in all sections of the country voted him the "Player of the Year."

Equally efficient in both the single wing and T-formation attacks, Horvath played under three head coaches during his varsity career, the late Francis Schmidt, the late Carroll Widdoes, and Paul E. Brown—the only Ohio State football player to have had that experience.

Horvath had the personality and quality of leadership to inspire his mates to almost unbelievable achievements. The best example was his direction of the winning touchdown against Michigan in 1944, the victory meaning the Big Ten title for the Buckeyes. With Ohio State trailing 12-14 and 8 minutes remaining, Horvath led a sustained march of more than 50 yards.

Calling his younger mates together in the huddle preparatory to launching the successful march, Horvath said, "We are not going to pass. We are not going to fumble. We are not going to give up the ball. We are going right in with a series of first downs. Now, everyone block as he never has blocked before."

The result was just as Horvath ordered—no passes, no fumbles—superb blocking through 4 first downs on short gains—1 first down being made on a "4th and 5" situation.

Leslie Horvath, modest and unassuming, will live in the minds and hearts of every Ohio State University supporter: always a gentleman, student, and athlete.

Season Of 1946:
One Of Peaks And Pitfalls

The season of 1946, when Paul O. Bixler served his one year as head coach after being an assistant under both Paul Brown and Carroll Widdoes, was one of peaks and pitfalls.

The peaks came in a fine 21 to 0 intersectional victory over Southern California at Los Angeles and a thrilling 39 to 27 triumph over previously-undefeated Northwestern at Evanston.

Inasmuch as this was the first year of the pact with the Pacific Coast Conference to permit the Big Ten winner to appear in the Rose Bowl, hopes were high for a championship team.

Wisconsin, however, pricked the bubble 20 to 7 at Madison; Illinois came from behind to win 16 to 7 at Champaign; and then Michigan really unloaded to hand the Buckeyes a 58 to 6 lacing in Columbus. Since it was the last game of the season and on the home field, at that, bitter memories lingered through the winter months.

The season had not been all bad, though, as the Buckeyes had tied Purdue and Missouri, and defeated Minnesota and Northwestern.

While the Northwestern games appeared to be nothing more than another Big Ten tilt, since both teams eventually finished in second division, it established a precedent in Buckeye football history as follows: BOTH TEAMS SCORED IN EVERY QUARTER.

This had never been done before and has not been matched since, despite some high-scoring games such as 46-34,

Paul O. Bixler was 39 years old when he assumed charge of the Ohio State football squad in 1946. He came to the university in 1941 as a member of Paul Brown's staff, coaching the ends and wingbacks. He served only one year as head coach.

44-20, 83-21, 34-32, and 35-34.

From the time Ohio State scored on the seventh play of the Northwestern game, when Bob Brugge went 13 yards, it was a parade of touchdowns and missed extra points which prevented a safe margin for either team.

Fullback Pete Perini, who was the only starter who scored for the Buckeyes, tallied in the second quarter, but this was

Fullback Joe Whisler was the star of the Ohio State's epic game with Northwestern at Evanston in 1946 when both teams scored in every quarter. It was an unprecedented feat and has not been repeated in the past 27 years.

matched by two Northwestern touchdowns, one in each period. Each team missed a conversion attempt, making it 13-13 at the half.

Northwestern went ahead 20 to 13 after 2 minutes and 35 seconds of the third period, but Jerry Krall, who like Brugge did not start, rambled 21 yards for 6 points. John Stungis missed the conversion attempt, keeping the Wildcats ahead 20-19. Moments later Krall scored again on a 20-yard pass, but for the third time Stungis missed the extra point.

With a precarious 25 to 20 lead going into the fourth period Joe Whisler, another non-starter, pushed the Buckeyes ahead, scoring from the 1-yard line. This time Stungis kicked the point for a 32-20 lead.

The Wildcats came right back with an 81-yard touchdown run by Fred Aschenbrenner, and the kick was good, so once more the Ohio State advantage was the unsafe margin of 5 points, 32-27. Only 2 minutes and 39 seconds had been played in the fourth period, so it was still anybody's game.

At that point the Buckeyes received a break when Tony Adamle intercepted a pass and returned to the Northwestern 30. Whisler caught a pass good for 19 yards, then, with the exception of 2 plays carried the ball the rest of the way, the last bolt for a touchdown. Stungis added the 39th point.

In the last 3 minutes and 25 seconds the Wildcats reached the Ohio State 30, and the Buckeyes went back to the Northwestern 8 when time ran out on the wild-scoring orgy.

Score by quarters of historical game;

Ohio State	7	6	12	14—39
Northwestern	7	6	7	7—27

Bixler recalls the flight to Los Angeles in three DC-3's as being more frightening than any of the football games in 1946.

"We had a big plane lined up, but at the last minute the government cancelled our plans. In the smaller planes we had to stop at St. Louis, Oklahoma City, and Albuquerque. The squad voted to practice there, so we stayed overnight at an Army base. Nearly everyone got sick from the stopping and starting. Oddly enough the sickest player was Hal Dean, a guard who had been a parachute jumper during the war. However he recovered rapidly and played a fine game against USC."

The Buckeyes won the game, 21 to 0.

Returning to Columbus the squad had planned to stay in Texas Sunday night, but fog forced another landing at Albuquerque. This caused an all-day flight Monday, with school classes being missed as well as the coaches missing a staff meeting.

To shorten the week further the team had to leave by train Thursday night for Madison, Wisconsin, where the Badgers thumped the Buckeyes on Saturday, 20 to 7.

Small wonder! It was a rough week.

The Fesler Regime

Following Bixler's resignation it was evident that the first choice of athletic director St. John was Wesley E. Fesler, then coaching at Pittsburgh.

Fesler, one of Ohio State's all-time great athletes, was a nine-letter winner, three each in football, baseball, and basketball. In addition he was a three-time all-American football selection, joining the great "Chic" Harley as Ohio State's only representatives in this category.

Versatile on the gridiron as an end or fullback, Fesler was even more so on the baseball diamond, where he played first base, second base, and center field. On May 18, 1931, Fesler had one of the greatest days at bat in the history of Ohio State baseball. He hit two doubles and three home runs, two of the homers coming with the bases full. With a total of sixteen bases he accounted for nine of ten runs as Ohio State defeated Illinois, 10 to 5.

In addition to being all-American in football, Fesler was all Big Ten in basketball. He also was named the most valuable player in the Big Ten in 1930.

Because Fesler began his college career in engineering, a course he followed for more than one year before transferring to commerce, his graduation was delayed until 1932. In the fall of 1931, and for one season following his graduation, Fesler was a member of the Ohio State football coaching staff. In 1933 he went to Harvard University as head basketball coach and assistant in football.

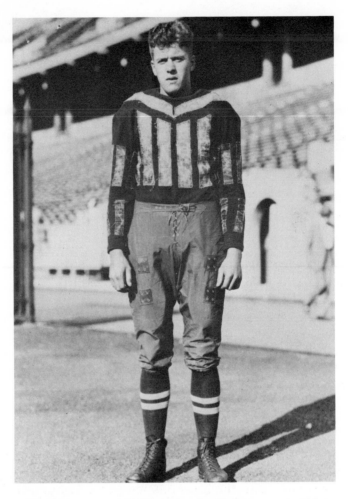

Wesley E. Fesler, one of Ohio State's all-time great athletes, was head football coach from 1947 through 1950.

In 1942 Fesler joined the staff of Connecticut Wesleyan University as head football and basketball coach and freshman baseball coach.

During 1944 Fesler received a leave of absence to join the Office of Strategic Services but in February of 1945 became head basketball and assistant football and baseball coach at Princeton University. In the spring of 1946 Fesler was named head football coach at the University of Pittsburgh, his last stop before coming to Ohio State.

Vic Janowicz: All-American

When Vic Janowicz, from Elyria, Ohio, enrolled as a freshman at Ohio State University in the fall of 1948, he had just finished being the most widely-recruited high school athlete in the history of the state. In 1947 Janowicz had led his high school football team to the championship of the Lake Erie League, a rugged circuit of good teams. He scored 101 points and ran away with all-Ohio honors. It was reported that 61 colleges and universities expressed interest in getting Janowicz' talents.

Vic said that he always wanted to go to the state university and play in the big stadium. He regarded it as a patriotic gesture, he said, indicating that Ohio boys should play in their home state. He added that he was impressed with Wes Fesler, who was beginning his second year as head coach. Since Janowicz also played baseball and basketball, he relished the opportunity to play these sports on the university level.

As a sophomore Janowicz played largely on defense, including safety. He also kicked off, punted, and booted extra points. Later he added field goals to his category of scoring.

Playing sparingly on offense in his first year, Vic scored only 14 points on 2 touchdowns and a pair of extra points. He rushed 30 times for 121 yards, caught 1 pass for a 24-yard touchdown, and punted 4 times for an average of 34.8. Injured in the third game of the season against USC, Janowicz missed the next four games but finished strong against Illinois, Michigan, and California in the Rose Bowl.

Vic Janowicz

Janowicz had his best year as a junior in 1950 when he received the Heisman award in a landslide vote, the first junior to win the honor. He also was a unanimous choice for first team all-American.

Vic played in all 9 games and scored 65 points, including 5 touchdowns, 26 extra points, and 3 field goals. In addition he passed for 12 touchdowns, including 6 against Pittsburgh and 4 against Iowa. He also punted 54 times for an average of 36.5 yards. In an incredible all-around performance, Janowicz carried the ball 114 times for 437 yards. It is true that he did everything except sell programs at half time.

In the game with Iowa, which Ohio State won 83 to 21, Janowicz established a record for points-after-touchdown with 10 in 11 attempts.

His place-kick against Michigan in the "Blizzard Bowl," described elsewhere, is an historical event among Buckeye fans.

In 1951, Woody Hayes' first year as successor to Fesler, Vic scored only one touchdown himself but passed for two others, kicked nine extra points, and booted three field goals. His punting average went up to 39.4, one of the best in the country. Carrying the ball 106 times, he averaged 3.5 yards per try.

During Vic's 3-year varsity career of 26 games he scored 8 touchdowns, gained 982 yards from scrimmage, and passed 102 times, completing 39 for 635 yards and 14 touchdowns. One of the most active kickers of that period, Vic punted 120 times for 4,532 yards, more than 2½ miles, for an average of just under 38. He also kicked 6 field goals, 2 of which won games from Pittsburgh and Northwestern in 1951.

Small wonder that he was a wanted young man in 1948.

Rose Bowl — January 1, 1950

Preparations for the first Rose Bowl trip in December of 1949 (first since the trip by invitation in 1920) caused quite a stir among members of the athletic board who had the responsibility of making all plans, paying the bills and selecting the personnel whose bills would be paid by the athletic department.

When the budget for the Rose Bowl was discussed, it was to include all expenses for 55 persons designated as the official party, plus all other related projects in connection with the Tournament of Roses. Estimated costs of these expenses were placed at $41,000, to be paid by the Tournament of Roses Committee.

Richard C. Larkins, then athletic director, submitted a list of 11 additional persons to be taken on the trip to properly take care of details of operation. These included ticket sales people, publicity man, auditor, an additional coach, 2 managers, an injured squad member, and an office manager.

Dr. Howard L. Bevis, then university president, now deceased, brought up the matter of the board of trustees' jurisdiction in the selection of the official personnel to represent the university at the Rose Bowl. These, he said, included the trustees, administrative personnel, and the athletic board representatives, all of whom would be subject to the state auditor's approval.

The auditor's office, he said, would conduct a post audit on Rose Bowl accounts, therefore all transportation expenses

Richard C. Larkins, former Buckeye football and basketball star, served as Ohio State's director of athletics from 1947 to 1971. Larkins, second director in the school's history, succeeded L. W. St. John, who pioneered activities from 1913. Larkins now is retired. Larkins built the varsity program up to 18 sports, one of the largest in the nation, and was widely-known as a leader in the intercollegiate field. He was active in NCAA, Olympic, and physical fitness programs as well as the National Association of Collegiate Directors of America. Under his supervision Ohio State University was the first to conduct a summer youth program, whereby hundreds of underprivileged children have benefited through use of the university facilities. The winner of the James J. Corbett Memorial Award, Larkins also was elected to the Helms Hall of Fame for athletic directors. Only two men in addition to Larkins have received the Corbett award to date: H. O. (Fritz) Crisler of Michigan and the late William R. Reed, commissioner of the Big Ten.

125

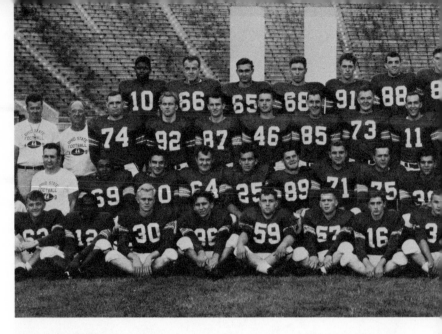

First Ohio State squad to play in the Rose Bowl under the modern agreement with the west coast was the 1949 team which defeated California, 17 to 14, on a fourth quarter field goal by Jimmy Hague. The team won seven, lost to Minnesota

would have to be officially approved before they could be expended. After considerable discussion it was decided that the matter of athletic board personnel selection representing the university at the Rose Bowl be left to the board of trustees.

Being consistent with rising prices, inflation, and increased costs the $41,000 budget of 1949 jumped to $119,535 in 1972, with the official traveling squad of players moving up from 44 to 60.

Ohio State's first appearance in the Rose Bowl in 30 years was achieved after a tie game with Michigan, 7 to 7. Since the Wolverines had gone to the Rose Bowl the previous year, they were not eligible this time, although the tie game gave them a share of the Big Ten title.

Close games, a 27 to 0 loss to Minnesota and a tie game with Southern California, in which several Buckeye players were injured, marked the season. Minnesota was the only team to shut out the Buckeyes, and Wisconsin was the only team that did not tally against Ohio State.

The tie game with Michigan was attained after it looked like a 7-6 loss, but the Wolverines were offside on an extra point

and had two ties, one of which was against Michigan, enabling the Buckeyes to gain the Rose Bowl invitation. Vic Janowicz, Heisman award winner, and all-American a year later, was a member of the team.

try that failed, and on the second attempt Jimmy Hague made it good.

Had Ohio State not gotten a clean shot at the Rose Bowl, it might have been a ticklish situation. Minnesota, next in line and in third place with a 4-2 record, had always opposed the postseason game and likely would have turned down a bid. That would have made Wisconsin, a fourth-place finisher, the choice to play. Fortunately this likely complication was eliminated.

Although the Buckeyes got off well offensively against the California Bears, they trailed at the half, 7 to 0. A 55-yard pass took the Bears to the Ohio 19, and they scored in 4 plays.

On a fourth and five situation in the third period and the ball on the California thirteen, Jerry Krall jump-passed to Ralph Armstrong for a first down on the six, and then Fred (Curly) Morrison, who put on an all-American performance that day, blasted over to tie the score. A moment later Bill Trautwein blocked a Bob Celeri punt, recovered by Jack Lininger, and Krall scored from two yards out.

Sportswriters voted Morrison the "player of the game."

Just before the third quarter ended, Bob Celeri lateraled

wide to Jim Monachino, who got away for a 44-yard touchdown run, and when the extra point was good the score was tied at 14.

Then came another big play by Jimmy Hague, whose extra point, after a miss, had tied Michigan to put the Buckeyes in the Rose Bowl. When Celeri was rushed on a punt try, he kicked left-footed, and it went out-of-bounds on the California thirteen. Three plays gained seven yards, but the Buckeyes were penalized five yards for delay of game trying to get Hague into the game. With the ball placed on the seventeen the kick was good for a 17-14 victory, and Ohio State had its biggest day in a long, long time.

The kick, briefly, avenged Ohio State's 28-0 loss to California 29 years earlier and ended the Bears' winning streak

Fullback and punter Fred (Curly) Morrison was named the most valuable player in the Rose Bowl game of January 1, 1950, when Ohio State defeated California, 17 to 14.

Ohio State's thrilling 17-14 victory over California in the 1950 Rose Bowl game came on this field goal by Jimmy Hague late in the fourth quarter. Several players of both teams forgot their blocking assignments and watched the ball clear the cross bar.

of 10. The boot also continued the Big Ten's domination of the bowl, this having been the fourth success in as many starts against the Pacific Coast under the new pact at that time.

The victory prompted the late Russ Needham, sports editor of the *Columbus Dispatch* who often quarreled with Fesler's coaching tactics, to write:

"Ohio State has known many glorious moments in its football life, but none to compare with this. This was the wow of all time and it came, as all will attest, when it could do the most good."

In appreciation of Wes Fesler's successful season in 1949 the Athletic Board commended the head coach and his staff in a letter, which read:

"The Athletic Board of The Ohio State University joins with a host of others in congratulating you and your associates upon a successful football season, climaxed by the great victory in the Rose Bowl. Because you and your staff exemplify so fully the type of coaching leadership under which we desire the young men of this university to train in competitive sport, the board is deeply gratified at your decision to remain as a part of the university community.

"That you would remain as head football coach, has, as you know, at all times been our earnest hope; in this hope the board had at no time authorized and consequently the director of athletics had not undertaken any consideration whatsoever of a possible successor.

"You may rest assured that you will have in the future, as you have had in the past, the respect and wholehearted support of the athletic board. We re-affirm our confidence in you as a leader in the field of sports, not alone because of the successes of your teams but even more because of your outstanding contribution to good character and citizenship through the development in those teams of fine sportsmanship and indomitable courage.

"Yours in loyalty to Ohio State"
(Signed) Ralph Paffenbarger,
(secretary)
Frank R. Strong, (chairman)

The Blizzard Bowl —
November 25, 1950

"...And the snow came down horizontally."

That was the late John McNulty's "lead" in the *New Yorker* magazine following the Ohio State-Michigan game of November 25, 1950.

You had to be there to believe it. Even then, some were not so sure they were viewing reality.

The game has been called the "blizzard bowl," "snow bowl," "ice bowl," and other names less complimentary.

"Blizzard" probably is the most appropriate. It almost obliterated vision between the field and stands. More than 82,000 tickets were sold, but only 50,503 fans showed up. Some of these hardy souls might not have come except that Ohio State was playing Michigan, with the Rose Bowl on the line for the Wolverines. Some fans may have been fooled at first by the weatherman. Because the weatherman, in turn, was completely fooled by the sudden polar conditions that hit Columbus Saturday morning. Weather conditions on Friday had been normal, cool, with no precipitation.

But by 10:00 a.m. Saturday the stadium looked like a scene from Admiral Byrd's expedition. Stadium seats were ice-covered and getting thicker by the minute as snow, accompanied by a biting wind, froze as it landed.

Nearly all of the spectators present were huddled in "B" deck, sheltered from the snow by the top deck. They were not protected from the wind, however, which swept in from the open end of the horseshoe and circled them like a giant lasso.

Fans were wearing all of the clothes they could use, some weighted down so much they could scarcely move. Some clear-thinkers covered their heads with cardboard boxes as a shield against the wind, now blowing 40 miles an hour. Slits, carefully cut on one side, allowed for what vision was available. The temperature, in the thirties early Saturday morning, dropped to five above zero during the game.

Scheduled to start at 2:00 p.m., the game was 20 minutes late getting under way, largely due to the ground crew having

great difficulty removing the tarpaulin, which had been left on the field until nearly noon. The snow-covered tarp, valued at $3,000, was then cut to shreds to facilitate removal. Boy Scouts, spectators, and game officials joined the ground crew which was forced to use a road grader with little success.

Meanwhile rival athletic directors, Richard Larkins of Ohio State and Fritz Crisler of Michigan, debated what to do: cancel, postpone, or play.

No Big Ten football game had ever been postponed, and

while weather conditions were bad at all other conference sites that day no thought was given to calling off the contests, rumors to the contrary.

Thousands of fans thought the game should not have been played, but they did not have any answers for the problems of refunding money. A postponement would have carried the game into December, and later events proved that the following Saturday was almost as bad, weather-wise.

A glance at the Big Ten standing prior to the game posed a few problems, too, and both athletic directors were aware of them. Ohio State was leading, 5-1, followed by Illinois, 4-1, and Michigan, 3-1-1, with Wisconsin also in contention with 4-2.

The Buckeyes were not Rose Bowl candidates but the other three were. Ohio State could have "backed into" the title by not playing and could cop the crown by winning. Later events proved that Illinois "blew" the Rose Bowl trip by losing to underdog Northwestern, and the Badgers were eliminated when Ohio State lost.

It was an incredible turn of circumstances that put Michigan on top as well as in the Rose Bowl.

Since Larkins was the home boss, it was his decision to make, and when he and Crisler were unable to contact commissioner Kenneth L. (Tug) Wilson relative to what action to take, the Ohio State athletic director said, "Let's play." For some time Larkins took a lot of "guff" from people who never would have said a word if Ohio State had won.

It was a great day for the second-guessers.

The play-by-play and statistics of the game were as bizarre as the weather.

The first scoring play not only put Ohio State ahead 3 to 0 but proved to be, in the judgement of veteran press box observers, the greatest field goal and single effort they had ever seen on a football field—if indeed the stadium ground could have been called a field that day.

With wind, snow, sleet, and numb hands as handicaps, Vic Janowicz kicked a field goal from the 28-yard line that had to have a lot of leg power to split the uprights. People are still talking about that one. Many writers said they would vote for Janowicz' effort as the biggest single achievement of the 1950 football season.

Shortly afterward, also in the first period, Janowicz cleared a spot in the end zone in an effort to punt out, but the kick was blocked and rolled out-of-bounds for a safety.

Then the game-breaker occurred, a play that has caused nearly a quarter century of discussion. With the ball in possession of the Buckeyes on their own 12-yard line and 40 seconds left to play in the half, Janowicz attempted to punt. It was blocked by Michigan's Tony Momsen, and he recovered for a touchdown. The extra point was good. It had been a third down punting attempt, and Fesler was roundly criticized for not stalling out the clock, a decision which reasonably could have accounted for a 3 to 2 Ohio State victory.

Desperation passing occupied the second half, and neither team came close to scoring.

The statistics defied reason. Michigan had won without making a first down and gained only 27 yards on the ground. Ohio State gained 16. Michigan threw 9 passes and did not complete 1. Ohio State threw 18 and completed 3 for 25 yards. There were 2 interceptions. Ohio State had 3 first downs, 2 by rushing and 1 by passing. Michigan fumbled 6 times and lost the ball once, while Ohio State fumbled 4 times, and likewise gave up the ball once.

There were 45 punts in the game, a Big Ten record. Janowicz kicked 21 times for a 32-yard average, but 2 blocked punts cost Ohio State 9 points. "Chuck" Ortmann of Michigan kicked 24 times for a 30-yard average. His only blocked punt gave Ohio State field position for Janowicz' first quarter field goal.

The Momsen brothers, Bob playing for Ohio State and Tony for Michigan, were big factors in the outcome. Bob blocked the first period kick, and Tony got the big one in the second period as well as the touchdown.

So the game that many said should not have been played was played, and the Buckeyes again lost to Michigan. Fesler, who objected to starting the game in the first place, had failed to beat the Wolverines in four tries. Once more it was the pressure of losing to Michigan that discouraged another Ohio State coach.

Wesley Fesler Resigns

When Fesler resigned in Chicago during the Big Ten meetings December 9, 1950, it created a precedent in Ohio State coaching circles. Never before had a coach resigned while outside Columbus. However President Howard Bevis, Athletic Director Richard Larkins and Faculty Representative Wendell Postle, who also were in Chicago, wanted Fesler to make up his mind. He had said that he "would not coach again for a million dollars," yet there seemed to be some doubt that he could be serious.

When, late Saturday night, it was determined that Fesler meant what he said, it created quite a stir in Chicago newspaper circles. The late Arch Ward, sports editor of the *Tribune,* who had departed for home, returned to the office to direct activities which resulted in a page one story. Newspapermen from other cities in the Big Ten bombarded the Ohio State headquarters in the LaSalle Hotel until early hours Sunday morning seeking details.

The athletic board accepted Fesler's resignation January 17, 1951, which was to become effective February 28. Immediately Fesler accepted the head coaching job at Minnesota, and two assistant coaches, Dick Fisher and Lyal Clark, went with him.

It became necessary to reorganize the football coaching staff, and president Bevis requested the chairman to appoint a screening committee to survey the field of eligible candidates and report to the athletic board.

After Fesler's coaching career ended at Ohio State, he told the author, "My entre into Ohio State football in 1947 was an experience I would not have missed for anything—but I would not want to repeat it for the world.

"It came at a really rough time. The records will show that the 1946 season, before I arrived, was a tough one, finishing with that horrendous loss to Michigan. Then the Cleveland Browns went to work, taking what was left. First went captain-elect Tommy James, then Adamle, Cline, and others.

"The 1947 spring practice was anything but hopeful, yet on the other hand was exciting. Even though our immediate future looked dismal, we all became sincerely dedicated to a goal. Every thought, every movement was pledged to that goal. In three years we were going to be in the Rose Bowl and have fun doing it.

"Football, by its very nature, means hard, brutally hard, work. Yet I know from my own undergraduate experience it can, and should be fun. There is plenty of room for laughter on a football field, and, as a coach, I have tried desperately hard to encourage it.

"I sincerely hope that the 1947, 1948, 1949, and 1950 men look back on those days with the fond memories I do."

Chairman Frank Strong presented the following resolution as an expression of the athletic board to Wesley E. Fesler:

"The athletic board keenly regrets, Wes, your decision to give up the position of head football coach at the university. You have exemplified fully the type of coaching leadership under which we desire the young men of this university to participate in competitive sport. It has ever been, as you know, the board's earnest hope that you would remain in this capacity as a part of the university community.

"Although you have now determined to sever this connection, you continue to hold our respect and sincere regard. Firmly assured that you will, in the years that lie ahead, retain for your alma mater that same outstanding loyalty which you have shown in the past, the board joins thousands of other well-wishers in hoping for you satisfying success and happiness."

The athletic council, at the suggestion of director of athletics Richard C. Larkins, should have a screening committee to study the backgrounds of all candidates interested in succeeding Wesley E. Fesler as head football coach.

Chairman Frank Strong then appointed Larkins; vice-president, registrar Bland Stradley, professor Hermann C. Miller, Fred C. Mackey, alumni member, and Walter Donham, student member. Strong also served on the committee.

The function of this committee, the board minutes said, will be to survey the entire range of possible candidates for the position of head football coach at the Ohio State University and to screen the names of those considered for presentation by the director of athletics to the athletic board.

The athletic board, after consideration, will transmit its nomination to the president of the university, who, in turn, will present it to the board of trustees for its final action.

It was the sentiment of the board that "much care should be exercised before giving statements to the press regarding the new head coach."

No information should be divulged to anyone, the board ruled, unless official approval was given through the proper channels.

Woody Hayes Selected

After Wes Fesler's resignation was accepted by the athletic board on January 17, 1951, to become effective February 28, forty candidates applied for the head coaching position. Included were five from the professional ranks, twenty-six from colleges, six from high schools, and three who were inactive at the time. Only eight were screened.

Inasmuch as four head coaches had been on the job since Paul Brown's last year in 1943, the screening committee established elaborate qualifications. They wanted the man selected to stick around awhile and remove Ohio State from the label of "graveyard of coaches." The man they selected not only is still around, but he has moved the "graveyard" to other premises.

The committee declared that the man "should be a person of both intellectual and moral integrity, a gentleman in the best sense of the word: that he be suited by temperament, interest, and background for productive work with young men, for cooperative advancement of the present sports program of the department of physical education and athletics, and for professorial membership in the university faculty. He is to be, by proven capacity and experience, skilled in football technique, in the effective teaching of the game, and in the organization and direction of a staff of coaching and administrative assistants."

There was more!

Personal qualifications included headings of personality,

character, conduct, and family. (He was to have a wife). Personal qualifications included headings of coaching ability, coaching attitude, and coaching reputation.

University qualifications came under three categories: departmental, all-university, and the public. Departmental included acceptability, cooperativeness, accountability to superiors, and genuineness of interest in the total sports program. The all-university was acceptability, cooperativeness in general university objectives, undivided loyalty to the university, attitude on football in total educational pattern, and educational background.

In regard to the public he was to have good press relations, be of ambassadorial capacity and, in general, have a good reputation.

It was evident that the committee had not forgotten anything.

Two candidates from the professional ranks wished their names to be held confidential, and their desires were respected. Paul Brown, Buckeye coach for three years, 1941, 1942, and 1943, and for five years after the war with the Cleveland professional team bearing his name, made an earnest bid to regain his old job.

Richard C. Larkins, director of athletics, stated flatly that he would resign if Brown was selected. This seemed to seal Brown out of contention, despite strong support of the *Columbus Dispatch* and other groups.

Larkins then offered the following proposal to the board: "That the athletic board recommend to the board of trustees, the appointment of Wayne Woodrow Hayes as head football coach for one year, at a salary of $12,500, with the possibility of advancement of $500 a year in succeeding years, until the maximum of $15,000 is reached."

A motion was made, seconded, and passed unanimously.

The late Lew Byrer, former sports editor of the *Columbus Citizen,* once told a cub reporter that information regarding Ohio State football, particularly the coaching staff, was the most important news in the city.

"We do not care," he said, "what happens in the statehouse, courthouse, city hall, or any place else by comparison. Ohio State football comes first."

Woody Hayes

There was evidence on Monday, February 12, 1951, to support Mr. Byrer's position. At least the board of trustees felt that the appointment of a new football coach required greater attention than had been focused on appointments of college deans.

A meeting of the athletic board had been called for 9:00 a.m. in the office of Vice-President Bland Stradley. It was for the purpose of relaying word to the trustees that Woody Hayes had been approved as head coach.

Word came back that "Because three members of the board of trustees have found it impossible to be present at today's meeting, and feeling that a matter of this importance should have the consideration of a larger representation of the board, a special meeting has been called for Sunday, February 18, at 4:00 p.m."

Thus, at an unprecedented Sunday meeting, Hayes was approved after considerable discussion, much of it still centering on Paul Brown.

Once more, Buckeye football was Page One news.

When Hayes was being screened for the head coaching job, he did not wait for members of the committee to ask questions. He started right in telling why he wanted the position, how he considered it his greatest opportunity and challenge, and expressing confidence he could handle all facets of the job.

He explained that since both his father and mother had been school teachers he was accustomed to the educational side of life. Hard work, sound fundamentals, and well-conditioned athletes would be adhered to, Woody seriously explained. He said he would pick assistants who would be willing to work at a fast pace or they would not be working at all. In recruiting, he said, education would be stressed above everything else.

Someone asked Hayes, "How about practice on Friday afternoons?"

Hayes replied, "There will be no practice on Friday. By that time, the hay is in the barn."

Vice-President Bland Stradley, an influential member of the committee, and a farming educator, seemed impressed by this homespun remark.

Hayes later said he felt he had the job won, judging from the expression on Stradley's face.

He was right.

Hayes came to Ohio State with an all-Ohio coaching career behind him, having started as an assistant at Mingo Junction, Ohio, High School. His first head coaching job came at New Philadelphia, Ohio, High. At this point he enlisted in the navy and served five years. Following his discharge he received his first opportunity to become a head college coach, and it was at his alma mater, Denison University, at Granville, Ohio, in 1946.

He coached for 3 years at Denison and 2 at Miami University, at Oxford, before coming to Ohio State. His Denison teams won 19 and lost 6, and the 1947 and 1948 teams were undefeated after a 1-6 season in 1946. At Miami his 1949 team was 5-4, and in 1950 the team won 9 of 10 games.

A 1935 graduate of Denison, Hayes majored in English and history. He played tackle for three years and was an outfielder in baseball. He holds a master's degree in education administration from Ohio State University.

Hayes, who has made four trips to Vietnam to discuss football with the United States military personnel, is a tireless worker in behalf of his job. He likewise is a fluent speaker, an outstanding recruiter, and a meticulous planner.

His 23-year record as he goes into the 1974 Buckeye season is 192-60-8 for .762, and in the Big Ten the record is 119-32-7 for a percentage of .788.

There have been 22 Big Ten football coaches who have served 10 or more years in the conference, and Hayes is the only one still active. Only 3 coaches were on the job longer than Hayes...Amos Alonzo Stagg at Chicago, 41 seasons; Robert C. Zuppke at Illinois, 29; and Fielding H. Yost at Michigan, 25.

Never one to downgrade his team, or the opposition either, Woody Hayes always has been an optimist. While some coaches have been known to build up the opponents to the point of making their own team an underdog and soliciting sympathy for the "down-trodden" home forces, Hayes always gives Buckeye fans a favorable trend.

"We figure to win," is his favorite, almost off-hand prediction.

Records show he has been right more than three-fourths of the time. He went into the 1973 season with a remarkable percentage of .753, based on 149 victories against 49 losses and

143

Woody Hayes on the sidelines

7 ties. Only Paul (Bear) Bryant among active college coaches has won more games. Three years at Denison University, his alma mater, and two at Miami of Ohio, gave him an overall record of 182-60 and virtually the same percentage of .752.

Hayes has been described as a man of many moods and contrasts.

He will be the first to say that he is difficult to work with, but he also will add, "I think I am fair."

Esco Sarkkinen, veteran end coach, who has been on the Ohio State staff since 1946, five years before Hayes arrived, and who has been with Woody each season, says, "You do not describe Hayes in one word, one sentence, or even one paragraph, but in chapter after chapter."

Hayes does not lose his poise too often during a game, probably less than the average head coach on the sidelines.

During practice, however, it is another story. He has broken countless watches and eye-glasses when a play goes wrong. He wears a baseball cap at all times, that is while it still is in one piece. The caps join the watches and glasses in being shredded. Once Woody had the equipment man slit the seams with a razor blade, making the cap easier to rip.

Hayes laughs off cold weather, usually wearing only a T-shirt at practice and games.

One player contends that it is always possible to tell when trouble is brewing. "He will whip off his cap with his right hand, shoot his hair back with his left (Woody is left-handed), and slam his cap back on. Then you know a play has gone haywire."

Hayes' many antics have made the headlines. Unfortunately his humanitarian deeds have not had as much exposure.

In recent years he has, in order, loaned money to players, which cost Ohio State a year of probation; evicted Big Ten writers and officials from preseason practice; had locker room battles with California sportswriters; ripped sideline down markers; had an altercation with a Los Angeles photographer; and has stuck by his ban on player interviews, which has infuriated many sportswriters.

Woody has had no trouble enlisting jeers and boos from the stands as his biggest cut-ups have been when the Buckeyes have played on the road. This has been particularly true at Iowa and Michigan where he has thrown his coat, kicked folding chairs, and booted a sideline marker which he thought was rubber. It turned out to be concrete, which must have pained him considerably, but he never limped to show it.

Woody's wife Ann, his best friend and severest critic, is proudest of his four Vietnam trips, and for his role in campus riots a few years ago. "He came back with several notebooks filled with names of parents, wives, and girlfriends. If he could not contact them by phone, he wrote to them. He did not overlook one person," says Anne.

Woody turned down a fifth opportunity to visit Vietnam in an effort to quell campus disturbances. According to Mrs. Hayes, Woody was on the campus every day and every night making speeches in dormitories in an effort to steer certain people in the right direction. He usually made his point.

Hayes is held in high regard by his fellow coaches, many of whom have wanted to join the Ohio State staff whenever there has been an opening. Seven of his former assistants hold prominent head coaching positions: John Pont of Northwestern; Carmen Cozza, Yale; Lou Holtz, North Carolina State; Earle Bruce, Iowa State; Bo Schembechler, Michigan; Bill Hess, Ohio University; and Bill Mallory of Miami of Ohio. Another assistant, Clive Rush, is a former head coach of the Boston Patriots.

Players as well as the assistant coaches know that he has their best interests at heart. He drives the players academically as well as physically. His irritation, call it temper, comes to the surface quickly when he detects a loafer, on or off the field. Someone asked what made Woody fly off the handle quicker than anything else. The answer is simple: when he saw someone not performing up to his potential.

Woody works seven days a week, 12 to 14 hours, and he cannot understand why everyone else cannot do the same.

Writing the foreword in Woody's recent book, *You Win With People,* Paul Hornung of the *Columbus Dispatch* says: "...this could only lead to Wayne Woodrow Hayes, my own nomination as the original "Most Unforgettable Character I Have Ever Met."

There is one thing about Woody on which everyone agrees. He will never be accused of being a phoney or something artificial, even if some people have, as Hornung points out, accused him of lack of diplomacy.

But returning to Woody's practice of not offering an alibi. Webster defines an optimist as: (1) "The doctrine that the world is the best possible world; (2) The doctrine that reality is essentially good; (3) The doctrine that the good of life overbalances the pain and evil of it; (4) An inclination to put the most favorable construction upon actions and happenings, or anticipate the best possible outcome."

With an English major behind him, as well as one in history, it has been said Woody knows the meaning of every word in the dictionary.

The above defines himself.

Woody Wins First One

As soon as Woody Hayes was hired as football coach, he went right to work preparing for his first opponent, Southern Methodist, a highly-regarded team with forward passing ace Fred Benners leading the attack. The Mustangs had a winning streak going, during which they had scored handily on all opponents, so it was with considerable surprise that the Buckeyes not only won but shut out the Texans 7 to 0. Benners completed 21 of 29 passes but never connected on a long one. Ohio State intercepted 5 passes, and, while Woody's T-formation was hit-and-miss, 1 touchdown stood up. A pass from Tony Curcillo to Bob Joslin accounted for the touchdown, and Vic Janowicz added the extra point.

The Buckeye victory prompted Wilfrid Smith, former sports editor of the *Chicago Tribune*, who covered the game, to say afterward, "Woody must have worked all summer on that game. He was really out to win the first one."

The next foe, Michigan State, had been admitted to the Big Ten, but its games were not to count in the standings until 1953. It was a rugged, high-scoring game, the Buckeyes losing 24 to 20 when the Spartans came from behind with a last-minute touchdown. While the outcome did not handicap Ohio State in the standings, fans groaned over losing to a team not yet a Big Ten neophyte. Later events proved that the Buckeyes had little to be ashamed of, as the Spartans finished the season undefeated, as they also did in 1952.

Hayes was far from satisfied with his first season of 4-3-2,

147

the same that Paul Bixler had had in 1946. Woody later said he feared that he might be asked to step down since he was on a one-year contract. "Fortunately, Director Larkins stuck with me, and I was determined to work all the harder to justify his confidence," Hayes said later.

The team lost to Indiana and Michigan, in addition to Michigan State, and the tie games were with Wisconsin, 6-6, and Illinois, 0-0. Woody was disappointed in the tie with Wisconsin as the team failed to move the ball as it had the previous week against Michigan State. The tie game with Illinois was the only contest the Illini did not win in an undefeated season that included a Rose Bowl victory over Stanford, 40-7. Wisconsin also had a great year of 7-1-1. On the other hand the one-sided loss to underdog Indiana was a shocker. The Hoosiers did not win another conference game and finished 2-7.

The second season saw a big improvement, a 6-3 year and 5-2 in the league. The big victory was over Michigan 27-7, the first one since 1944. Following on the heels of a 27-7 victory over Illinois the previous week, fans were inclined to forget annoying losses to Purdue, Iowa, and Pittsburgh, games that could have been won as easily as they were lost. The team featured a dazzling freshman named Howard (Hopalong) Cassady and one of Ohio State's most admired quarterbacks, John Borton.

The same record, 6-3, was repeated in 1953, and the three losses were no flukes. Illinois' halfback combination of J. C. Caroline and Mickey Bates ran the Buckeyes dizzy in front of the home folks, 41 to 20. Ray Eliot, Illini coach at the time, said it was one of his greatest victories.

Michigan State, now having its games counted in the standings, defeated the Buckeyes 28 to 13 to tie Illinois for the championship and represent the Big Ten in the Rose Bowl, where it defeated UCLA, 28 to 20. The other loss was to nemesis Michigan, 20 to 0.

This was the year of elimination of the platoon system and of offensive and defensive specialists, at least for the time being. Hayes made numerous shifts to get the best football players in the game for the greatest length of time. His linemen, Dick Hilinski, George Jacoby, Jerry Krisher, Mike Takacs, and Jim Reichenbach, were strong and durable. Often the Buckeyes played with the fewest substitutions in the Big Ten. Backfield men Borton, Bobby Watkins, Dave Leggett, and Cassady, were just as rugged.

Despite fair success with the new rules Hayes was angry about the necessity of playing "one-way" football. He insisted that the rule was ill-advised and made effective too quickly. The players agreed with him, as a vote revealed a 40 to 2 count in favor of the two-platoon system.

But, in spite of "one-way" football, Hayes was working hard toward developing a championship team. Writing in his column, "Letters From Home," Jack Fullen, editor of the *Alumni Monthly*, said "While other coaches are hunting, fishing, playing cards or golf, Woody Hayes is running off pictures and plotting strategy...He is one of the most persuasive and forceful recruiters of talent we have ever had."

Later, Hayes and Fullen were to feud violently, but there was no indication of that here.

National Championship: 1954

The Buckeyes hit the jackpot in 1954. An improvement had been expected over the previous season, but just how much had been anybody's guess. The 1953 team had given up 164 points with all opponents scoring from 6 to 41 points. The Buckeyes had totaled 182. Obviously the defense had to be improved.

An important addition to the offense was Hubert Bobo, a tough sophomore, who could run, block, and play defense. He fitted in well with Cassady, Leggett, Borton, and Watkins.

The Buckeyes swept by Indiana 28-0, California 21-13, and Illinois 40-7 before being pushed to the hilt to stop Iowa, 20-14. The Buckeyes had to stop the Hawkeyes on the five-yard line to preserve the decision.

That brought Wisconsin to Ohio Stadium in a showdown between two of the nation's leading teams. Little Tad Weed kicked a field goal for the Buckeyes for a 3 to 0 lead, but before the half the Badgers scored on a 35-yard pass and kicked the extra point for a 7-3 lead at intermission.

Toward the end of the third period a play occurred that turned the game around, sky-rocketed Cassady toward all-American fame, and started the Buckeyes to the 1954 pinnacle. With Wisconsin on the Ohio State 20, "Hopalong" intercepted Bob Miller's pass on the 12 and returned 88 yards in one of the most thrilling runs in stadium history. He zig-zagged, feinted and, with what Woody called "down field vision," left a flock of would-be Badger tackles scattered all over the field.

150

Anticipating a great game, the press box was loaded with the nation's leading writers. Cassady made the all-American team right then and there.

With the Buckeyes leading 10-7 at the end of three periods, the Badgers folded to the extent of giving up three touchdowns, the first of which was set up by another long run by Cassady, one of 39 yards. Bobo, Jerry Harkrader, and Leggett added touchdowns before Wisconsin scored with four minutes left. The 31 to 14 decision came right in the middle of the season, and now there was no looking back.

There was a natural letdown the following week at Northwestern, and injuries to Bobo, guard Jim Parker, and end Dick Brubaker added to the difficulties. Cassady played the entire game with a bruised leg. With the score 7-7 going into the final period the Buckeyes pulled out the decision on a pass from Leggett to Watkins, and the latter kicked the extra point for a hard-fought 14-7 verdict.

Pittsburgh was blanked 26 to 0, the first shutout since the opener with Indiana, and Purdue was jolted 28 to 6. The Boilermakers were beaten with long runs by Cassady and Watkins, a 79-yard scoring march, and a pass from Leggett to Brubaker, one of just nine thrown that afternoon.

That brought on the showdown with Michigan in Ohio Stadium, where all tickets had been sold for several weeks. The Buckeyes were leading the Big Ten with a 6-0 record, and the Wolverines were 5-1 with a chance to tie for the title, if they could win. All other contenders had been eliminated.

The Associated Press rated Ohio State No. 1 in the country, followed by UCLA and Oklahoma. The UPI had UCLA first, followed by Ohio State, with Oklahoma third.

As is so often the case, bad weather haunted the game, and rain fell during the morning hours. Hayes wanted the bands kept off the field to preserve the turf, but he was overruled by the university presidents, Dr. Howard Bevis of Ohio State and Dr. Harlan Hatcher of Michigan.

When Michigan took the opening kickoff and scored without losing the ball in 6 minutes and 28 seconds, Buckeye fans were stunned. Nothing like this had happened to their favorites in a long time.

An intercepted pass by Jack Gibbs put the Buckeyes back

151

The 1954 team was a national champion contender following seven conference victories and intersectional triumphs over California and Pittsburgh. Led by all-American and Heisman

in business with less than 3 minutes left in the half. Gibbs caught the ball on Ohio's 43 and returned to Michigan's 10 before he was caught. After a penalty for delay of game, Leggett passed to Fred Kriss for a touchdown, and Weed kicked the tying point. Both Gibbs and Kriss were third stringers going into the game, but at half time they were real heroes.

Neither team scored in the third quarter, but momentum was going Michigan's way and when the final period opened, Michigan had a first down on Ohio's four-yard line. It looked like bad news for the Buckeyes, but four cracks at the line left the Wolverines one foot shy of the goal line, big Jim Parker leading the stonewall defense.

The events which followed have caused Hayes to describe

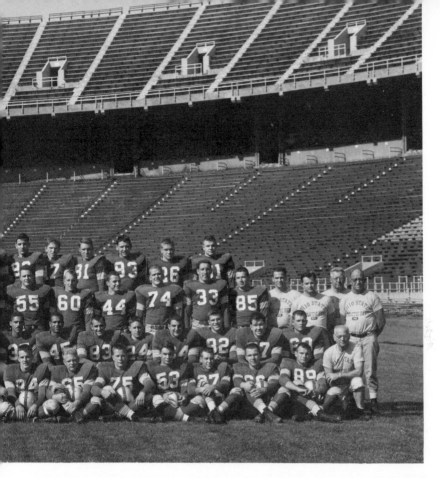

award winner Howard (Hopalong) Cassady, the team defeated Southern California in the Rose Bowl 20 to 7.

them many times as "the greatest thing that has happened in my coaching experience."

What did happen was a march of 99 yards and 2 feet for a touchdown. As usual Cassady supplied the important punch, a 61-yard run from the Ohio 2 to the Michigan 37. After 2 first downs worked the ball to the Michigan 8, Leggett passed to Brubaker for a touchdown and Weed again made the extra point.

The Wolverines suffered a case of jitters at this point and not only fumbled but were penalized for offside. In addition passers slipped while throwing, and Cassady intercepted one, returning it 13 yards. That was the clincher. The Buckeyes never gave up the ball until Cassady scored from the one-yard line. Again Weed split the uprights.

Thus the Buckeyes had their first undefeated, untied team since 1944 and became the second Big Ten team to go through a seven-game conference schedule without defeat. The other was the Chicago team of 1913, the year Ohio State entered the conference.

After the game Hayes not only was carried off the field but was dunked, fully clothed, in the shower. Once in a dry suit Hayes told the press that Cassady had been the big difference with his long runs and pass interception while Parker had supplied the defensive strength.

"Michigan won the first half," Hayes pointed out, "but the second was the reverse. You have to be lucky to go through a season undefeated, and luck came our way. Cassady is a true all-American. He should get the Heisman award."

Statistics showed that Michigan made 15 first downs to 13 for Ohio State and outgained the Buckeyes 303 yards to 254. But, as Hayes said in the post-game conference, Ohio State's defense was geared to stop touchdowns. There was no question about it, stopping Michigan at the one-foot mark turned the game around.

Michigan out-punted the Buckeyes by an average of 42 yards to 24, but 3 pass interceptions were returned for 62 yards, 2 leading to touchdowns. Michigan also lost the ball twice on fumbles. Cassady was the leading ground gainer, netting 94 yards in 14 carries for an average of 6.7. Bobo netted 52 in 7 tries for 7.3. The Buckeyes again played it "close to the vest" personnel-wise. With fullback Watkins out of the game with an injury, only 5 backs were used, compared to 8 by Michigan.

After four years both Hayes and Ohio State football were "tops."

Rose Bowl — January 1, 1955

Never before had it rained on a Rose Bowl crowd, but the first day of January, 1955, spiked the record with a vengeance. Not only did it pour all day, but fog and cool weather added to the woes of the players and fans alike. The miserable conditions were more depressing to Trojan followers, however, as the Buckeyes won the mud battle, 20 to 7.

Whereas Ohio State was undefeated over a nine-game schedule, the Trojans had played 11 games, winning 8. Two of their three losses came in the last two games of the season against UCLA and Notre Dame. UCLA, ranked No. 1 nationally but ineligible to play in the Rose Bowl, had trounced the Trojans 34 to 0, and many west coast fans were annoyed with the rule that prevented the Uclans from tackling the Buckeyes. They had appeared in the bowl the year before, losing to Michigan State. The late "Red" Sanders, UCLA coach, was named coach of the year, Hayes being runnerup. Woody did not complain about playing second fiddle to Sanders, but he was disturbed about the Uclans being No. 1 in the polls. He was positive he had a point that Ohio State had played a stronger schedule than UCLA. Even some of the west coast critics agreed with him.

After both teams oozed around in a scoreless first period, the Buckeyes, thanks to a recovered fumble by Jim Parker, went 69 yards without giving up the ball. On the second play of the second quarter Leggett sneaked over from the three. The Trojans were offside, but the penalty was declined and Tad

Rain, fog, mud, and cool weather met Rose Bowl fans on January 1, 1955. Here quarterback Dave Leggett of the Buckeyes is scoring on a line smash 35 seconds into the second quarter. Leggett was named the most valuable player in the game, won by Ohio State over USC 20 to 7.

Weed booted the extra point.

Following the ensuing kickoff Joe Contratto's slippery pitchout to Jon Arnett went wild, and Leggett recovered on the Trojan 35.

Bobby Watkins smashed through tackle for 14 yards and on the next play caught a pass from Leggett for a touchdown. He grabbed the ball on the 7 while running at full speed and carried a couple of Trojans over the goal with him. Weed kicked the 14th point, and the Buckeyes had gotten all of their points in 1 minute and 20 seconds.

With 9 minutes left in the half Bobo punted to Aramis Dandoy on the Trojan 14 and, with fine blocking ahead of him, went 86 yards for a touchdown. When Sam Tsagalakis kicked the extra point the Trojans were back in the game, they thought.

The field, now muddier than in the first half, held the offenses down in the third quarter, neither team scoring. With 2 minutes and 10 seconds gone in the fourth quarter, Leggett took charge and directed the team for 77 yards, passing to Jerry Harkrader from the 9-yard line for a touchdown. This time Weed's kick was blocked.

The Buckeyes again were knocking at the door with three minutes left, but Leggett's pass was intercepted on the USC 10-yard line. It was the only time during the game that a Trojan had stepped in front of a Buckeye receiver.

Statistics were top-heavy in favor of the winners, who piled up 22 first downs to 6 for USC. Total yards gained

Dave Leggett

favored the Buckeyes 360 to 206, and Leggett, who was named "player of the game," completed 6 of 11 passes for 65 yards. The Trojans were able to complete only 3 of 8 for 29 yards. Ohio State lost the slippery ball only once, but the Trojans gave up 3 fumbles. Punting was outstanding considering the playing conditions, and the Trojans had this average edge, 46 to 38.

Ohio State rushed the ball 69 times compared to the

Coach Woody Hayes (left) does not seem to be as happy as he should be. His Buckeyes have just defeated Southern California 20 to 7 in the rain-drenched Rose Bowl game of January 1, 1955. However Hayes is telling reporters that the bands should not have been permitted on the field at half-time because playing conditions then became intolerable.

Trojans' 28, with Cassady carrying 21 times for a net of 92. Leggett carried 16 for 67, gaining every time he handled the ball. It was his perfect ball-handling that earned him the "most valuable" award and was a tremendous factor in the victory. Watkins was right behind with 64 yards in 15 tries. Bobby was a ball of fire all afternoon and seemed oblivious to the hazardous running conditions. Harkrader had the highest average of 7 yards, with 49 gained in 7 trips.

After the game Hayes had the first of many controversies with the west coast writers. He said that at least five teams in the Big Ten could have defeated the Trojans, and this was taken in some quarters as an insult to west coast football. He was merely giving an honest answer to an honest question, but it was not accepted in that light.

Hayes also criticized the bands being on the field at half time. He made it clear that he thought that the musicians chopped up the grass too much for second half play. Since the university had gone to great expense and much trouble to get the 120-piece marching band to Pasadena, this even back-fired on the home front.

Ohio State fans went back to the Huntington Hotel wet but happy. Many of them never dried out until they returned to Columbus where the cleaners made extra revenue trying to get coats, suits, and dresses back in shape.

The date of January 2 dawned warm and clear with no sign of the previous day's disturbance. The day was made even brighter when word was received just before the squad left for the depot that the Football Writers' Association, ignoring the opinion of wire service polls, had voted Ohio State No. 1 for 1954.

1955 — Another
Big Ten Championship

Many of the stars of 1954 were back again, so it was with great optimism and fanfare that the 1955 campaign was welcomed. Cassady was ready to go again and so was Don Vicic, a powerful fullback, who made people scatter when he barged into them. All-American Jim Parker was set to anchor the forward wall; Fred Kriss was available for place-kicking chores; and some good-looking sophomores were considered to have enough talent to start.

After a 28 to 20 win over Nebraska, Stanford stopped the Buckeyes cold at Palo Alto, 6 to 0. It was just the second time the Buckeyes had been shut out since the Iowa game of 1952. The Cardinals trained on Cassady, who was held to 37 yards in 11 carries. Stanford took the opening kickoff and went 69 yards for the touchdown, something few teams had done to the Buckeyes in recent games. The score came on a 2-yard pass, breaking Ohio State's 11-game winning streak.

The Buckeyes were ready for Illinois at home the following Saturday, stopping the Illini 27 to 12, with Cassady scoring 2 touchdowns.

It was a real oddity that this powerful team should lose another non-conference game, but Duke took the measure of the Buckeyes, 20 to 14. It was the first showing of the Blue Devils in Ohio Stadium, and they made the most of their opportunity. Hayes was disappointed after the game but praised Duke and said that the visitors deserved to win.

Getting back on the Big Ten winning streak again, the

Buckeyes rolled over Wisconsin, Northwestern, Indiana, and Iowa to make it 12 league victories in a row. The Badgers and Wildcats did not present too many problems, but Indiana and Iowa applied the pressure, striving for an upset. The Hoosiers finally bowed 20-13, and Iowa was out-lasted 20 to 10.

Both Michigan and Michigan State were in the running to go to the Rose Bowl when Ohio State invaded Ann Arbor for the season's finale. The Buckeyes were in front with 5-0, followed by Michigan with 5-1, and Michigan State at 4-1. The Spartans, who had plenty of fans in Ann Arbor that day, needed an Ohio State victory to send their favorites to Pasadena for the second time in three years.

Hayes had said that the 1954 game with Michigan was his favorite victory, but the 1955 battle with the Wolverines must have given it a run for the money. The first game featured offense and this one defense, for Michigan was to cross the midfield stripe only once this afternoon, that on a penalty.

Wearers of the Maize and Blue seemed completely frustrated, particularly in the fourth quarter when they were penalized three times for unsportsmanlike conduct and once for unnecessary roughness. One player was expelled from the game and near fist-fights occurred on the field. Meanwhile, Michigan State fans in the stands were gleeful and shouting "unpack," just in case Wolverine followers had ideas of preparing for a Rose Bowl trip.

With 5:10 left in the half Kriss kicked a 24-yard field goal that was the only scoring before intermission. The Buckeyes put on a sustained drive midway in the third period, and Cassady scored from 2 yards out. The point was missed by Don Sutherin. With only 2:20 on the clock Bob Barr was thrown for a safety by Bill Michael, running the score up to 11-0. The real clincher came with only 1:15 remaining on the clock. Penalties moved the ball to the 1-yard line, and Vicic dove into the end zone. It mattered not that Sutherin again missed the extra point, as the score now was 17 to 0.

Fans flooded the field, and the Michigan goalposts came down.

Statistics were overwhelming in support of the Buckeyes except for punting, a category in which the Wolverines always have excelled. First downs were 20 to 5, and the net yards gained were 333 to 95. The Buckeyes attempted only 3 passes, completing 1 and intercepting 2. The Wolverines completed 3 of 9 attempts.

Cassady, with 146 yards, outgained the entire Michigan team by 51 yards, and hard-running Vicic averaged just under 5 yards with 81 in 17 tries. Sophomore Don Sutherin, who later was to be a big factor in Ohio State's kicking game, averaged better than 4 yards per try with 75 in 18 trips.

With two successive championships behind them, the players were as happy as any group of college players could be—and the happiest of all was Woody Hayes, who has said many times that the 1955 victory over Michigan comes close to being a "perfect game."

As usual Hayes did not flood the field with substitutions, only 21 players seeing action. Sutherin and Michael played the entire 60 minutes; Cassady missed only 30 seconds, the same as tackle Francis Machinsky; and Ellwood played 59. This was quite in contrast to the way 1955 had started, as 43 out of 44 players saw action in the Rose Bowl. Quarterback and co-captain John Borton voluntarily declined to play due to an injured finger on his right hand. Although Hayes wanted him to play, so that all members of the traveling squad would make an appearance, Borton said that he might make a ball-handling mistake which could prove costly. Besides, he said, Leggett was playing too well to be removed.

Such an attitude reflected the quality, dignity, and leadership of the 1955 team.

Howard Cassady — An Inspiration

Howard (Hopalong) Cassady, described by coach Woody Hayes as "the most inspirational player I have ever seen," came to Ohio State as a 150-pound freshman in 1952. He wound up being an all-American in successive years as well as the Big Ten's most valuable player in 1955.

In making the *Chicago Tribune's* Most Valuable Award to Cassady in January of 1956, Wilfrid Smith, former sports editor of that newspaper, said that "Howard Cassady is the greatest college football player I have ever watched."

Cassady scored three touchdowns in his first varsity game against Indiana and then gained 113 yards against Wisconsin in an upset victory over the Badgers. Avoiding injury during nearly all his varsity career, Cassady played in 36 of 37 games. During Cassady's four years on the varsity, Ohio State won 29 games and lost 8.

In Cassady's freshman season he rushed for 293 yards in 65 tries for an average of 4.5. Scoring 6 touchdowns he caught 13 passes for 192 yards, his total yardage being 485.

His sophomore year indicated what was to come later. He rushed for 514 yards in 86 carries for an average of 5.9, scored 8 touchdowns, caught 16 passes for 273 yards, and had a total yardage of 787.

When Cassady first made all-American in 1954 (a unanimous choice), he had total yardage of 849, based on 701 yards in rushing, 13 pass receptions for 148 yards, 8 touchdowns, and an average of 5.7. The 1954 team was undefeated in 10 games,

Howard (Hopalong) Cassady, described by Coach Woody Hayes as the most inspirational player, as well as the greatest Ohio State player he has had, twice was named all-American and was the Heisman Award winner in 1955. Cassady excelled in the art of "downfield vision."

including a 20-7 decision over USC in the Rose Bowl and was named No. 1 in several polls.

In Cassady's 1955 season, when he repeated as all-American and won the Heisman award, he starred in all games and helped the Buckeyes gain a 13-game winning streak in the Big Ten, later stretched to 17, a conference record. Cassady's 1955 yardage was his greatest—964 yards total, when he ran his

TD count to 15, bettering by one his combined freshman-sophomore total.

In addition to playing football Cassady was a shortstop-outfielder on the Ohio State baseball team for three years. He came to Ohio State from Columbus Central high school where he starred in basketball as well as baseball and football. After graduation Cassady played professional football with the Detroit Lions, Cleveland Browns, and Philadelphia Eagles.

CASSADY'S FOUR-YEAR STATISTICS

Year	Games	No. Of Rushes	Yds.	Ave.	TD	Passes Caught	Yds.	Total Yds.
1952	9	65	293	4.5	6	13	192	485
1953	9	86	514	5.9	8	16	273	787
1954	9	123	701	5.7	8	13	148	849
1955	9	161	958	5.9	15	1	6	964
4 Yr. Total	36	435	2466	5.6	37	43	619	3085

An amusing incident occurred toward the end of the 1955 season when the Buckeyes won their second straight Big Ten title and Howard (Hopalong) Cassady again was everybody's all-American. A long distance call came to the sports information office and the young lady on the phone introduced herself as being identified with a Catholic newspaper in Chicago.

"I thought you would like to know," she explained, "that your Mr. Howard Cassady has been named on the all-Catholic all-American team."

"I regret to tell you," a publicist informed her, "but Cassady is a Lutheran."

"Oh my God," the girl exclaimed, "that makes him ineligible."

It was the only time during Cassady's career that he was ineligible.

The following week he won the Heisman Trophy.

Probation In 1956

Probation came in 1956. It followed an investigation by Commissioner K. L. (Tug) Wilson into alleged irregularities by Ohio State football players and the "job program."

At a special meeting on January 22, 1956, the Ohio University athletic board met with Director Larkins and Coach Hayes for a discussion of plans, procedures, and problems of administering the intercollegiate football program. No action was taken, it was reported by Dr. James Pollard in his book, *Ohio State Athletics*.

Part of the difficulty, it was pointed out by Dr. Pollard, arose from the fact that Hayes had personally advanced small sums of money to individual players for immediate needs. The coach insisted it was a personal matter, freely admitting what he had done. It also was charged that varsity players received pay for jobs they did not do, in some cases merely appearing for their pay check. About 30 players were involved.

The matter was cleared up before the 1956 football season began by having the players do the work they were supposed to have completed. Meanwhile, the conference placed the Buckeyes on probation and made them ineligible to participate in the Rose Bowl, even if the team did win the title. Under the terms of the probation, all athletes who were involved in irregularities in the work program of 1955 had to repay fully in services the wages they had received. All of them did so before fall practice began.

The university accepted the punishment without protest,

but many felt that the infraction had been minor. Hayes, at the time, did not see any harm in giving some needy players a few dollars for essentials.

Writing in his book, *Hot Line to Victory*, Hayes devoted a paragraph to discipline. "Football," he wrote, "is discipline, discipline which starts with the coach, but must become the player's own discipline. Discipline is more than merely imposing plays, tactics, and techniques upon a player. For us discipline implies disciple, for the player will first believe in the coach as a person before he will fully accept the teachings of that coach. Obviously, the player-coach relationship is of paramount importance."

Hayes proved to be a good example of a man who not only demands discipline, but one who can accept it.

Jim Parker, one of Ohio State's all-time great guards and an all-American in 1955 and 1956, won the Outland trophy as a senior. He was all-pro nine years with the Baltimore Colts and recently was enshrined in the National Professional Football Hall of Fame at Canton, Ohio. Coach Woody Hayes credits Parker with having much to do with the Buckeyes' dynamic offense of that period. Parker was picked on the all-time team for the first 100 years of college football.

For the third time in a five-year period the Buckeyes were heading for a 6-3 season, this one coming in 1956. Despite the probation penalty hanging over their heads, the players were experiencing a great campaign, and at the end of seven games the only loss had been 7-6 to pesky Penn State, whom the Buckeyes never have defeated. The last two games, however, resulted in white-washings from Iowa 6 to 0 and Michigan 19 to 0. For many players the loss to Iowa was the first Big Ten defeat they had ever experienced.

Guard Jim Parker repeated as all-American just as Cassady had in 1954-55. With end Dean Dugger having been selected in 1954 the Buckeyes were represented for three consecutive years on the mythical team.

With probation lifted and an opportunity to play in the Rose Bowl possible, the Buckeyes went to work in 1957. This year proved to be an even greater season than 1954 in that Woody Hayes was named coach of the year. Only Carroll Widdoes, in 1944, had brought such an honor to Ohio State.

A fine Texas Christian team stung the Buckeyes in the opener, 18 to 14, and many thought the absence of Parker, Michael, Ellwood, Dick Guy, and Jim Roseboro might be felt more than met the eye. Eighteen lettermen were back, but only

The 1957 team, which lost only the opening game to Texas Christian 18 to 14, went on to win another Big Ten title. This led to the Rose Bowl and a 10-7 victory over a fine Oregon

three linemen and two backs, Don Clark and Galen Cisco, were considered regulars. It was Ohio State's first opening game loss since 1950 and the first for Hayes. This extended the losing streak to three.

It was not long, however, before Hayes and his aides had the right men in the right places. Russ Bowermaster was paired at end with little Leo Brown; John Martin and Dick Schafrath formed the tackles; and Aurelius Thomas, who was named all-American, was one of the guards along with Bill Jobko. Dan James was the center, the biggest man on the squad at 258 pounds. Frank Kremblas won the quarterbacking job; Dick LeBeau and Clark were the halfbacks; and Cisco, now the pitching coach for the Kansas City Royals, was the fullback.

After defeating the Buckeyes, coach Abe Martin of Texas Christian said, "Don't worry about Ohio State this season. They'll be OK."

Any thought that Ohio State would be a "patsy" as a result of the opening game loss was a misnomer. A trip to Seattle resulted in a 35 to 7 victory over the University of Washington. A punt return for a touchdown by Don Sutherin 'broke the game open, and Hayes later said that the play gave everyone a big lift.

team. Guard Aurelius Thomas was named on the all-American team.

When the Big Ten season opened, Illinois and Indiana were defeated handily 21 to 7 and 56 to 0, but Wisconsin posed a different problem. Both teams scored 13 points in the first period, and it was a field goal by Sutherin in the third quarter that won the game, 16-13. Northwestern was beaten soundly, 47 to 6, but Purdue was more of a problem, 20 to 7. The Buckeyes scored all of their points before intermission, and then Purdue dominated the second half completely.

This brought on a showdown with Iowa at home. The Hawkeyes had broken the Ohio State 17-game winning streak over conference foes the year before, and the Buckeyes were eyeing revenge. They got it, 17 to 13, after a long afternoon with fullback Bob White the hero. Carrying the ball seven times out of eight midway in the final period, White gained 65 of the 68 yards needed to cross the goal line. LeBeau gained the other three yards.

Iowa coach Forest Evashevski was dumbfounded after the game. "That's the first time I ever saw one player gain so much ground in such a short period of time," he said. "And we knew what he was going to do, too."

For one of the few times in recent years the Big Ten title was won regardless of the final week's outcome. The Buckeyes still had Michigan to play at Ann Arbor, but they were the only undefeated team. They had one more game in the victory column than Michigan State, the leading contender after Iowa had been removed. The Buckeyes played seven games that year, and all others playing that number lost at least three times.

Rose Bowl — January 1, 1958

The season's-ending game with Michigan was somewhat of an anticlimax with the title already in the bag, but nonetheless Hayes and the players were elated with the 31 to 14 victory. Though Michigan led at the half 14 to 10, the Buckeyes dominated the play from then on, scoring twice in the third period and again in the fourth. It was the eighth straight win of the season and enabled Hayes to take the "rubber" game of seven from the Wolverines since he had become head coach.

After the season there was quite a division of opinion as to the No. 1 team in the national rankings. Auburn had won 14 straight games and got the nod from the AP, but UP and INS (before it merged with UP to form UPI) favored Ohio State. Guard Aurelius Thomas, who played his high school football at Columbus East, was named on four major all-American teams.

Woody was loud in his praise of the team as a unit. "We have had more stars before (obviously referring to the 1954-55 group), but all of these fellows have worked hard, not only on the playing field but in their attitude toward training."

Hayes was rewarded himself by being named coach of the year by his colleagues, members of the American Football Coaches Association. The speaker at the coaches' banquet in Philadelphia was none other than Richard M. Nixon, who was vice president of the United States at the time. He and Hayes since have become close friends.

In an off-to-the-side remark, Nixon said to one of Hayes' co-workers from Ohio State, "You have a good product, one of

The Ohio State football team of 1957 was given an enthusiastic welcome by the Tournament of Roses queen and her court upon arrival at the Los Angeles Airport. The Buckeyes defeated Oregon in the Rose Bowl game, 10 to 7.

the best. Stay with it."

When the Buckeyes reached Pasadena to play Oregon in the Rose Bowl, they read about a team that was being downgraded about as badly as any they had ever faced. They also were about to meet a group of players, mostly seniors, who were fighting mad about their image. Oregon, in a preseason rating, had been ranked seventh in the conference, and apparently many writers and fans thought they really belonged there.

Oregon was eager and aggressive from the start, but the Buckeyes moved right in with a first-quarter touchdown, Frank Kremblas going over on a one-yard quarterback sneak. Oregon tied the score in the second quarter on a five-yard run following a pitchout to Jim Shanley. That is the way the score stood until late in the fourth period when Sutherin place-kicked from the 24 yard line—a 34 yard boot.

Sutherin, whose only punt in the game had gone only 14 yards, said after the game, "I was sure I would make it good. I kept my head down, but I did not know it was good until Kremblas, who was holding the ball, told me."

Oddly, from that very same spot on the field, Jack Morris of Oregon had missed earlier in the game.

Oregon coach Len Casanova admitted that the pre-game ballyhoo in favor of the Buckeyes had irritated his players. "Nobody can be humiliated like our boys and take it. I think we have the best team in the country."

Coach Hayes praised Sutherin as the Ohio State star, adding that his kicker had been bothered by a bad back and leg for some time. "He had not kicked for a long time until a week before the game," Hayes said.

"We intercepted two passes and recovered two fumbles. Whenever we can get the ball four times on turnovers we figure we can win," Hayes added in a post-game chat.

Statistics were interesting. Ohio State gained 283 yards running to Oregon's 95, but the Webfoots led in first downs, 21 to 19. Ohio State, as usual, threw only 6 passes, 2 being completed for 59 yards. Both were caught by Jim Houston. Oregon, on the other hand, threw 21, completing 13 for 191 yards. Jack Crabtree threw 17 of Oregon's passes, completing 10 for 135 yards, but he threw the 2 interceptions. Oregon did

For the second time in three Rose Bowl appearances, covering just an eight-year period, Ohio State won the Pasadena Classic by the margin of a field goal. Here Don Sutherin, right, is kicking a 34-yarder to edge Oregon 10 to 7 in the 1958 game. In the 1950 game the Buckeyes had defeated California 17 to 14.

not have to punt once, and neither of Ohio State's 2 punts was returned, both going out-of-bounds.

Although the game was hard-fought from start to finish, it was one of the cleanest in Rose Bowl annals. Each team was penalized three times, but total yardage assessed was 15 against Ohio State and 25 against Oregon.

One sportswriter following the Buckeyes said that Oregon had won everything but the score, but the fact remained that Ohio State held onto the ball. The Buckeye backs, headed by Kremblas, were sticky-fingered as they had been in the 1955 Rose Bowl game against Southern California.

Bob White carried the ball 25 times, well over one-third of the team's 61, and was the game's leading ground-gainer with 93 yards. Don Clark carried 14 for a net of 82. Shanley led Oregon with 59, followed closely by Morris with 57.

Ohio State used only 23 players in the game, and 4 of them, Kremblas, Thomas, Jobko, and Houston, played all but one-half minute.

Sutherin remarked after the game that Ohio State simply could not "get up" for it. Yet the Buckeyes held on long enough to win.

High Ranking In The Classroom

Since 1953, sports information directors of the Big Ten have been sponsoring all-conference academic teams, thus calling attention to achievements in the classroom as well as on the gridiron. In this category the Buckeyes have ranked high, indeed, with 34 representatives, many being chosen for more than one year. By positions, quarterbacks and fullbacks have led the group, but linemen and defensive players also have claimed their share of prestige.

Heading the list is fullback Bob White, who was selected 3 times—the seasons of 1957-58-59. As a sophomore White is well remembered for his ball-carrying exploits against Iowa. Lugging the ball 7 times, all but once in a march of 68 yards, White was largely responsible for a 17-13 victory which eventually put the Buckeyes in the Rose Bowl. His gains ranged from 3 to 29 yards.

Two-time honorees on the scholastic teams have been quarterbacks John Borton and Frank Ellwood; center Ray Pryor; guard Dave Cheney; linebacker Mark Stier; tackles Dave Foley and Dick Himes; and safety man Rick Seifert.

White, Pryor, and Foley achieved all-American recognition on the field, as did defensive back Arnie Chonko, who also was an all-American baseball player. A first baseman of tremendous agility, Chonko had numerous offers from professional clubs in both sports but spurned all to enter medical school, where he promptly became the No. 1 man scholastically in his class.

Two other football players, quarterbacks Don Unverferth

177

Bob White, Ohio State's fullback in 1957-58-59, was selected those years on the Big Ten's first all-scholastic football team. White came to Ohio State from Lexington, Kentucky.

and John Darbyshire, matched Chonko's feat. Darbyshire was prevented from playing when a physical examination revealed that he had developed a heart murmur.

Coach Woody Hayes, who always has been justifiably proud of these men heading their respective classes, likewise has been embittered that such a fine story, although released

Two outstanding athletes, Arnie Chonko and Don Unverferth,
became No. 1 students in their respective medical college
classes. Chonko was an all-American in both football (1964)
and baseball (1965), while Unverferth quarterbacked the
Buckeyes in 1963-64-65.

through proper university channels, failed to receive the exposure he felt it deserved.

"The dope addicts make page 1 but these fine young men get little or nothing," he complains.

One-time selections have included Fred Kriss, quarterback, 1955; Billy Wentz, halfback, 1961; Tom Perdue, end, 1961; Dave Katterhenrich, fullback, 1962; Arnie Chonko, halfback, 1964; Bill Ridder, guard, 1965; Tom Portsmouth, safety, 1966; Dick Himes, tackle, 1967; John Muhlbach, center, 1968; Bill Urbanik, tackle, 1969; Doug Adams, linebacker, 1969; Rex Kern, quarterback, 1970; Mike Sensibaugh, safety, 1970; Rick Simon, tackle, 1971; and Randy Gradishar, linebacker, 1973.

Time Out: Matte,
Warfield, Ferguson, Snell

One of Ohio State's most underrated players of the 1958-60 era was Tom Matte, described by coach Woody Hayes as a "winner." Hayes says that Ohio State never had a better man when it came to running the option. Matte was a little-used sophomore, carrying the ball only once, but he did intercept a pass for a 36-yard return and brought back 4 punts for 30 yards.

In the 1959 season as a junior, Matte moved up fast, carrying the ball 92 times for a net of 190 yards. He completed 28 of 51 passes for 439 yards and had only 2 intercepted, scoring 4 touchdowns. He led the team in total offense with 629 yards, punted 5 times, intercepted a pass, had 1 punt return of 15 yards, and returned 4 kickoffs for 66 yards.

Matte's versatility was solidified in 1960 when he again performed triple threat duties. Rushing 161 times he netted 682 yards, averaging 4.2 yards per carry and scoring 2 touchdowns. He passed 95 times, completing 50 for 737 yards, and having only 4 intercepted as he threw for 8 touchdowns. He led the team in total offense with 1,419 yards and 10 touchdowns, punting 29 times for an average of 35.2.

Matte starred for the Baltimore Colts for 10 years, retiring last year.

Tom Matte, Option Expert

A superb athlete, and a gentleman on and off the field. This was the reputation of Paul Warfield, Ohio State's all-around performer in 1961-62-63. Always ready and always in condition, Warfield played in every game for three years and went on to become the ace pass receiver for the world champion Miami Dolphins.

As a sophomore Warfield played 300 minutes and netted

Paul Warfield: Athlete and Gentleman

420 yards in 77 carries, averaging 5.4 yards and scoring 5 touchdowns. Showing the all-around ability which he has carried to the heights as a professional player, Warfield caught 9 passes for 120 yards and 1 TD; returned 10 kickoffs for 196 yards; and returned 11 punts for 88 yards.

As a junior Warfield led the team in playing time with 373 minutes, netted 367 yards in 57 tries for an average of 6.4; and scored 2 TD's. He caught 8 passes for 139 yards and 2 more touchdowns and returned 4 kickoffs for 123 yards, an average of 30.7. His 14 punt returns were good for 99 yards, an average of 7.1.

Warfield again led the team in playing time as a senior, seeing action for 376 minutes. Maintaining his art of catching passes, he received 22 for 266 yards and 3 touchdowns. His kickoff returns totaled 15 for 383 yards, an average of 25.5, while his punt returns added up to 10 for 101. He intercepted 2 passes for 23 yards, and carried the ball 62 times for a net of 260, an average of 4.2.

Despite playing both offense and defense and doing everything on a football field except carry water, according to many observers, Warfield failed to make any of the leading all-American selections. However, he was named to the all-Big Ten team in his junior and senior seasons.

Outstanding defensive players say that it is impossible to play Warfield "one on one."

Coach Woody Hayes describes Warfield as "the most graceful athlete I have ever seen."

Bob Ferguson, a real bulldozer of a fullback, moved into Coach Hayes' offense as a sophomore. Carrying the ball 61 times, he gained 374 yards, losing only 3, for a net of 371, an average of 6.1.

Scoring only 2 touchdowns as a sophomore, Ferguson hiked this category to 13 in his junior year. Carrying the ball 160 times, he gained on every occasion except 1, when he lost 1 yard. His net was 853 for an average of 5.3.

Ferguson was a real workhorse in 1961, carrying the ball 202 times for a net of 938 yards. His average per try was 4.6, and he crossed the goal line 11 times.

Matt Snell, a super star with the New York Jets until his recent retirement, was one of Ohio State's most versatile

Bob Ferguson: A Bulldozer

Matt Snell: Versatile Star

football players. As a sophomore he was a running halfback and a year later was playing defensive end, despite a weakened knee. As a senior he was an outstanding fullback.

Snell, who played with the Buckeyes in 1961, '62, and '63, wanted to get a degree in dentistry, but the financial lure from pro football was too great for him to turn down. Since retiring from the Jets, Snell has been identified with a Wall Street brokerage house.

Eleven Years
Between Bowl Games

In the 61 years of Big Ten membership, Ohio State has become a football power. Most of the non-championship seasons have been winning ones, and every coach—eight of them—has had moments of glory and satisfaction.

Although 11 years went by between the Rose Bowl appearances of 1958 and 1969, many successful seasons and many all-Americans dotted the Buckeye football map.

After the 10 to 7 victory over Oregon by the 1957 group, the holdovers from the championship team, and another promising group of sophomores, went through a 6-1-2 season in 1958. The only loss was to Northwestern, 21 to 0, and tie games were played with Purdue, 14-14, and Wisconsin, 7-7.

A real novelty occurred in the Purdue game when tackle Jim Marshall scored both touchdowns, first by blocking a punt and running it over and then by deflecting a pass which he held onto again running the play into the end zone.

Iowa won the title, but Ohio State inflicted the only loss on the Hawkeyes, 38 to 28, in the season's highest-scoring game.

This was the year, September 11 was the exact date, when Hayes ordered Commissioner Kenneth L. "Tug" Wilson and a group of touring sportswriters from the Buckeye practice field. His explanation was that he wanted to criticize his players for a poor drill and that he did not want to do this in front of outsiders.

"It would not be fair to the boys," he explained.

He granted a lengthy post-practice interview in which he apologized many times for his actions, but many of the writers never forgave him. Nearly all of the stories involving Ohio State's 1958 prospects, to be exposed in print during the following week, dealt with Hayes' order instead of an outline of the players' abilities.

Three all-Americans heaped prestige on the team and themselves—tackle Marshall, fullback Bob White, and end Jim Houston, with Houston repeating in 1959.

The season of 1959 was to be Ohio State's poorest under Hayes up to that point. It was the first time any of his teams had lost as many as 5 games. Only Michigan State and Purdue were defeated in the conference, and Wisconsin beat the Buckeyes for the first time since 1946. Other losses were to Southern California, Illinois, Iowa, and Michigan. Indiana, which had been defeated 7 straight years, held the Buckeyes to a scoreless tie. As it turned out, there was a second tie, as these 2 teams finished in a deadlock for eighth place with a 2-4-1 record.

For the first time in the modern era (1939–) a team won the Big Ten title with two defeats against its record. Wisconsin was the champion with a 5-2 mark, nosing out Michigan State's 4-2. The Badgers also were unimpressive in the Rose Bowl, losing to the University of Washington, 44 to 8.

The 1960 season saw Iowa and Minnesota tie for the title with 5-1 marks, the Buckeyes finishing third at 4-2. Since Iowa had been in the Rose Bowl two years earlier, Minnesota got the bid and had the same fate as Wisconsin, losing to Washington 17-7. Ohio State won 7 games decisively due largely to pile-driving Bob Ferguson, who won the all-American fullback spot, repeating in 1961.

Hayes regarded his "forgotten" squad of 1961 as a team as dedicated as the championship teams of 1954 and 1957. After a 7-7 tie with Texas Christian, UCLA was topped 13 to 3, after which both Illinois and Northwestern were blanked, 44 to 0 and 10 to 0. Wisconsin, showing the best offense the Buckeyes were to face all season, ran up 21 points, but Ohio State tallied 30. Iowa was the next victim, 29 to 13, followed by Indiana 16-7. The Hoosiers did not win a conference game and finished with a 2-7 record, yet gave the Buckeyes a stubborn battle. Oregon,

The 1961 squad won the Big Ten title and wound up the season with a 50-20 victory over arch-rival Michigan but was denied the opportunity to go to the Rose Bowl. The Ohio State faculty

which had been scheduled because of the congenial Rose Bowl meeting 4 years before, was defeated, 22 to 12.

The windup against Michigan at Ann Arbor saw the Buckeyes score 50 points, highest number in history against the Wolverines who wound up with 20. Bob Ferguson finished his career with 4 touchdowns; sophomore quarterback Joe Sparms passed for 200 yards; and Paul Warfield made a dazzling 69-yard run, longest of the day among many big gains.

After the Buckeyes were turned down by the Ohio State faculty to appear in the Rose Bowl, Minnesota represented the Big Ten for the second straight year. It had better luck this time, defeating UCLA, 21-3. The Gophers provided the confer-

council voted 28 to 25 against participation. No formal pact existed between the Big Ten and Pacific Coast rivals.

ence oddity during the long Rose Bowl negotiations. Always voting against the postseason game, Minnesota not only wound up going to Pasadena twice but in successive years at that.

The ramifications of the 1961 football season never had been experienced in the Big Ten, nor were they likely to be repeated. It was a story of Ohio State winning the conference title and being denied permission to play in the Rose Bowl.

The winning team was not without its detractors, however, even at Ohio State. John B. (Jack) Fullen, editor of the *Alumni Monthly*, blasted the Buckeye football program editorially. Also Woody Hayes was standing in the line of fire as he and Fullen had been feuding ever since the editor had asked, editorially, "for a balance on the campus."

"We have small-time support for the true mission of the university and big-time support for athletics," Fullen wrote in the *Monthly*. "You are not going to have a very good house if you put all your money in the game room and ignore the rest."

Fullen also accused the football players of being a "bunch of pros," to which Hayes objected strenuously.

Since there was no contract binding the Big Ten to supply a team in the Rose Bowl, it was not known whether Ohio State's faculty committee would approve the Rose Bowl trip, even if the Buckeyes did win the title. The faculty council took the final vote in a meeting said to have attracted a record attendance of 53 out of a possible 57.

The bid was turned down, 28 to 25. If 2 voters had changed their minds, the bowl trip would have won by 1 ballot. Hayes was bitter, and so were the players, but the coach said that he respected the integrity of the faculty men and that there would be no demonstrations by squad members. In fact, co-captains Tom Perdue and Mike Ingram addressed protesting groups, urging them to accept the verdict peacefully.

The athletic board carried the decision to the trustees who determined that the decision of the council should be final, otherwise Ohio State's status in the Big Ten might be in jeopardy.

Athletic Director Dick Larkins was chagrined but realized that there was no use pressing the point any further. "We have no recourse now," he said.

The issue was the subject of editorial comment in newspapers of Ohio and other midwest points. Opinion was divided, some attacking the outcome as being an injustice to the team while others said it was a wise academic decision.

In rebuttal Fullen said that he was opposed to the Rose Bowl venture because of the high rental fee charged for the facilities and for the manner in which tickets, both complimentary and saleable, were allotted.

Professor Roy A. Larmee, current faculty representative, tells a story which reflects an attitude of many of the off-campus people regarding the "turndown." Larmee joined the faculty in 1962, the year after the bowl refusal. Going to one of the neighborhood banks, he informed the teller that he was from out of the city, wished to open an account, and that he was going to be a member of the faculty.

The teller gave him an evil eye and said, "The faculty, eh? Do you know what those so-and-so's did last fall? Voted down the Rose Bowl game. I hope you're not going to be like one of them."

Wisconsin regained the pedestal in 1962 with a 6-1 record, nosing out Minnesota that was completing a fine three-year record during which the Gophers won 16 conference games and lost only 4. The Buckeyes tied Northwestern for third place with 4-2, losses being to Iowa, 28-14, and Northwestern, 18-14. A non-conference game was lost to UCLA, 9 to 7.

The 1963 season found the Buckeyes tying Michigan State for second place with a 4-1-1 mark, Illinois winning with 5-1-1, the extra victory paying off. After shutout victories over Texas A&M, 17 to 0, and Indiana, 21 to 0, the Buckeyes had a sensational 20-20 tie with Illinois. Former Illini coach Ray Eliot has always regarded this game as one of his personal highlights.

Southern California gave the Buckeyes one of their worst defeats in years, a 32-3 decision, so the team was hard-pressed the following week to edge Wisconsin, 13-10. The same was true against Iowa, a 7-3 squeaker. Another close game followed, but this time the Buckeyes were on the short end, as usual, against Penn State, 10-7. Northwestern, returning to the Buckeye schedule, won 17 to 8, but Michigan was defeated in the finale, 14 to 10, resulting in a 5-3-1 mark for the year.

President Kennedy's assassination had delayed all Big Ten games, and the Ohio State-Michigan contest was played after Thanksgiving. With gloom covering the nation, coupled with the fact that the game's outcome had no bearing on the title picture, the usual Buckeye-Wolverine excitement was missing. To complicate matters further, the postponement was not announced until shortly before noon on Saturday. Consequently, special trains and motorists arrived in Ann Arbor not knowing that the game had been called off.

With the team and followers making another round trip the next weekend in inclement weather, a listless game was no surprise. Attendance fell off and so did enthusiasm. Everyone seemed to wish that the season could have ended the week before.

Michigan returned to the top in 1964 for the first time since 1950 when it won the title by taking the famous "blizzard bowl" game 9 to 3. The record was 6-1, with the Buckeyes second with 5-1.

Three all-Americans dotted the Ohio State scene, those honored being tackle Jim Davidson, center Ike Kelley, and defensive halfback Arnold Chonko, who scored a double by being named to the all-American baseball team as well. Chonko was an outstanding first baseman.

The overall record was 7-2, losses being to Penn State (again), 27 to 0, and Michigan, 10 to 0.

The intersectional loss to Penn State was offset somewhat by two victories in the same category, 27-8 over Southern Methodist and 17-0 against Southern California. Biggest victory of the year was a 26-0 triumph over Illinois.

The season of 1965 was another of those 7-2 seasons, the fourth in 10 years. When North Carolina won the opening game 14 to 3, and Washington was barely nosed out 23 to 21 by virtue of a last-minute field goal by Bob Funk, it looked like the Buckeyes were in trouble.

The first-game loss was the first since 1957, when the 18-14 decision was dropped to Texas Christian. Illinois was defeated 28 to 14, but the following Saturday at East Lansing, Coach Duffy Daugherty was going to present one of his better teams.

The Spartans led only 7-0 at the half, but with all-American Ike Kelley injured in the second half the home team went to work offensively and won going away 32-7. Led by "Bubba" Smith, the Spartans stopped the Buckeyes cold as they showed a minus 22 yards on the ground.

It was the first time in Hayes' coaching career that his fullback offense did not move.

The next three games resulted in 10 points for each of the opponents, but the Buckeyes won all: 20-10 over Wisconsin, 11-10 over Minnesota by virtue of a 2-point conversion, and 17-10 over Indiana. Iowa was defeated for the third straight year 38 to 0, and Michigan was shaded 9 to 7 on another winning field goal effort by Funk. Ike Kelley repeated as all-American, and he was joined by tackle Doug Van Horn.

The 1966 campaign was another long season, five losses

194

being suffered for the second time in eight years. Ray Pryor was honored as all-American center but there was little else to cheer about. Although Michigan State had lost the Rose Bowl game to UCLA 14 to 12 in what was termed an upset, the Spartans were on top again with a second straight undefeated conference season.

Three consecutive Ohio State defeats occurred early in the year to Washington, 38-22, Illinois, 10-9, and Michigan State, 11-8. Although considerably outmanned the Buckeyes gave the Spartans their toughest game of the season. Point-after-touchdown plays had much to do with the outcome. Michigan State connected on a two-pointer after the Buckeyes missed a conversion attempt. This was the only time in Hayes' career that the Buckeyes had lost three straight in one season.

After Wisconsin was defeated 24 to 13, Minnesota inflicted a 17-7 loss in a disappointing showing at Minneapolis. Indiana was defeated in the rain 7 to 0, and Iowa was shaded 14 to 10 at Iowa City, a sputtering pass attack failing for the Hawkeyes in the final minute when they had a chance to put over the winning tally.

After Michigan won the finale 17-3 before a jam-packed Ohio Stadium crowd, the old challenge, "Wait 'til next year," was heard once more.

Purdue, with a 6-1 record, represented the Big Ten in the Rose Bowl and nosed out Southern California 14 to 13. It was the 15th victory in 20 games for the mid-westerners at Pasadena.

It had been six years since the "forgotten" title season of 1961, and Hayes and his staff were determined to do something about moving toward the top again. The overall record during that time was 29-15-1, not exactly shabby, but still well below the pace to which the Buckeyes had been accustomed.

The policy had been to concentrate on Ohio boys in recruiting, as the "crop" had been good, and likewise the kind of disciplined athletes Hayes desired. Now it was evident that too many were leaving the state. So, in an effort to point to the immediate future, the Buckeye staff went out of the state, too.

While the varsity was going through a 6-3 season in 1967, a talent-laden freshman team was defeating Indiana's frosh 26 to 7 and Pittsburgh 36 to 20. A few boys from "far-a-way" places were getting to be pretty well-known before the snow fell. These included Jack Tatum of Passaic, New Jersey, Jan White of Harrisburg, Pennsylvania, Bruce Jankowski of Fair Lawn, New Jersey, John Brockington of Brooklyn, New York, and Tim Anderson of Follansbee, West Virginia.

Headed by Rex Kern from nearby Lancaster, the Ohio contingent was both large and dripping with ability. Soon 17 sophomores would be starting for Ohio State. Blood pressures were moving up to the point that 1967 losses to Arizona, Purdue, and Illinois were almost forgotten, not entirely, however, as all three defeats occurred in Ohio Stadium and fans really could not believe what they had been seeing in the 14-7 setback to Arizona and the 41-6 trouncing by a powerful Purdue team.

Ernie Godfrey: Kicking Coach

No story of Ohio State football would be complete without including Ernest R. (Ernie) Godfrey, supreme teacher of place-kicking and line coach.

"Keep your head down" and "Keep your eyes on the ball" may sound like instructions from a golf pro, but on the Ohio State practice field it was Ernie working patiently with a kicking prospect. Godfrey joined the Buckeye staff in 1929, following an enviable coaching record at Wittenberg College. He retired in 1962.

Immediately games were won by the margin of a successful extra point or field goal, largely through Godfrey's tutoring. During the next decade 6 decisions were gained in this manner, and before he retired in 1962, 17 more kicking triumphs were recorded, including 2 Rose classics. These were 17 to 14 over California, January 1, 1950, and 10-7 over Oregon, January 1, 1958.

Godfrey continued to coach the kickers on his own time after retirement, and all of them are credited with university records. Gary Cairns kicked three against Illinois in 1966, one of them being 55 yards, a Big Ten record. Dick Van Raaphorst kicked eight in 1963, a school mark which was tied by Bob Funk in 1965. Stan White kicked a former season's record total of thirty-nine in 1969, and Fred Schram set a record for most consecutive extra points with forty in 1970-71.

Two of Godfrey's pupils were little fellows, Dave Kilgore and Tad Weed weighing less than 150 pounds, but another one,

197

E. R. (Ernie) Godfrey was a member of the Ohio State football staff from 1929 until his retirement in 1962.

Lou Groza, was not so small. The all-pro star played freshman football at Ohio State, then entered the service before joining the Cleveland Browns. He became the greatest kicker in NFL history, and always gave Godfrey credit for his success.

"I want to see the ground give and the grass fly." These were the stern commands of Godfrey as he instructed his linemen in preparation for a game.

Ernie also had some expressions which puzzled his listeners. When he was coaching at Wittenberg, he told the players to "pair off in threes," and on another occasion urged them to "line up alphabetically and according to size."

In neither case could they accommodate him.

After coming to Ohio State, he was known to have said, "The best way to fly is by plane" and "Never advance the ball backward."

When it came to turning out all-American guards and tackles, however, his candidates knew exactly what he was talking about.

Four tackles and eleven guards fall into this exclusive category.

The tackles included Charles Csuri, 1942; William Willis 1944; Warren Amling, 1946; and Jim Marshall, 1958.

Guards started with Joe Gailus, 1932, and followed with Regis Monahan, 1934; Inwood Smith, 1935; Gust Zarnas, 1937; Lindell Houston, 1942; William Hackett, 1944; Warren Amling, 1945 (Amling made all-American in successive years at two positions); Bob Momsen, 1950; Mike Takacs, 1952; Jim Parker, 1955-56; and Aurelius Thomas, 1957.

Godfrey was inducted into the National Football Hall of Fame for coaches, joining two previous Ohio State selections, Dr. John W. Wilce and Francis A. Schmidt.

1968 — "Best College Team Of The Sixties"

Perhaps the best way to describe the strength and versatility of the 1967 freshmen would be to say that 19 earned letters as sophomores. Another way would be to write that Jack Tatum, twice an all-American in 1969 and 1970, could not earn a special award as a frosh player. In any event football talent was solid at every position and, in most instances, the backup man was capable of starting on nearly every other team in the Big Ten.

This 1968 squad was not all sophomoric, however. Co-captains Dave Foley, tackle, and Dirk Worden, linebacker, were outstanding football players, as were 1967 holdover tackles Rufus Mayes, Chuck Hutchison, Paul Schmidlin, Brad Nielsen, and Bill Urbanik; ends Nick Roman and Dave Whitfield; guards Alan Jack, Vic Stottlemyer, and Tom Backhus; and centers John Muhlbach and Jim Roman, who also was a place-kicker.

In the backfield from the 1967 squad were quarterbacks Bill Long and Kevin Rusnak; halfbacks Dave Brungard and Ray Gillian; fullback Jim Otis; and defensive players Ted Provost, Mike Polaski, Mike Radtke, and Mark Stier. In all, 28 lettermen returned, 15 from offense and 13 defense.

This, indeed, was a formidable group. Otis was the leading ground-gainer in 1967 with 530 yards, followed closely by Brungard with 515. Gillian showed promise with an average of 4.1 yards per carry. While the 1967 team scored on all opponents, it tallied only one touchdown against Arizona,

Northwestern, and Purdue for 155 points in 9 games. All teams scored against the Buckeyes, except Oregon, for a total of 120—not too much spread. It was obvious that more punch must be sought. The defense might be adequate.

Some concern was expressed whether quarterback Rex Kern, one of the prize sophomores, would be available early in the season as he had submitted to a spinal disc operation in mid-June. However he was ready and played 26 minutes with the offensive unit against Southern Methodist in the opener. The Buckeyes won, 35 to 7, quite a reversal from the first game of the year before when Arizona won, 14-7. Twenty sophomores played, the tip-off on what was to come. Nine of them, including Kern, played more than 25 minutes. Sophomore safety Mike Sensibaugh played 30, one less than the game leader, Dirk Worden.

Hayes and his assistants liked what they saw from their young newcomers, and 12 of them had as much game time or more in the second game with Oregon, defeated 20 to 6. The Buckeyes watched SMU attempt the amazing number of 76 passes, a stadium record, and Oregon contributed 21, yet only 3 touchdowns were scored. Seven of the aerials were intercepted. Ohio State was conceding short gains both on the ground and in the air as the opposition showed 33 first downs in 2 games. However, the Buckeyes had 40.

The biggest game of the season was about to be played in Ohio Stadium. Purdue, which had scalped the Ohioans 41 to 6 the year before, figured to roll over the younger Buckeyes. After all, the Boilermakers had Heisman award candidate, Leroy Keyes, and a big veteran line. They were a 13-point favorite.

When the game was over, they were 13 points behind and whitewashed at that.

Tom Keys, sports editor of the *Columbus Citizen Journal*, writing in his column following the game, said: "Beautiful is the only way to tag Saturday's super, super special upset registered by Woody Hayes' young Buckeyes over No. 1 Purdue. It has to gain a place with all-time classics spanning 79 seasons at Ohio State."

He wrote on: "If Keyes has been knocked out of the Heisman box in this one, his first regrets should be forwarded to sophomore Jack Tatum, who seemed to wear numbers 32 and

The 1968 Ohio State team was voted the "outstanding college football team of the sixties." Led by all-American tackles Dave Foley and Rufus Mayes and directed by fabulous ball-handling

23 all afternoon...his and Leroy's."

A 35-yard run, following a pass interception by defensive back Ted Provost, proved to be the game-breaker, but a second touchdown was added by senior quarterback Bill Long who, not finding a receiver, darted into the end zone. The point after touchdown, which was missed after the first score, causing great concern, was good this time.

Many regarded the Purdue victory as the turning point in the season. One player who felt so was sophomore end Jan White, who said: "We had to win that one to keep going, and after we did win, we felt we could beat any team we had to play. Both the offense and defense had complete confidence in what we could do."

Ohio State outgained Purdue in total yardage, 411 to 186.

Rex Kern, the Buckeyes rolled over nine opponents before upsetting Southern California in the Rose Bowl, 27 to 16. The Trojans were led by all-American O. J. Simpson.

Northwestern was defeated 45 to 21 in a free-scoring game in which the Buckeyes rolled up their biggest yardage total of the season—565. The Wildcats totaled 288.

Illinois was the next victim, but it was not easy. The Buckeyes led at the half 24 to 0 and it looked like a romp, but by midway in the third period the score was tied at 24 all. Three Illini touchdowns had been accompanied by as many incredible 2-point conversions. Each was a rushing play, and there was no doubt about any of them. With less than 3 minutes left, a Buckeye drive of 74 yards was good for the deciding touchdown in a 31-24 thriller. Again the Illini charged back, but Mike Sensibaugh intercepted a pass to end the threat.

Illinois finished the season 1-6 in the conference and 1-9 overall, but for 30 minutes they gave every indication of scoring the upset of the year.

Michigan State, always a tough nut for the Buckeyes to crack, was edged, 25 to 20. Bruce Jankowski, sophomore end, caught 8 passes to highlight the game. The Buckeye scouting report showed that the Spartans could be passed against so a season's high of 26 were thrown, 16 being completed for 215 yards and 10 first downs. Only 214 yards were gained rushing. It was the first time since the opening game of 1967 that passing yardage was greater than rushing.

The statistic of 26 passes thrown stood out like a beacon, too. In the early days of Hayes' coaching career there were entire seasons when 26 passes were not thrown. Mediocre passers and fumbling receivers did not make for a good passing attack, Hayes correctly figured.

Wisconsin was defeated for the ninth straight year, 43 to 8. With Kern injured, Ron Maciejowski, who had directed the winning touchdown against Illinois, was at the throttle. The Badgers were held to 88 yards on the ground and 99 in the air. "Mace," the "super sub," completed 15 of 25 passes as the Buckeyes continued to put the ball in the air.

Iowa was troublesome on its home field, but the game was not quite as close as the final score would suggest. Jim Otis and John Brockington carried the offensive brunt in the 33-27 victory, and Jack Tatum keyed on Ed Podolak, Iowa's fine runner, at critical times. Iowa scored in the last few seconds to narrow the gap to 6 points.

For the second time in 7 years the Buckeyes scored 50 points on Michigan, the last being the championship team of 1961. Tatum and Tim Anderson took care of the defense while Otis powered the offense. Hard tackling led to 9 fumbles, 5 by Michigan, as the Buckeyes matched their season's high with 28 first downs. Kern connected on 6 of 9 passes for 46 yards while the rushing yardage of 421 was the highest of the season, surpassing the gains against Northwestern by 74.

Considering that this was a championship game between two previously undefeated teams, it seems amazing that the Wolverines were so outclassed. But Kern's passing, team direction, pitch-outs, and hand-offs, coupled with Brockington's long gainers and Otis's terrifying line smashes, kept Michigan off-balance all afternoon.

Ohio State's national champions of 1968 were voted the "Outstanding College Football Team Of The Sixties." Many Buckeye fans have said that the two all-American tackles, Dave Foley and Rufus Mayes, "put the show on the road." Few have disputed the assertion.

Tackle Rufus Mayes, Brockington, and Kern played 31 minutes, while Otis was only one minute behind. Coach Hayes used all 48 members of the traveling squad, who not only were smelling roses but holding a large bouquet, it was said. It was just like Jan White had said. "We think we can beat anyone we play."

So, this young team, now being watched nationwide, had scored 44 touchdowns, gaining 4,402 yards, representing 2½ miles of ground. Offensive tackles Dave Foley and Mayes were named on several all-American teams. They paved the way for the Buckeye backs, Otis in particular. As veteran coach Ernie Godfrey often said, "Show me a squad with good offensive tackles and I will show you a winning team."

Now for the first time in 11 years the Buckeyes had earned the right to return to Pasadena. There they could give Ohio State a fourth straight victory over coast elevens.

Trojan Coach Is Impressed

By the time the Buckeyes reached the Rose Bowl, the word had gotten around that Ohio State had a defense, particularly against passing, as well as an offense. Twelve different players had figured in 23 interceptions, and Jack Tatum, with three of them, was feared the most. The Trojans reasoned that with Tatum's blinding speed (9.5 for the 100 in high school), he could return one for the distance any time.

When John McKay, USC coach, was asked what he felt was most impressive about Ohio State, he replied, "Nine wins and no losses." He then went on to say: "Ohio State has fine balance on offense and an excellent defense. The team has excellent personnel and is extremely well-coached. We are impressed with the quarterback-fullback type of offense they use."

Woody Hayes was equally as complimentary about the Trojans.

"I think John McKay uses the tailback offense better than any coach in the country. He has gotten a lot of mileage out of his tailbacks ever since he began coaching."

The Buckeyes' season record was beginning to impress coast scribes. Writing in the *Pasadena Star-News*, sports editor Joe Hendrickson said: "A strategic phase to the game will center around the defensive tactics which USC will employ to check the Ohio State 'moving' offense. The Buckeye quarterbacks like to work the option. When a team has good bolting power straight ahead to keep a defense honest, such as Ohio

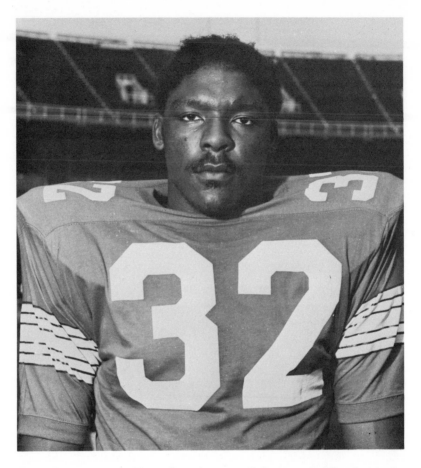

Jack Tatum was Ohio State's star defensive halfback in the 1968-70 era when the Buckeyes lost only two games in three years. An all-American in 1969 and 1970, Tatum's great speed and ability to diagnose opponents' plays kept the Ohioans in many a game.

State has with fullback Jim Otis, the quarterback-pass-run stuff is difficult to handle."

"Kern loves to roll outside," Hendrickson wrote on. "Whether an injured left shoulder will prevent this remains to be seen. It would seem probable that Rex would be handicapped, especially going to his left. But USC will have to figure on Kern, Ron Maciejowski, or Bill Long high-tailing it to the

Jim Otis was an all-American fullback in 1969 and a powerful factor in the Buckeyes' 1968 Big Ten and national championships. Otis, described by Coach Woody Hayes, as the quickest-starting fullback he has ever seen, was a regular as a sophomore in 1967. He led the team in rushing with 530 yards for a 3.7 average, his total offense was 622 yards, and his average was 3.9. As a junior on the team that was termed the "best college eleven of the Sixties," Otis again led the team in rushing with 985 yards, an average of 4.5, and scored 17 touchdowns, which made him the leading scorer with 102 points. He was second to Rex Kern in total offense and caught 10 passes in his fullback role for 82 yards. In his senior year Otis went over the 1,000 mark with 1,027 yards rushing for an average of 4.5, scored 16 touchdowns to again head the scoring with 96 points, and once more was second to Kern in total offense. He caught 5 passes for 36 yards, one good for a touchdown.

outside."

Tatum gave one of his rare interviews, brief as it was, to Hendrickson, saying: "I am looking forward to playing against O. J. Simpson, and I am also looking toward our victory party afterwards. I started thinking about O. J. after our win over Purdue. I figured we would make it here after we beat the Boilermakers."

For Tatum, this was a long speech.

Tatum's concentration on Leroy Keyes had been largely responsible for the Buckeye victory, and the Purdue star said afterward, "Tatum is a monster."

The word also had arrived from the east that Tatum, after being knocked down in the Northwestern and Michigan games, had gotten up and caught ball-carriers from behind. Bob Olsen and Ron Johnson were the respective victims as they appeared headed for touchdowns.

This prompted Hendrickson to write, "Tatum is Jack-be-tough, Jack-be-quick."

Comparison of the passing statistics of Kern and the Trojans' Steve Sogge revealed an amazing fact. Both had completed 57 percent of their tosses during the season, Sogge with 103 of 177 and Kern, throwing less, 75 of 131. Sogge connected for 8 touchdowns; Kern for 7. Sogge had 8 interceptions; Kern 6.

Though playing 2,500 miles apart, it was obvious that the 2 quarterbacks had learned their lessons equally well.

With 102,063 watching, the first quarter was a punting duel between Trojan John Young and Ohio State's Mike Sensibaugh. The Buckeye had an edge, two kicks going for 41 and 47 yards while Young, kicking three times, booted 47, 38, and 34.

When the second period opened, Bill Long held the ball on the USC 17-yard line for an attempted place-kick by Larry Zelina, but the ball sailed wide. The Trojans then put on a march that carried to the Buckeye three-yard line and a first down. Three plays lost a yard and, with Sogge holding, Ron Ayala kicked from the 11-yard line for a 3-0 lead.

Ohio State came back to midfield and Sensibaugh, forced to punt, booted one for 51 yards. However, it mattered little, as Simpson took a pitchout to his left, cut back to his right, and

Mike Sensibaugh, weighing only 187 pounds, has been regarded as Ohio State's premier safety man, a position he played during the amazing three-year winning period of 1968-70. Missing only one game in three years, that because of an injury, Sensibaugh intercepted 22 passes to establish a school career record. On six occasions he played the entire game on defense. His playing time ranged from 217 to 231 minutes, and, as the team's punter, he had the amazing consistency of a 37-yard average each season.

went 80 yards for a touchdown. When Ayala's kick was good, the Buckeyes were in the hole, 10 to 0. Leo Hayden returned the Trojan kickoff 18 yards, and the Buckeyes did not quit until Otis barged over from the one. Five first downs were made in succession with Kern's pass to Ray Gillian for 18 yards being the longest gain. Jim Roman's place-kick made it 10-7.

When Polaski made a fair catch of Young's ensuing punt, the Buckeyes were off again. Taking the ball on their own 40, they went right down to the Trojan 10, the longest gain again being Kern's pass to Gillian for 19 yards. With Long holding on the 16, Roman's field goal made the score 10-10 at the half. Only three seconds were left to play.

Someone called it a Roman holiday. This was not far from the truth as all of the players and coaches felt better about starting all even again instead of being three points behind.

Half-time statistics showed that Kern and Sogge were maintaining their usual pace and staying close together. Each completed five of ten passes, Kern's for 61 yards, Sogge's for 65. Simpson, as expected, netted 137 yards to lead both teams, an average of 7.61. Otis gained 68 to lead Ohio State, but Hayden had the best average of 7.58. The Buckeyes seldom have an edge in punting, but this time Sensibaugh's average was 46.3 to 37.7 for the Trojans and it was a factor in keeping Ohio State even at half-time.

In the third quarter a drive started on the Ohio 46, and after three first downs Roman booted another field goal from the 15 for a 13-10 lead. The Buckeyes were on fire now, and Kern passed to Hayden for a touchdown. When Roman again converted it was 20 to 10.

After Simpson fumbled Sogge's pass, Polaski recovered, and again the Trojans could not cover Gillian as a pass receiver. He caught another for 16 yards, this time for a touchdown, and when Roman converted it was 27 to 10 and out of the Trojan's reach.

With 45 seconds left, a disputed pass reception was ruled good for a Southern Cal touchdown. Officials decided that Trojan Sam Dickerson had more of the ball than interceptor Polaski. The game ended after Ohio State was penalized 15 yards for having unauthorized personnel on the field.

To nobody's surprise Kern was named the most valuable player in the game, the third such honor for an Ohio Stater, following selection of Fred (Curly) Morrison in 1950 and Dave Leggett in 1955.

National syndicated columnist Jim Murray wrote: "Rex Kern missed his calling. He should have been a pick-pocket."

This seemed to sum up how well the Buckeyes were directed in a sleight-of-hand performance.

Now the Buckeyes were national champions, and Woody Hayes was coach of the year.

1969 — Another Awesome Team

At the conclusion of the 1969 season coach Woody Hayes, who dislikes making comparisons, was asked which team he regarded the better, the undefeated team of 1968 or the high-scoring unit of 1969 which often decided the outcome of a game in the first quarter.

Hayes' reply was, "Even though the 1969 team scored a lot of points and only lost one game (to Michigan) I guess you would have to say that an undefeated team is better than one that loses a game."

The average fan accepted this solution, yet the fact remained that the predominately junior squad was awesome in its accomplishments.

Rewriting the record book by scoring 383 points in 9 games, breaking the 10-game record of 337, this explosive outfit scored 121 points in the first quarter to a mere 14 by opponents. Fourteen players figured in scoring a record 56 touchdowns. A total offense record was set of 4,438 yards, and fullback Jim Otis hit a single season mark of 1,027.

Hayes' former conservative passing offense blossomed to the point that 14 players figured in receptions, 17 resulting in touchdowns. Of the first downs 74 were by passing, and the 250 total first downs were school records.

The Big Ten winning streak, which had started with the Michigan State victory in 1967, reached 17 before being snapped in the season's finale at Michigan when the Wolverines won, 24 to 12. The streak matched the 17-game string of the

Jim Stillwagon is regarded as one of Ohio State's all-time great middle defensive linemen. He won both the Lombardi and Outland awards in 1970. He was all-American in both 1969 and 1970.

1954-56 era.

The team boasted four all-Americans in guard Jim Stillwagon, fullback Jim Otis, and defensive backs Ted Provost and Jack Tatum.

The least number of first downs made by the Buckeyes was 20 against Michigan, when a pregame injury to Rex Kern not only handicapped him but the team as well. He played only 22 minutes, smallest time of the year. With Michigan putting pressure on the defense, linebacker Doug Adams, defensive back Tim Anderson, safety Mike Sensibaugh, defensive end Dave Whitfield, and cornerback Jack Tatum played the entire game.

In prior games the Buckeyes had held the ball an unbelieveable number of times against their opponents. Whereas total plays against Michigan numbered only 79 (more than an average number for a team), ball control numbered 101 against both Illinois and Texas Christian; 99 against Wisconsin; 95, Northwestern; 93, Michigan State; and 91, Purdue.

Michigan not only spoiled a second undefeated season but hurt the Buckeyes statistically. The 24 points represented the greatest scored against the team, and the 12 total was the poorest offense.

Probably the biggest setback of all was a tremendous opportunity to be national champions for the second straight year.

Seniors Take A Vow

After Michigan put an end to a 22-game winning streak, which included 17 straight in the Big Ten, a senior group that had played together since freshman days vowed to close out their college careers with another undisputed championship. They were to succeed, including the Rose Bowl, where the venture was not as enjoyable as two years previously.

With virtually the same key men in their respective positions, the team scored 273 points during the conference season compared to 383 the year before. Defense also slipped from 93 points surrendered in 1969 to 120 in 1970. However there were two prominent absentees on offense, Jim Otis and Ray Gillian. Missing from the defense were Dave Whitfield on the line and Ted Provost and Mike Polaski from the backfield.

Michigan State was the only team shut out, 29 to 0, but five teams, Minnesota, Northwestern, Wisconsin, Purdue, and Michigan, were held to one touchdown. Only the Purdue game was close, and the Buckeyes were fortunate to win in the snow, 10 to 7 on Fred Schram's field goal.

As was the case in 1968, Illinois reached a season's high in effort and dedication. This time the team rallied for and around coach Jim Valek, whose dismissal had been sought for some time by certain factions.

In a most unusual announcement made just before the game, Valek's resignation was demanded. The players countered by declaring they would not finish the season unless Valek did too. The reaction scared the daylights out of the Buckeyes (48

J. Edward Weaver, director of athletics at the Ohio State University, is only the third man to hold the position. He assumed the duties October 14, 1970, succeeding Richard C. Larkins. As head of the department, Weaver made a move to increase revenue rather than cut the budget. The first accomplishment was to schedule a 10th football game, and in addition a professional game was played in the stadium in both 1972 and 1973. Permission later was granted to play an 11th game, and this was scheduled for the 1974 season. Artificial turf was installed in the stadium and on the practice field in 1971. Two projects were finalized in 1973—a new varsity tennis court complex and installation of fiberglass covering for 53,805 stadium seats.

to 29), and it carried over to the following Saturday when the Illini upset a heavily-favored Purdue team.

Against Michigan it was a case of ball control again. The Wolverines had only 56 plays, smallest number by an opponent during the season. Ohio State had 77 and more than doubled the net gain in yardage, 329 to 155. Michigan had only 37 yards on the ground. Even Texas A&M, walloped 56 to 13, showed 50.

The Buckeyes were heavily-favored over Stanford in the Rose Bowl, January 1, 1971. Undefeated, compared to a Stanford record that showed three losses, Ohio State followers were confident of the outcome and another victory celebration to go along with that of two years before when Southern Cal was downed, 27 to 16.

Just as the Trojans had done, Stanford took an early lead when Eric Cross got away for 41 yards, setting up a touchdown by Jackie Brown on a four-yard smash. Steve Horowitz kicked the first of two field goals, and now the Indians, now known as the Cardinals, had done exactly what the Trojans did on January 1, 1969—they took a 10-0 lead. Then Ohio State put the ground power in action, and Rex Kern pitched, John Brockington and Leo Hayden smashed, and the Buckeyes took a 17-13 lead. Nearly all press box occupants thought that the lead would be increased and that the Buckeyes would be home free despite a Rose Bowl record field goal by Horowitz of 48 yards.

One play seemed to turn the game around and give Stanford the momentum it needed. With fourth down and inches to go on Stanford's 19 Brockington attempted the first down, but instead of making inches he lost a yard when he was met head-on by linebacker Ron Kadziel.

Then Jim Plunkett, Stanford's Heisman trophy winner, went to work with a dazzling display of passing. Up to that point Kern had been overshadowing his quarterback opponent and actually was the No. 1 candidate for "player of the game," an award he had received in 1969.

Connecting to Randy Vataha and Bob Moore, Plunkett passed for two fourth-quarter touchdowns that spelled doom for the Buckeyes. Moore seemed to make an "impossible" catch between two defenders on the four-yard line that set up another

John Brockington, who is making a success of professional football with the Green Bay Packers, gained a mile and 100 yards while playing with the Buckeyes in 1968, 1969, and 1970. His 378 carries, 261 of which were in his senior year, netted 1,663 yards and his 37 pass receptions were good for 197, totaling 1,860 yards, 100 beyond the mile mark. As a senior, his best year, when he was named all-American, Brockington returned 6 kickoffs for 160 yards, an average of 26.7. His three-year per carry average was 4.4. Brockington scored 24 touchdowns during his career, 17 of them as a senior, a Buckeye record until another fullback, Harold Henson, scored 20 in 1972, to lead the nation in both touchdowns and point-making. Brockington is the fifth Buckeye fullback to be named an all-American.

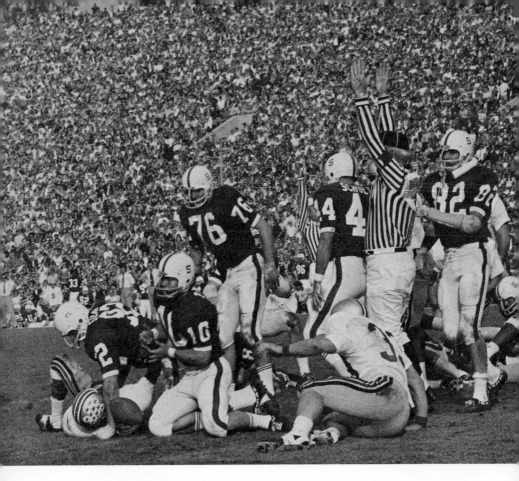

John Brockington scores for the Buckeyes against Stanford in the 1971 Rose Bowl, but Ohio State lost, 27 to 17.

touchdown by Brown.

The Buckeyes outgained their opponents 439 to 408, but poor pass defense hurt as Stanford picked up 265 yards in the air.

Time Out: Rex Kern

Why Rex Kern was not a consensus all-American in at least one of his three years as an Ohio State quarterback is a question often asked. Kern directed, ran, passed, and inspired the Buckeye offense to 27 victories in 29 games, including a Rose Bowl victory over USC on January 1, 1969, in which he was named the most valuable player. Rated as one of the finest quarterbacks in Buckeye history, Kern had the intangible quality of leadership which aroused his mates to superior heights.

A master in taking advantage of broken plays, Kern also often concealed the ball so well that opponents despaired of finding it until the play had been completed. Always imaginative, his ball-handling likewise was faultless.

In addition to his exploits on the field, Kern was one of 12 scholar-athletes honored by the National Football Foundation. He received a graduate fellowship and has earned a master's degree in athletic administration. Just recently he joined the Ohio State athletic department on a parttime basis to learn all facets of the operation.

As a youngster Kern's first interest in athletics leaned toward baseball, then basketball, and finally football. Although Kern did not play varsity baseball at Ohio State, he was drafted in an early round by a major league club, an opportunity he did not pursue.

A native of Lancaster, Ohio, Kern had the rare distinction of winning all-Ohio honors in football, basketball, and baseball.

Rex Kern, the Buckeyes' multi-talented quarterback

At the same time he turned toward religion which led to his
leadership in work for the Fellowship of Christian Athletes. In

this he had joined Bart Starr, Bill Glass, Bobby Richardson, Don Shinnick, Carroll Dale, Willie Richardson, Bobby Mitchell, and two of his own Buckeye teammates, John Muhlbach and Mark Stier.

Kern gives numerous speeches in behalf of the movement. He says that he has three approaches: "My main one is how I compare athletics with the Christian way of life, how in athletics we have to have faith in our teammates, and we have to have desire and dedication and enthusiasm. Then I tie it in with the Christian way of life, how we need faith in the Supreme Being as we have faith in our teammates and coaches, and have to be dedicated in the summer to work and strive and sweat for our goal, just as we have to be dedicated Christians, and then I try to bring in some of the Bible verses with Paul on the road to Damascus and the conversion there. Then I draw symbols, with the goal line being the gate to Heaven, first down being rebirth, loss of game, loss of life, faith in God, faith in the coach."

When Kern was 19 he was the speaker at a high school commencement, his audience being only a year or two younger than himself. He pointed out four principles as being basic in athletics: having a goal, sacrifice, dedication, and unity. His audience was attentive and responsive.

"Toward the end of my freshman year I was not certain that fall I would even be in shape to try out for the squad," Kern relates. "I was having trouble with my back, and one doctor said I would have to have a spinal disc operation. But another specialist refused to recommend it. I had to decide, knowing full well that my playing career might hang in the balance. I prayed about it, then made up my mind to go ahead with the operation. I put myself in the hands of the Almighty and stopped worrying.

"As it turned out the surgery was successful, and I got my chance. Prayer such as this is an indispensable part of my life. So is Bible reading. And I do not hesitate to let people know it."

Kern's yardstick is more than remarkable. He is the single-season total offense leader with 1,585 yards (1969) and is the career total offense leader with 4,158 yards during his three varsity seasons.

Kern's table:

Year	Carries	Net Yds.	TD's	Passes Att.	Comp.	Yds.	TD's
1968	131	534	8	131	75	972	7
1969	109	583	9	135	68	1,002	9
1970	112	597	7	98	45	470	3
Career	352	1,714	24	364	188	2,444	19

Rushing - 1,714
Passing - 2,444
Total Offense - 4,158

1971 — Poorest In Six Years

The 1971 season was the poorest, won-lost-wise, since 1966, four losses being sustained against six victories—a winning season, yet a disappointment.

After a 52-21 victory over Iowa in the season's opener, which represented the biggest scoring punch of the season, the Buckeyes lost an intersectional game to Colorado, 20 to 14. Ohio State won everything but the long end of the score. First downs favored Ohio 24 to 19; total yardage was 444 to 382 and the Buckeyes had the ball for 90 plays compared to 59 for the winners. Ohio State also completed a season's high of 21 passes in 34 attempts and had none intercepted, while Colorado completed four of nine and had two snatched away. The Buckeyes did not fumble while Colorado erred twice, recovering once. Even in yards penalized, Ohio State had an edge of 59 to 47. Only in punting did Colorado have an advantage, and it was a mere 39.7 to 38.5. The answer was that the Buffaloes made their wishbone offense move at strategic times, the 285 yards rushing almost doubling the Buckeyes' 145.

Intersectional-wise, the Buckeyes lost no time in getting even as the California Bears were defeated the following week 35 to 3. The sunshine of the west was over-matched by the Columbus humidity, and the Bears seemed to suffer more from the 90-plus temperature than did the Ohioans, who rolled up a season's high first downs of 28. For the third straight game the Buckeyes totaled more than 400 yards in net gain rushing. However, it was the last time during the season that the team was to achieve this figure in moving the ball.

A four-game winning streak followed against Illinois, Indiana, Wisconsin, and Minnesota. Only the Gophers provided trouble. They piled up 14 first downs to 11 for the Buckeyes and outrushed Ohio State 273 to 198. A two-point conversion try following a last-minute Minnesota touchdown missed by inches, preserving a 14-12 victory.

In the next two games the Buckeyes could get only 10 points from their offense and bowed to Michigan State 17-10 and Northwestern 14-10. The Michigan State loss was the first to the Spartans since 1966, while Northwestern had been defeated every season since 1963.

This brought the season to the closing game with Michigan at Ann Arbor where Woody Hayes made his widely-publicized

Woody Hayes invades playing field.

invasion of the playing field—and justifiably so, according to Ohio fans—to protest a "call" by an official that was "not called."

With the fourth quarter rapidly ticking away, the Buckeyes had the ball in midfield. A pass was thrown to Dick Wakefield who was so completely interfered with that Woody could not restrain himself from dashing onto the field. While there he smashed the yard markers to dramatize what he considered an injustice to his team which was trailing 10 to 7 at the time. That is the way the game ended, too.

Hayes admitted later that he probably should not have gone onto the field but he said, "After seeing the pictures, I would have been ashamed of myself if I had not registered a protest."

The Buckeyes were a decided underdog prior to the game and were making a tremendous effort to score an upset. Woody never said that his team would win or tie, but he felt that an opportunity had been denied his players.

Michigan coach "Bo" Schembechler, when asked to comment about Woody's action said: "That's a personal thing with him. On occasion, I have been aroused, too."

Don Canham, Michigan athletic director, said: "If Woody ever stops his antics our games will draw 30,000 fewer people. We need his showmanship."

No criticism of Woody's actions was ever released from the Big Ten office. Buckeye adherents assumed from this that the commissioner agreed with the movies and that Hayes had made his point.

Michigan won the title with an 8-0 record and 11-0 overall, the first undefeated, untied season for the Wolverines since 1902. Stanford, however, won the Rose Bowl game, 13 to 12.

The Buckeyes finished in a three-way tie for third place with Illinois and Michigan State with a 5-3 mark. Center Tom DeLeone was chosen on the all-American team, the fifth Buckeye to be honored at the pivot position.

Halfback Don Lamka had an outstanding year. He led the team in touchdowns with eight; passing, with 54 completions in 107 attempts for 718 yards; total offense with 1,026 yards; and tied for first in scoring with 48 points. On defense he tied for the lead in recovered fumbles with three.

Ohio — Michigan:
A Ping-Pong Match

Ever since Indiana went to the Rose Bowl unexpectedly after the 1967 season, Ohio State and Michigan have made a ping-pong match of winning the Big Ten title and going to Pasadena.

The Buckeyes have defeated USC twice and lost to Stanford and the Trojans, while Michigan has lost twice, one to USC and the other time to Stanford. Thus in six years only four teams have represented both conferences, and the Buckeyes and Trojans have matched with four appearances, the Wolverines and Stanford with two.

In conference play over the six-year period of 1968-73, Michigan and Ohio State finished almost in a dead heat. The Wolverines had the edge of 40-4-1 for a percentage of .909 while the Buckeyes played at the rate of .889, with 39-5-1, exclusive of the tie.

Two-team domination has been the name of the game.

Until 1973 Ohio State and Michigan had not played a tie game since 1949, but Wolverine fans thought there should have been one in 1972. A field goal in Michigan's 14 to 11 defeat would have given the Maize and Blue an undefeated season as well as an undisputed Big Ten title, but the Buckeye victory created a two-way tie at 7-1.

Three magnificent goal line stands inside the five-yard line prevented Michigan from scoring. A Wolverine touchdown appeared to be within easy reach so often that coach "Bo" Schembechler gave no thought of going for a tie. Coaches have been criticized for playing for a deadlock. In this case an 11-11 tie would have been very pleasing to Michigan followers. The final standing then would have appeared:

	Won	Lost	Tie
Michigan	7	0	1
Ohio State	6	1	1

It was obvious before the 1972 season opened that Buckeye fans could count on another winner. Fourteen lettermen had been lost from the previous year, including eight regulars, four from each unit, but thirty-six veterans were available. There was an extra incentive, too, as historic Ohio Stadium was about to have its golden anniversary, covering 50 years of exciting football since its dedication in 1922.

Seven offensive regulars and the same number of defensive veterans were ready to go. The group included offensive stars Rick Middleton, Merv Teague, Jim Kregel, Chuck Bonica, Rick Galbos, Morris Bradshaw, and John Bledsoe. In addition there was all-American John Hicks, who missed the 1971 season due to surgery. From the defense were Tom Marendt (later ruled out due to a knee injury), George Hasenohrl, Shad Williams, Vic Koegel, Randy Gradishar (a concensus all-American), Jeff Davis, and Rick Seifert.

The team staged a seven-game winning streak, and there were no threats to victory as the offense rolled up 210 points and the defense yielded only 85. However the margin of triumph tightened in games six and seven (28-20 versus Wisconsin and 27-10 versus Minnesota).

Perhaps this was a tip-off on what was to follow the next Saturday when the Michigan State Spartans, emotionally keyed by the announced resignation of Coach Duffy Daugherty, upset the Buckeyes 19 to 12. A walk-on place-kicker from the Netherlands, no less, stole the spotlight. Kirk Krijt, who never had participated in a varsity game, kicked four field goals, all in the first half, matching Ohio State's game total. This tied a Big Ten record, oddly enough established only one month before by Chris Gartner of Indiana. Krijt since has dropped out of school and returned to Holland, one year too late to please Ohioans.

Daugherty likes to tell about his soccer-style kicker, the favorite story being Krijt's query as to whether the ball should

229

go under or over the crossbar. When informed that the ball should go over the bar, Krijt went to work on his specialty. His fourth field goal, which came seconds before the end of the half, struck the bar after traveling 22 yards and toppled over for three points. It tied the score and enabled the Spartans to enter the dressing room all even at 12-12. Krijt, who never had seen a football game until he came to America, was successful on earlier kicks of 40, 31, and 24 yards.

Some of the doldroms carried over to the next week as Northwestern's undermanned squad gave the Buckeyes all they

Ohio State's 1972 squad won the Big Ten title by defeating Michigan in the season's finale 11 to 8 but lost to USC's national champions in the Rose Bowl, 42 to 17.

could handle before losing, 27 to 14. Fullback Harold Henson established a new Ohio State rushing record of 44 carries, good for 4 touchdowns and 153 yards. This surpassed by 2 tries John Brockington's 42 of 1970, also against Northwestern.

Henson led the nation in scoring with 20 touchdowns, an Ohio State single-season record, breaking the previous mark of 17, held jointly by Brockington and Jim Otis. For the seventeenth time more than one Buckeye made the all-American. They were linebacker Randy Gradishar and offensive tackle John Hicks.

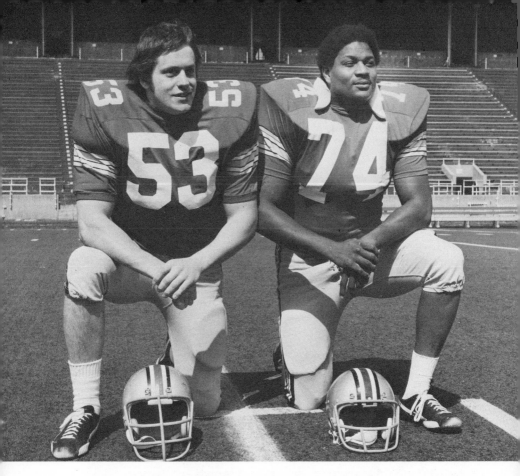

Seniors Randy Gradishar, left, and John Hicks joined Ohio State's two-time all-American group in 1973. The 6-3 236-pound Gradishar, showing speed, strength, and consistency from his linebacking spot was a unanimous choice for the second straight year. He also was runnerup in the "Player of the Year" sweepstakes. Hicks, 6-3, 258, has been described by Coach Woody Hayes as the "best interior lineman I have ever had." Hicks won both the Outland and Lombardi trophies and was named the UPI Lineman of the Year in 1973. When the Associated Press all-Americans met at the season's end, Gradishar was named captain of the defensive squad and Hicks received the same honor from the offense.

When the first half of the 1973 Rose Bowl game ended 7 to 7 after the Trojans got a break in recovering a fumble to help them score, it seemed that the Buckeyes were in the tilt as much as their opponents. But tailback Anthony Davis shredded

Ohio's defense with his brilliant running and quarterback Mike Rae passed with precision as the Trojans broke the tie with three touchdowns in the third period and won going away. Two more were added in the fourth quarter while the best the Buckeyes could do after intermission was a field goal in the third period by Blair Conway and a last-minute score in the fourth stanza on a five-yard run by John Bledsoe.

Coach Hayes used all 48 eligible players in the game with Rich Parsons, Rick Middleton, and Van DeCree leading in playing time with 31 minutes each. Merv Teague was next with 29. The Trojans won 42 to 17.

The Buckeyes actually had one more play than the Trojans, 73 to 72, and out-rushed the winners 285 to 207, but the passing difference was shocking, 244 to 81. The west coast aerial game hurt the Buckeyes as it did two years before when Stanford cut the Ohioans down. Completing 19 of 27 passes, with none intercepted, the Trojans kept on the move despite 48 yards in penalties to only 7 by Ohio State. The Buckeyes gave the ball twice on interceptions and conceded a 5-yard edge in punting, 41 to 36.

The Buckeyes were rated third nationally behind the Trojans and Oklahoma.

A Truly Magnificent Team

There were some great ones that went before, a half dozen claiming a piece of the mythical national championship, but perhaps the best-of-all in 84 years of football materialized with the 1973 team.

It really was not until January 1, 1974, however, that Woody Hayes would admit that his swashbuckling 23rd team, seen by more fans than any other college team in history, was his best despite that frustrating knot at Michigan which was the only blemish in 11 games. The only blemish, that is, if you discount the verbal beating the Buckeyes and others in the Big Ten took from Michigan mentor Glenn E. (Bo) Schembechler.

Like a bad case of indigestion was that 10-10 Bo-tie, but it was relieved almost majestically in the Rose Bowl where the Buckeyes came back full bloom, to manhandle Southern California 42-21. There were 105,267 live fans and the biggest TV audience this side of the Super Bowl on New Year's Day to obliterate the b'ad taste of both Michigan and the 1973 mis-adventure with virtually the same Southern Cal team.

That was the frosting on the cake, making amends for the misery in Ann Arbor where some said Woody's conservatism almost "did in" a truly magnificent team.

In the beginning 1973 was particularly impressive, in fact awesomely ominous because this team started with much the same perfection it displayed at the uproarious conclusion in Pasadena, California. What the Buckeyes did for openers was annihilate a reviving Minnesota Gopher team that was supposed to have new teeth ready to sink into the whole league. They did it with astonishing ease, 56-7, and second-year Minnesota Coach Cal Stoll paraphrased an old Hayes trademark when he solemnly noted after the carnage, "They are no longer three yards and a cloud of dust—now they are twelve yards and a mass of humanity."

Stoll, unquestionably, was shell-shocked in terms of the game because he had spent the entire spring, summer, and early fall building for this revenge shot at a Buckeye team his first Gopher gang nearly caught before bowing, 28-20. This time, however, Ohio State had 14 points on the board before Minnesota's touted offense ever touched the football, and it soon became a track meet. A crowd of 86,005 watched as the Buckeyes rolled to 383 rushing yards and 25 first downs. They put the ball in the air only 5 times.

Saying it even better than Stoll was his predecessor, crusty Murray Warmath, a Minnesota administrator and advance man who had come to bury an old adversary but wound up praising Woody. He said, "Never have I seen a team execute better so early in the season."

There were some old reliables leading the way, like junior fullback "Champ" Henson, the 1972 national scoring champion with 20 touchdowns, starting strongly in 1973 with 3 touchdowns and 81 yards. And the incredible sophomore tailback Archie Griffin, picking up where he left off after a dazzling freshman year.

With almost equal dispatch, but certainly more consistent defense than offense, did the Buckeyes handle the non-conference part of their 10-game schedule—a 37-3 rout of Texas Christian before 87,439 and nearly a carbon copy 27-3 job on Washington State with 87,425 witnesses.

The record crowd at the TCU Horned Frog game added their own tears to the worst rainstorm to hit Ohio Stadium in history when the 228-pound block-buster from Teays Valley, "Champ" Henson, was felled with a damaged knee midway in the second quarter. It was shortly after his fourth TD of the young season had given his mates a 14-0 edge. The Bucks went on to score 17 more the second quarter, then buttoned things up, still piling up 433 yards and 20 first downs to 151 yards and 8 first downs for the Frogs.

Harold (Champ) Henson, Ohio State's brilliant fullback, suffered a knee injury in the second game of the season against TCU and was lost for the season. Henson led the nation in scoring in 1972 with 20 touchdowns, a new Buckeye scoring record. His 44 carries against Northwestern set a school record and his 4 touchdowns in the same game tied a university mark.

It was a bit tougher doing in Coach Jim Sweeney's Washington State Cougars in a game that launched linebacker Bruce Elia's fullbacking career with a pair of touchdowns and 57 yards in 11 carries. But once again it was indomitable Archie Griffin who carved up the Cougars with 128 yards in just

When fullback Harold Henson was lost for the 1973 season with a knee injury, Bruce Elia, another junior, moved into the position. Elia started the 1972 season as a reserve fullback, but was shifted to linebacker. Although preferring to play defense, Elia took full advantage of the opportunity to succeed Henson and scored 6 touchdowns in his first 3 appearances, finishing the season with 14. Elia's success at the position indicated the depth of the Ohio State squad.

15 trips, one a 26-yard dart in the third quarter to make a tense situation relaxed. And like Woody acknowledged, "Having Archie around is a pretty good thing."

Archie also nabbed a six-yard pass from Cornelius Greene for a touchdown on a broken play that dumbfounded Sweeney.

Sophomore halfback Archie Griffin proved to be Mr. Spectacular for the Buckeyes in 1973. Not only was he the first sophomore ever to win the Big Ten's "most valuable" award (Chicago Tribune), *but he rushed to a new conference record of 1,577 yards. This surpassed the previous mark of 1,464 by Eric (the Flee) Allen of Michigan State, set in 1971. Both appeared in 11 games. Griffin's two-year record is 2,334 yards, third among Ohio State's all-time ball-carriers. He trails only fullback Jim Otis, 2,542 yards in three seasons, and Howard "Hopalong" Cassady, 2,466 yards in four campaigns. Named on several all-American teams, Griffin gained more than 100 yards in each of the 1973 games, including the Rose Bowl, where he rambled for 149. At the end of the season it was announced that Archie's brother, Ray, would enter Ohio State in the fall of 1974. Ray had been his high school's rushing leader for the past two seasons.*

"That is the stuff that beat us—a busted play," he moaned. But only in the mid-section of the game, when they scored all 27 points, were the Bucks impressive, leading Woody to comment "we did not play as well as we did in the first two," though he left unsaid his paramount point—he saves everything for the Big Ten.

Now the Buckeyes were back to the real business at hand, the Big Ten, and the Badgers of Wisconsin. Camp Randall stadium was overflowing with 77,413 fans dreaming of an upset of the then No. 1-ranked Buckeyes. They became downright rabid at the outset when they took it to the visitors, and at the conclusion when the Bucks had done them in 24-0. Sticks, stones, marbles, eggs, bottles, tennis balls, ice-filled towels, and verbal insults were hurled at the Bucks and their coach by part of the fifth largest crowd in Camp Randall history, but none of it deterred the Ohioans.

The Buckeyes forced yet another team to change courses in the middle of its screams when it made a second straight road trip, this one to Bloomington where it convinced Indiana Coach Lee Corso, if not an over-loaded Memorial Stadium collection of 53,183 sun-bathers.

Corso, the rookie coach who quickly became the king of gimmickery because of a curious string of weird innovations, played it totally straight, noting on Friday: "I admire Coach Hayes too much. He has a great team and I do not want to get him mad. I even think I will have my wife go down and give him a big kiss before the game because I do not want him mad at her either."

The Bucks did a workmanlike job on Corso's troops, jumping out front 24-0 at halftime, then coasting home as they took the opportunity to re-establish their fullback attack for a final score of 37-7.

The 60-0 homecoming rout of Northwestern was shattering to Woody's old Miami player and aid John Pont, in his first year with the Wildcats, as well as to a record crowd of 87,453 fans who saw a record 82 players gather another record 87 Buckeye leafs (citations for outstanding play).

Pont was solemn—"It was just one of those games when everything went right for Ohio, everything we did was wrong; you cannot explain them; you just try to pull yourself together for next week."

Ohio State scored nine touchdowns on just seven possessions, a strange statistic brought about when the remarkable Neal Colzie intercepted and raced 19 yards for a touchdown the second straight week and when sophomore cornerback Tim Fox blocked a Wildcat punt, then covered it for a 12-yard touchdown play.

Maybe they were looking ahead, maybe the hometown inspiration of Ray Eliot Day (honoring Illini grid coach of 1942-59), or maybe just the midseason "blahs" caught up with them, but the Bucks had a real hassle initiating a 30-0 win over Illinois at Champaign for their seventh victory.

Hayes admitted that his offense "lacked consistency early," credited a "sticky" Illini defense for doing "the best job of any team yet on our option," and cited a "tough break on the opening kickoff" (a touchdown called back) for the sluggish early performance that saw Ohio State held to a 3-0 advantage on Conway's first-quarter, 35-yard field goal.

Hayes became convinced that "this is the best defense I have had in 23 years" after his Bucks squared a lot of accounts with Michigan State in front of another record crowd of 87,600.

The 35-0 shiner dished to rookie Coach Denny Stolz' Spartans was the Bucks' third straight shutout, squared the all-time series with the Spartans at 7-7 (leaving Michigan the only Big Ten team with an edge on the Bucks), and atoned for 19-12 and 17-10 Spartan victories in the two previous years. It also was the widest margin of victory in the series, surpassing Ohio State's 54-21 win in 1969.

After having their two-game victory streak snapped and being held to just four first downs and 94 total yards, five Spartan players, who also had lost to Michigan in a rainstorm, put their heads together and agreed that Ohio State's remarkable offensive line gave it a decided edge over the Wolverines.

Hayes saluted Colzie as "the greatest punt return man I have ever seen," but took the occasion to single out 255-pound senior John Hicks as "the best lineman I have ever had—and that includes Jim Parker. Hicks has NEVER had a bad game."

Iowa certainly took nothing away from the Buckeyes in their home finale before 87,447 fans, least of all terrific tailback

240

Griffin, who ripped them for a school record of 246 yards in 30 carries which wiped out the 239 he had set as a freshman.

The Hawks, folding 55-13 in a game that was the forerunner of Coach Frank Lauterbur's departure from the school, did succeed in getting Woody's goat and causing him to take some wrath out on the reserves. Iowa scored two late touchdowns that matched the total scoring output of Ohio State's first eight victims.

"I had a notion to make the Bombers (reserves) shower in the back room for lousing up a good effort by the first defensive unit," Hayes said.

All of this, though, as everybody knows, was just so much trimming for the real thing—that season windup at Ann Arbor.

And what a windup!

Both teams unbeaten, Ohio State in nine games, Bo Schembechler's Wolverines in ten. It was strangely, for Ann Arbor, a mild day, 50 degrees, overcast and a touch of wind—but still wild as an all-time record crowd of 105,223 jammed into the Wolverine bowl, largest gathering ever to see a regular season game under NCAA auspices.

Then came the most talked-about 10-10 tie since the 1966 Michigan State-Notre Dame knot, a game in which Ohio State dominated the first half with a 10-0 lead, and threatened to run the Wolverines out of their own orchard, and Michigan coming back to dominate the last two quarters.

And Schembechler making a bigger scene in the post-game hullabaloo than Hayes ever dreamed in his best yard-line-shredding form.

If you did not care who won—and the nation's television audience may have felt that way—it was a slam-bang performance by both teams.

The teams thus tied for the conference title, and the decision as to which went to the Rose Bowl was up to a Sunday morning vote of the league's athletic directors. This eventually brought critical remarks from the disappointed Schembechler.

When the directors' vote went to the Buckeyes, rumored 6-4, Schembechler made comments for the better part of a week in a manner, to say the least, not complimentary to the directors of the league.

Both coaches had made impeccable preparations for the

championship, sealing off practice areas for a week, and Hayes had said he had never had a team better-prepared mechanically and emotionally. Woody was criticized for his conservative offense but stated after the game, "Now it can be told....our passing is no good....has not been good all season. We can't pass." He explained that Greene did not pass because of a sore finger.

But between that game in Ann Arbor and the brilliant one in Pasadena six weeks later, the passing game made a miraculous recovery because the Buckeyes came out throwing against Southern California and quite effectively, at that.

For the first time all season the Buckeyes fell behind in their Rose Bowl rematch with John McKay's vaunted Southern Cal Trojans. In fact they lagged twice, 3-0 on Chris Limahelu's 47-yard field goal in the first period, and again 14-7 midway in the second quarter when rifle-armed junior quarterback Pat Haden pitched to tailback Anthony Davis on an apparent sweep, only to have Davis drop back and loft a 10-yard scoring pass to flanker J. D. McKay. To complete the trickery, the Trojans then went for a two-point conversion pass from Haden to McKay, and the Buckeyes sagged, 14-7.

Freshman Pete Johnson, that 244-pound fullback, softened the Trojans plenty with a one-yard touchdown burst that set up a 14-14 halftime tie, and when Davis dove a yard for a touchdown, capping an 84-yard march early in the third period, the 105,267 fans and a national TV audience of 128 million might have sensed another Trojan rout, similar to the 1973 game that was tied 7-7 at half.

They were half right. It was a rout, but that was USC's last gasp as the Buckeyes then exploded for 27 points while holding McKay's men at bay.

McKay's worst fears were realized because before the game he had said, "If anybody makes a rout of the game, I'm afraid it might be Ohio State." He also said that "Nobody can outrun us, of this I am sure." And then he had to swallow those words painfully as the Buckeyes rolled up the third highest total by a Big Ten team in this series when the incomparable Griffin snaked through his team, faked four of the Trojans out of position, out-ran three others, and carried two more into the end zone on a 47-yard touchdown scamper that put the nail in the Trojan coffin.

It was a remarkably good game offensively, the Trojans doing it mostly through the air with Haden's bombs, the Buckeyes surprising by traveling all routes, including that familiar game-breaker Colzie, who lit the fuse for the explosion once again with a daring 56-yard punt return late in the third quarter that carried to the USC nine. This set up the go-ahead touchdown on a one-yard keeper by Greene on fourth down after he handed off to Pete Johnson the first three times.

Griffin was worth 149 of Ohio State's 320 rushing yards in only 22 turns; Johnson hammered 94 in 21 trips; Greene added 45 in 7; and Elia 27 in 8. More surprising was Greene hitting the Trojans with six completions in eight passes for 129 yards, four of them to senior tight end Fred Pagac, who had caught only five in ten previous games.

The Trojans' 27 first downs were 7 more than the Bucks, but came primarily as Haden threaded 21 of 39 passes for 229 yards. On the ground USC settled for 167 yards, 74 by the touted Davis in 16 trips.

Strangely, if Woody was to be criticized for not putting the ball in the air enough in early games, McKay might be cited for throwing it too much because eventually the Buckeye defense absorbed all of Haden's shots.

Hayes was ecstatic and cordially greeted the press after the game with a thank you, adding that "I have great respect for you, you know. ....this is the greatest victory I have ever had....the greatest we have ever had."

McKay was subdued but gracious and said, "I will not get into that argument about who is No. 1. I will just say Ohio State is the best team we played."

Most of his players concurred, and in a post-game survey they generally agreed that Ohio State was the toughest, Oklahoma second, and that both Ohio and Oklahoma were tougher than Notre Dame.

Hayes said he thought that the biggest play was Colzie's 56-yard punt return, and after that he figured victory was in sight.

Hayes was impressed with the appearance of the Trojans' Haden, Lynn Swann, linebacker Dale Mitchell, and defensive tackle Art Riley in the Buckeye locker room after the

Junior Pete Cusick (6-2, 244) and Senior Fred Pagac (6-1, 210) have played so many positions since their high school days they must feel they are qualified to coach. Cusick, who plans to enter law school, played five positions in high school—fullback, tight end, guard, linebacker and defensive end—just about everything except defensive tackle, where he has been starring for the past two years for the Buckeyes. Tackle Coach Chuck Clausen, who says defensive tackle is not a glamorous position,

points out that Cusick "has the ability to overpower anybody and has super techniques." Pagac (pronounced Pugitch, as in Polish-Lithuanian), came to Ohio State hopeful of being a running back. He became a defensive end as a freshman and then was switched to fullback. During spring practice he moved to tight end, and, while he had some tough opposition, became the No. 1 man. In high school, he was a fullback and linebacker. Pagac is regarded as the top blocker among the tight ends.

game—"One of the most sportsmanlike acts I have seen." But he was just as impressed with his entire offensive line that eventually out-toughed the Trojans, blew them so far off the scrimmage line that you could have pushed the Rose Bowl press box through a couple of the holes.

Maybe the toughest, most overlooked was 252-pound junior center Steve Myers, who played Trojan all-American linebacker Richard Wood off his feet.

Just about as devastating was the Buck defense, though coordinator George Hill sheepishly confessed that the unrealistic shutout he had set as the team goal "was a bit egotistical."

It was the finest hour, for certain, for what many say is the greatest Buckeye squad of all.

Appendix

THIS IS THE OHIO STATE UNIVERSITY

The Ohio State University is an active center of higher education for more than 50,000 students. The replacement value of the land, buildings, and equipment of the university is $700 million.

The university's program of off-campus instruction includes regional campuses at Lima, Mansfield, Marion, and Newark, where the first two years of undergraduate education are provided. The Agricultural Technical Institute at Wooster offers Ohio State's first associate degree program. Graduate and advanced undergraduate instruction is available at the Ohio State University Graduate Center at Wright-Patterson Air Force Base.

The university offers approximately 5,000 courses in more than 250 programs of study. The teaching faculty numbers 3,500, 80 percent of whom hold doctoral degrees. The composition of the university is complex. There are 16 colleges, 10 schools, 18 academic faculties, 13 divisions, and 80 departments. A master's degree is offered by 96 study areas, and 76 offer a Doctor of Philosophy.

There are 10 undergraduate colleges and 6 professional colleges. The undergraduate colleges are Administrative Science, Agriculture and Home Economics, The Arts, Biological Sciences, Education, Engineering, Humanities, Mathematics and Physical Sciences, Social and Behavioral Sciences, and University College. The professional colleges are Dentistry, Law, Medicine, Optometry, Pharmacy, and Veterinary Medicine.

Ohio State has a Columbus campus of 3,290 acres.

TREE PROVIDES NICKNAME

The buckeye tree, which is native to the State of Ohio, provides the nickname of the "Buckeye State" and consequently the moniker of Ohio State athletic teams. The Indians called the buckeye "Hetuck," meaning the eye of a buck, because of the striking resemblance of the seed in color and shape to the eye of a buck. Early settlers used the wood for building purposes. A law, effective October 2, 1953, adopted the buckeye as Ohio's official tree.

Brutus Buckeye, (right), symbol of the university's mascot, is greeted by Bucky Badger of Wisconsin during an Ohio State game.

BRUTUS BUCKEYE

Brutus Buckeye is a familiar sight cavorting at Ohio State football games. Worn by a student, the giant likeness of the seed of Ohio's symbolic buckeye tree first appeared at the 1965 Minnesota game.

Now the ward of the "Block O" cheering section, the famous Ohio State mascot was the idea of Ray Bourhis, a College of Arts student at the time. Bourhis was a member of the student service organization, Ohio Staters, which persuaded the athletic council to adopt the symbol as the university's mascot.

The name resulted from a contest won by an arts college senior, Kerry Reed, and a trial model was constructed of papier mache for the game.

Too heavy to be worn comfortably, Ohio Staters arranged to have a fiber glass model made from a mould which students fashioned from styrofoam, just in time for the season's final game. The project later was passed on to "Block O," which designates a committee to choose the students who wear the model at games.

BUCKEYE LEAF AWARDS

Buckeye leaves first were awarded to football players during the 1968 season as an acknowledgement of merit for outstanding performances.

They are given for a particular play, such as a recovered fumble, an intercepted pass, or an excellent run. They are also presented for an outstanding game performance.

The leading offensive and defensive player receives a leaf each week, and others are awarded based on the coaching staff's evaluation of the game films. A player may receive several leaves each week or even part of a leaf.

A presentation ceremony takes place before each Monday evening practice at a meeting of the full squad. The psychological effect of the award is difficult to determine since this particular athlete is of such football caliber that good performances would be expected. However, the leaves are a matter of pride to those who have earned them.

BUCKEYE "FIRSTS"

FIRST FOOTBALL SONG

The first football song was written just before the game with Kenyon College in Columbus in 1894. It was sung to the tune of "My Sweetheart is the Man in the Moon." The song proved inspirational. Ohio State won the game, 20 to 4, the finale of the season, which enabled the Buckeyes to have a 6-5 season's record.

FIRST VICTORY PARADE

The first downtown parade celebrating what was supposed to have been a football victory was staged in 1893. Ohio State was playing its greatest rival at the time, Kenyon College at Gambier, Ohio. A telegram of misinformation was sent to the Ohio State training quarters from Kenyon, stating that the Buckeyes had won the game. Hundreds of rejoicing students organized a parade to meet the team at the railroad station. Then they marched down High Street, the main thoroughfare of the city, to the state capitol building. As the parade approached its destination, official word reached the marchers that Ohio State had lost the game, 10 to 8, thus forcing abandonment of the parade.

FIRST PERFECT DEFENSIVE SEASON

First team to finish a season with its goal line uncrossed was the 1906 eleven, coached by A. E. Herrnstein and captained by James F. Lincoln. The 14 points scored by Michigan and Ohio Medical came on field goals and safeties. The team lost to Michigan 6 to 0 but defeated Ohio Medical 11 to 8 for an 8-1 season.

FIRST FORWARD PASS

Ohio State attempted its first forward pass in the 1906

250

season, and the Ohio championship was won by its use. In the title game with Wooster College, quarterback "Rink" Barrington threw a 10-yard pass to Harry Carr who went over for the second touchdown in a 12 to 0 victory.

FIRST RECOGNITION BY WALTER CAMP

First Ohio State player to gain recognition from Football Writer Walter Camp was fullback Millard Gibson of the 1908 team. Gibson was given honorable mention by the gridiron expert, who, eight years later was to name Charles W. (Chic) Harley as Ohio State's first all-American.

FIRST "ROOTERS" CLUB

The first organized "rooters" club was formed in 1905 with Harry E. (Mother) Ewing as head cheerleader. Fraternities were the organizations back of the movement.

LIKE FATHER, LIKE SON

The first son of a former Ohio State football player to win his gridiron letter was Nelson Dunlap, a guard on the teams of 1921, 1922, and 1923. His father, Renick Dunlap, also a guard, was captain of the 1895 team after having played the three previous years.

FIRST FOOTBALL INJURY

The first injury to an Ohio State football player occurred in 1890 before the team was ready to go to Delaware, Ohio, 25 miles away, to meet Ohio Wesleyan University. Edward D. Martin sustained a broken collar bone in practice, which made it necessary for the team to play without the services of a regular.

FIRST "DEMANDS"

Present-day pressures for an "all out" performance were preceded by 80 years.

In 1893 football rivalry between Ohio State and Kenyon College had increased to the point that newspapers were demanding an "all out" effort to make the game a "gala" event. The *Lantern*, Ohio State's student daily, stated that the band was there to stir up the great throng of 2,800 spectators.

FIRST HONORARY VARSITY "O"

The first honorary Varsity "O" to be presented to a non-athlete went to Elliott Nugent, playwright and actor. In a scenario of *The Poor Nut*, Nugent, an alumnus of the university, class of 1919, directed attention to Ohio State football. He was presented an honorary degree by the university in 1965.

FIRST WOMAN IN PRESS BOX

First woman to have a working place in the Ohio State press box was Loraine Clayton, a coed from Akron, Ohio. Miss Clayton, being the first sports editor of the student daily, the *Lantern*, in 1944 when male counterparts were in service, was placed in a radio booth as a compromise with the rule against women in the "press box proper."

FIRST FOOTBALL TITLE

Ohio State won its first undisputed football championship of Ohio in 1899. The deciding game was played on Ohio Field on Thanksgiving Day against Kenyon, the Buckeyes winning 5 to 0. It was Coach John Eckstorm's first season. Captain D. B. Sayers was the star of the game.

FIRST "YOU MUST HAVE A SEAT"

Even as early as 1909, fans demanded that anyone had a right to see the game—if he paid for a ticket.

Fans had been coming to games in tallyhos, buggies, and surreys and, even after bleachers were constructed, persisted in watching the action from their horse-drawn vehicles. Persons who paid for seats in the bleachers protested that "free-loaders" in buggies were blocking their view of the game.

After that, horses were banned from the area of the playing field, and anyone wishing to see the games had to buy bleachers seats.

This might have been the era of the first "free-loaders."

FIRST VARSITY "O" ORGANIZATION

The first Varsity "O" organization was formed in 1903. Doctor Roy O. McClure and James R. Marker, captain of the 1903 team, formulated plans. Interest was high until 1928 when enthusiasm waned and meetings ceased to be held. Interest returned in 1939 and a reorganization was effected, with the athletic board offering support.

FIRST CHEERLEADER

The first Ohio State cheerleader was Fred A. Cornell, so recognized in 1902. Mr. Cornell also was author of Ohio State's official alma mater song, "Carmen Ohio." He wrote the lyrics on a train returning from Ann Arbor after Ohio State had been crushed 86 to 0.

FIRST CAPTAIN'S BREAKFAST

The first breakfast of football captains was held in 1934 at the suggestion of Columbus manufacturer Walter Jeffrey. Mr. Jeffrey felt that former football captains should be so honored and that reunions would give them an opportunity to replay games of the past. The first breakfast was held at Scioto Country Club with Mr. Jeffrey as host. Twenty captains and two former coaches attended. The custom has continued with each captain having a mug indicating his name and year. Whenever a captain passes away, his cup is turned upside down and placed in the center of the speaker's table.

FIRST BUCKEYE TOUCHDOWN

The first Ohio State touchdown was scored by Joseph H. Large in the spring game of 1890 against Ohio Wesleyan. The Buckeyes won, 20 to 14.

FIRST DRESSING ROOM

The basement of a men's dormitory was used as the first football dressing room. The "shower" was a tub, also located in the basement.

FIRST FOOTBALL BANQUET

The first annual banquet for a football team was held in the "Busy Bee" Candy Kitchen on the Saturday following the end of the 1894 season. All of the players were guests of the board of directors. About 60 persons were seated around the long tables arranged in the form of a hollow square. Speakers included Coach Jack Ryder and Captain W. G. Nagel. Tickets were $1 each.

FIRST ATHLETIC ASSOCIATION

The first Athletic Association among the students was organized in 1881 at a meeting called by Professor A. H. Tuttle. The first athletic constitution was written by this association, but no record has been found of its details.

FIRST ELIGIBILITY RULES

The first eligibility rules were passed by the faculty in 1893 in its attempt to regulate athletic participation. In 1896 eligibility rules of the Ohio Conference were put into effect, and faculty supervision became a reality.

FIRST ATHLETIC BOARD

The first athletic board, appointed February 14, 1912, was made up of five faculty members, two alumni, and two student members. This numerical division and total has remained unchanged for more than six decades. Only names are different.

FIRST ATHLETIC TREASURER

Ray M. Royer was the first and only treasurer of the Athletic Association from 1912 until 1927 when the university assumed the responsibility of handling the financial affairs in its business office.

FIRST EXTRA POINT RECORD

Homer Howard of the 1896 team held the record of 19 for the most consecutive extra points made until Fred Schram kicked 40 in a row during the 1970 and 1971 seasons.

FIRST STADIUM CONCESSIONAIRES

First and best concessionaires in Ohio Stadium were William and Elizabeth Belknap, a couple of hard workers who knew all of the players and most of the customers. Bill, who lived to be 85, was a master at providing service. It has been said that he started out with a kettle, stand, and some wieners, a homespun project he built into serving crowds of more than 80,000. In 40 years of doing business his word was his bond. He and his wife served the best and tried to be the quickest. It has been said that Mrs. Belknap probably served more hot dogs than any woman in history. Their son, Dave, succeeded them and maintained the same service and dignity of operation.

FIRST COED IN MARCHING BAND

After a half century of tradition, during which no women had participated in the marching band, Karen Griffith, 21, of Pomeroy, Ohio, was selected to play in the trumpet section for the 1973 season. She and four female alternates survived the cut to join the 180-member band.

FIRST SPECIAL TRAIN

The first special train conveying rooters to an out-of-town game was in 1899 when 300 fans followed the team to Oberlin where the teams played a scoreless tie. It was difficult to get a special train as the railroads did not care for that kind of business, a situation duplicated a half-century later. A student store, operated by A. W. Kiler, financed the trip. The project was such a success that the following year a train was sponsored to Ann Arbor for the Michigan game. Fifteen hundred fans followed the team, and a second train was necessary. Chair car seats were $3 for the round trip. The day-coach fare was $2. Oddly, the result of the game was the same as the year before with Oberlin, a scoreless tie.

FIRST HEISMAN WINNER

Leslie Horvath, 1944 all-American, was Ohio State's first Heisman award winner. He also was elected captain of the all-American team by vote of the members of the squad at San Francisco.

FIRST COACH OF THE YEAR

Carroll Widdoes was Ohio State's first "Coach of the Year." He was elected in 1944 after a Big Ten championship season. The team was declared national "civilian" champions.

FIRST BIG TEN SCORE

Captain James M. (Boss) Kittle made Ohio State's first touchdown against a Big Ten team in the Indiana game of 1901. The Hoosiers won 18 to 6.

FIRST FOUR-LETTER WINNER

Ohio State's first all-American, "Chic" Harley, also was the first to win four letters in one year. He made them in football, baseball, basketball, and track.

FIRST GAME ON OHIO FIELD

First football game on old Ohio Field was against Heidelberg, October 1, 1898. The Buckeyes won the game 17 to 0. The field was not completed for several years and not dedicated until November 21, 1908, in a game with Oberlin. Mrs. W. O. Thompson, wife of the university president, christened the field with a flask of water from the campus spring, with this statement: "In the name of clean athletics and manly sport, I christen this 'Ohio Field.'"

Oberlin won the game 14 to 12. Fourteen years later Ohio State also lost its stadium dedication game to Michigan, 19 to 0.

FIRST OUT-OF-STATE OPPONENT

The Buckeyes' first out-of-state football foe was the University of Kentucky at Lexington, November 15, 1895. The score was 8 to 6 in favor of the Ohioans. The Kentuckians substituted their coach for a player they claimed was hurt. Centre College also was played at Danville on the following day, Centre winning 18 to 0.

FIRST PHYSICAL EXAMINATIONS

First physical examinations were conducted in 1907. Doctor H. Shindel Wingert inaugurated the plan after he became head of the athletic and physical education work. This was compulsory for all students and assured physical fitness for the athletes.

FIRST TACKLING MACHINE

The first tackling machine, now known as a dummy, was purchased in 1897 and used in practice for the game with Case.

FIRST CONFERENCE MEDAL WINNER

First winner of the Western Conference medal for proficiency in athletics and scholarship was Arthur S. Kiefer, a member of the 1915 football team.

FIRST UNIVERSITY CHEER

The first Buckeye cheer was: "Wahoo, Wahoo, Rip, Zip, Bazoo. I Yell, I Yell, OSU."

FIRST SCORE AGAINST MICHIGAN

The first touchdown against Michigan was scored by Bill Marquardt in 1904, but Michigan won, 31 to 6. "Tex" Thrower, Buckeye captain, snatched the ball after the game and made off with it. It required an angry plea from Michigan Coach Fielding Yost to retrieve it.

258

FIRST USE OF STADIUM

First use of Ohio Stadium was not for football but for the opening of a drive for Children's Hospital funds. Requested by Franz Huntington, the entertainment was held there Sunday, October 1, 1922.

FIRST SECRET PRACTICE

Secret practice was first introduced in 1894 when three workouts each week were closed. Only university officials and the press were admitted.

FIRST FOOTBALL PROFIT

First profit from a football gate was the Kenyon game of 1893. The attendance was 2,800, and $1,000 was cleared, from which a $400 debt had to be paid.

FIRST ADMINISTRATORS

First administrators under reorganization of the athletic department in 1912 were Professor Thomas E. French as faculty representative, John Richards as athletic director and football coach, and L. W. St. John as athletic manager. Six months later St. John succeeded Richards as athletic director.

FIRST VISITING SCOUT

First visiting football scout was Frank Stewart, Kenyon coach and manager in 1906. He witnessed Ohio State's game with Wittenberg.

FIRST RESERVE FOOTBALL TEAM

The first reserve football team played a schedule of five games in 1928. Four games were won and one tied. Nineteen sweaters were awarded. Reserve teams were discontinued at the close of the 1931 season but resumed in 1945 under the name of junior varsity.

FIRST ROSE BOWL TRIP

The first Rose Bowl trip was made in December, 1920, with the team losing January 1, 1921, to California, 28 to 0.

●
OHIO STATE COACHES' RECORDS

Coach	Years	Won	Lost	Tied	Pct.
Alexander S. Lilley	1890–1891	3	2	0	.600
Jack Ryder	1890				
	1892–1895				
	1898	22	24	2	.479
Charles A. Hickey	1896	5	5	1	.500
David F. Edwards	1897	1	7	1	.166
John B. Eckstorm	1899–1901	22	4	3	.810
Perry Hale	1902–1903	14	5	2	.714
E. R. Sweetland	1904–1905	13	7	2	.636
A. E. Herrnstein	1906–1909	28	10	1	.731
Howard Jones	1910	6	1	3	.750
Harry Vaughn	1911	5	3	2	.600
John R. Richards	1912	6	3	0	.667
John W. Wilce	1913–1928	78	33	9	.687
Sam S. Willaman	1929–1933	26	10	5	.695
Francis A. Schmidt	1934–1940	39	16	1	.705
Paul E. Brown	1941–1943	18	8	1	.685
Carroll C. Widdoes	1944–1945	16	2	0	.889
Paul O. Bixler	1946	4	3	2	.555
Wesley E. Fesler	1947–1950	21	13	3	.608
W. W. Hayes	1951-1973	159	49	8	.755
All-Time Record		486	205	46	.701

OHIO STATE'S ALL-OPPONENT RECORD—1890-1973

Team	G.	OSU W.	OSU L.	T.	Pct.
Akron	5	4	1	0	.800
Antioch	1	1	0	0	1.000
Arizona	1	0	1	0	.000
Auburn	1	0	0	1	.500
California	6	5	1	0	.833
Camp Sherman	1	1	0	0	1.000
Carlisle Indians	1	0	1	0	.000
Case	23	11	10	2	.522
Central Kentucky	1	0	1	0	.000
Chicago	14	10	2	2	.786
Cincinnati	11	9	2	0	.818
Colgate	2	1	0	1	.750
Colorado	1	0	1	0	.000
Columbia	2	2	0	0	1.000
Columbus Barracks	3	2	1	0	.667
Cornell	2	0	2	0	.000
Dayton YMCA	1	1	0	0	1.000
Denison	16	14	1	1	.906
De Pauw	1	1	0	0	1.000
Drake	1	1	0	0	1.000
Duke	3	2	1	0	.667
Fort Knox	1	1	0	0	1.000
Great Lakes	2	1	1	0	.500
Heidelberg	3	3	0	0	1.000
Illinois	62	39	19	4	.678
Indiana	51	37	10	4	.765
Iowa	34	22	10	2	.671
Iowa Seahawks	2	1	1	0	.500
Kentucky	3	3	0	0	1.000
Kenyon	22	16	6	0	.727
Marietta	7	6	1	0	.857
Miami	2	2	0	0	1.000
Michigan	70	26	39	5	.406
Michigan State	14	7	7	0	.500
Minnesota	17	12	5	0	.706
Missouri	9	8	0	1	.933
Mount Union	1	1	0	0	1.000
Muskingum	7	7	0	0	1.000
Navy	2	2	0	0	1.000
Nebraska	2	2	0	0	1.000
New York University	2	2	0	0	1.000
North Carolina	3	2	1	0	.667
Northwestern	47	33	13	1	.712
Notre Dame	2	0	2	0	.000

OHIO STATE'S ALL-OPPONENT RECORD—1890-1973—Cont'd

Team	G.	OSU W.	OSU L.	T.	Pct.
Oberlin	26	13	10	3	.558
Ohio Medical	9	5	2	2	.667
Ohio University	4	4	0	0	1.000
Ohio Wesleyan	29	26	2	1	.914
Oregon	5	5	0	0	1.000
Otterbein	18	13	2	3	.806
Pennsylvania	3	3	0	0	1.000
Pennsylvania State	4	0	4	0	.000
Pittsburgh	18	13	4	1	.750
Princeton	2	0	1	1	.250
Purdue	25	16	7	2	.680
Seventeenth Regiment	1	1	0	0	1.000
Southern California	16	9	6	1	.578
Southern Methodist	6	5	1	0	.833
Stanford	3	1	2	0	.333
Syracuse	1	0	1	0	.000
Texas A. & M.	2	2	0	0	1.000
Texas Christian	6	4	1	1	.750
U.C.L.A.	2	1	1	0	.500
Vanderbilt	4	3	1	0	.750
Virginia	1	1	0	0	1.000
Washington	5	4	1	0	.800
Washington State	2	2	0	0	1.000
Western Reserve	12	5	6	1	.458
West Virginia	4	3	1	0	.750
Wilmington	1	1	0	0	1.000
Wisconsin	43	32	7	4	.820
Wittenberg	15	12	3	0	.800
Wooster	8	4	2	2	.625
Total	737	486	205	46	.703

*Tie games count .5 (half-game won, half-game lost)

OHIO STATE'S ANNUAL WON-LOST RECORD

Year	Won	Lost	Tied	Pct.	Coach
1890	1	3	0	.250	A. S. Lilley—J. Ryder
1891	2	2	0	.500	Alexander S. Lilley
1892	5	3	0	.625	Jack Ryder
1893	4	5	0	.444	Jack Ryder
1894	6	5	0	.545	Jack Ryder
1895	4	4	1	.500	Jack Ryder
1896	5	5	1	.500	Charles A. Hickey
1897	1	7	1	.125	David F. Edwards
1898	3	4	1	.429	Jack Ryder
1899	9	0	1	1.000	John B. C. Eckstorm
1900	8	1	1	.889	John B. C. Eckstorm
1901	5	3	1	.625	John B. C. Eckstorm
1902	6	2	2	.750	Perry Hale
1903	8	3	0	.727	Perry Hale
1904	5	5	0	.500	E. R. Sweetland
1905	8	2	2	.800	E. R. Sweetland
1906	8	1	0	.889	A. E. Herrnstein
1907	7	2	1	.778	A. E. Herrnstein
1908	6	4	0	.600	A. E. Herrnstein
1909	7	3	0	.700	A. E. Herrnstein
1910	6	1	3	.857	Howard Jones
1911	5	3	2	.625	Harry Vaughn
1912	6	3	0	.667	John R. Richards
1913	4	2	1	.667	John W. Wilce
1914	5	2	0	.714	John W. Wilce
1915	5	1	1	.833	John W. Wilce
1916	7	0	0	1.000	John W. Wilce
1917	8	0	1	1.000	John W. Wilce
1918	3	3	0	.500	John W. Wilce
1919	6	1	0	.857	John W. Wilce
1920	7	1	0	.875	John W. Wilce
1921	5	2	0	.714	John W. Wilce
1922	3	4	0	.429	John W. Wilce
1923	3	4	1	.429	John W. Wilce
1924	2	3	3	.400	John W. Wilce
1925	4	3	1	.571	John W. Wilce
1926	7	1	0	.875	John W. Wilce
1927	4	4	0	.500	John W. Wilce
1928	5	2	1	.714	John W. Wilce
1929	4	3	1	.571	Sam S. Willaman
1930	5	2	1	.714	Sam S. Willaman
1931	6	3	0	.667	Sam S. Willaman
1932	4	1	3	.800	Sam S. Willaman
1933	7	1	0	.875	Sam S. Willaman
1934	7	1	0	.875	Francis A. Schmidt
1935	7	1	0	.875	Francis A. Schmidt
1936	5	3	0	.625	Francis A. Schmidt
1937	6	2	0	.750	Francis A. Schmidt
1938	4	3	1	.571	Francis A. Schmidt

OHIO STATE'S ANNUAL WON-LOST RECORD—Cont'd

Year	Won	Lost	Tied	Pct.	Coach
1939	6	2	0	.750	Francis A. Schmidt
1940	4	4	0	.500	Francis A. Schmidt
1941	6	1	1	.857	Paul E. Brown
1942	9	1	0	.900	Paul E. Brown
1943	3	6	0	.333	Paul E. Brown
1944	9	0	0	1.000	Carroll C. Widdoes
1945	7	2	0	.778	Carroll C. Widdoes
1946*	4	3	2	.555	Paul O. Bixler
1947	2	6	1	.278	Wesley E. Fesler
1948	6	3	0	.667	Wesley E. Fesler
1949	7	1	2	.800	Wesley E. Fesler
1950	6	3	0	.667	Wesley E. Fesler
1951	4	3	2	.555	W. W. Hayes
1952	6	3	0	.667	W. W. Hayes
1953	6	3	0	.667	W. W. Hayes
1954	10	0	0	1.000	W. W. Hayes
1955	7	2	0	.778	W. W. Hayes
1956	6	3	0	.667	W. W. Hayes
1957	9	1	0	.900	W. W. Hayes
1958	6	1	2	.778	W. W. Hayes
1959	3	5	1	.389	W. W. Hayes
1960	7	2	0	.778	W. W. Hayes
1961	8	0	1	.944	W. W. Hayes
1962	6	3	0	.667	W. W. Hayes
1963	5	3	1	.611	W. W. Hayes
1964	7	2	0	.778	W. W. Hayes
1965	7	2	0	.778	W. W. Hayes
1966	4	5	0	.444	W. W. Hayes
1967	6	3	0	.667	W. W. Hayes
1968	10	0	0	1.000	W. W. Hayes
1969	8	1	0	.889	W. W. Hayes
1970	9	1	0	.900	W. W. Hayes
1971	6	4	0	.600	W. W. Hayes
1972	9	2	0	.818	W. W. Hayes
1973	10	0	1	.913	W. W. Hayes
Totals	486	205	46	.703	

* Starting in 1946, Big Ten counted ties as half-game won and half-game lost

OHIO STATE SCORES THROUGH THE YEARS
(Ohio State Score Listed First)

1890

20	Ohio Wesleyan	14
0	Wooster	64
0	Denison	14
10	Kenyon	18

Won 1, Lost 3

1891

6	Western Reserve	50
0	Kenyon	26
8	Denison	4
6	Akron	0

Won 2, Lost 2

1892

0	Oberlin	40
62	Akron	0
80	Marietta	0
32	Denison	0
0	Oberlin	50
42	Dayton YMCA	4
18	Western Reserve	40
26	Kenyon	10

Won 5, Lost 3

1893

16	Otterbein	22
36	Wittenberg	10
10	Oberlin	36
6	Kenyon	42
16	Western Reserve	30
32	Akron	18
32	Cincinnati	0
40	Marietta	8
8	Kenyon	10

Won 4, Lost 5

1894

6	Akron	12
0	Wittenberg	6
32	Antioch	0
6	Wittenberg	13
30	Columbus Barracks	0
4	Western Reserve	24
10	Marietta	4
0	Case	38
6	Cincinnati	4
46	17th Regiment	4
20	Kenyon	4

Won 6, Lost 5

1895

14	Akron	6
6	Otterbein	14
8	Kentucky	6
0	Oberlin	12
8	Ohio Wesleyan	8
4	Cincinnati	0
0	Central Kentucky	10
0	Marietta	24
12	Kenyon	10

Won 4, Lost 4, Tied 1

1896

24	Ohio Medical	0
6	Cincinnati	8
12	Otterbein	0
0	Oberlin	16
30	Case	10
4	Ohio Wesleyan	10
10	Columbus Barracks	2
0	Ohio Medical	0
6	Wittenberg	24
12	Ohio Medical	0
18	Kenyon	34

Won 5, Lost 5, Tied 1

1897

6	Ohio Medical	0
0	Case	14
0	Michigan	34
12	Otterbein	12
0	Columbus Barracks	6
0	Oberlin	44
0	West Virginia	28
0	Cincinnati	24
0	Ohio Wesleyan	6

Won 1, Lost 7, Tied 1

1898

17	Heidelberg	0
0	Ohio Medical	0
34	Denison	0
0	Ohio Medical	10
5	Case	23
0	Kenyon	29
0	Western Reserve	49
24	Ohio Wesleyan	0

Won 3, Lost 4, Tied 1

1899

30	Otterbein	0
29	Wittenberg	0
5	Case	5
41	Ohio University	0
6	Oberlin	0
6	Western Reserve	0
17	Marietta	0

265

12	Ohio Medical	0
34	Muskingum	0
5	Kenyon	0

Won 9, Lost 0, Tied 1

1900

20	Otterbein	0
20	Ohio University	0
29	Cincinnati	0
47	Ohio Wesleyan	0
17	Oberlin	0
27	West Virginia	0
24	Case	10
6	Ohio Medical	11
0	Michigan	0
23	Kenyon	5

Won 8, Lost 1, Tied 1

1901

0	Otterbein	0
30	Wittenberg	0
17	Ohio University	0
24	Marietta	0
6	Western Reserve	5
0	Michigan	21
0	Oberlin	6
6	Indiana	18
11	Kenyon	6

Won 5, Lost 3, Tied 1

1902

5	Otterbein	0
17	Ohio University	0
30	West Virginia	0
34	Marietta	0
0	Michigan	86
51	Kenyon	5
12	Case	23
0	Illinois	0
17	Ohio Wesleyan	16
6	Indiana	6

Won 6, Lost 2, Tied 2

1903

18	Otterbein	0
28	Wittenberg	0
24	Denison	5
59	Kenyon	0
30	Muskingum	0
0	Case	12
34	West Virginia	6
0	Michigan	36
27	Oberlin	5
29	Ohio Wesleyan	6
16	Indiana	17

Won 8, Lost 3

1904

34	Otterbein	0
80	Miami	0
47	Muskingum	0
24	Denison	0
6	Michigan	31
16	Case	6
0	Indiana	8
0	Illinois	46
2	Oberlin	4
0	Carlisle Indians	23

Won 5, Lost 5

1905

6	Otterbein	6
28	Heidelberg	0
40	Muskingum	0
17	Wittenberg	0
2	Denison	0
32	DePauw	6
0	Case	0
23	Kenyon	0
0	Michigan	40
36	Oberlin	0
15	Wooster	0
0	Indiana	11

Won 8, Lost 2, Tied 2

1906

41	Otterbein	0
52	Wittenberg	0
16	Muskingum	0
0	Michigan	6
6	Oberlin	0
6	Kenyon	0
9	Case	0
12	Wooster	0
11	Ohio Medical	8

Won 8, Lost 1

1907

28	Otterbein	0
16	Muskingum	0
28	Denison	0
6	Wooster	6
0	Michigan	22
12	Kenyon	0
22	Oberlin	10
9	Case	11
23	Heidelberg	0
16	Ohio Wesleyan	0

Won 7, Lost 2, Tied 1

1908

12	Otterbein	0
0	Wooster	8

16	Denison	2
0	Western Reserve	18
6	Michigan	10
20	Ohio Wesleyan	9
7	Case	18
17	Vanderbilt	6
14	Oberlin	12
19	Kenyon	9

Won 6, Lost 4

1909

14	Otterbein	0
39	Wittenberg	0
74	Wooster	0
6	Michigan	33
29	Denison	0
21	Ohio Wesleyan	6
3	Case	11
5	Vanderbilt	0
6	Oberlin	26
22	Kenyon	0

Won 7, Lost 3

1910

14	Otterbein	12
62	Wittenberg	0
23	Cincinnati	0
6	Western Reserve	0
3	Michigan	3
5	Denison	5
10	Case	14
6	Ohio Wesleyan	0
0	Oberlin	0
53	Kenyon	0

Won 6, Lost 1, Tied 3

1911

6	Otterbein	0
3	Miami	0
0	Western Reserve	0
0	Michigan	19
3	Ohio Wesleyan	0
0	Case	9
24	Kenyon	0
0	Oberlin	0
0	Syracuse	6
11	Cincinnati	6

Won 5, Lost 3, Tied 2

1912

55	Otterbein	0
34	Denison	0
0	Michigan	14
47	Cincinnati	7
31	Case	6
23	Oberlin	17

0	Penn State	37
36	Ohio Wesleyan	6
20	Michigan State	35

Won 6, Lost 3

1913

58	Ohio Wesleyan	0
14	Western Reserve	8
0	Oberlin	0
6	Indiana	7
0	Wisconsin	12
18	Case	0
58	Northwestern	0

Won 4, Lost 2, Tied 1

1914

16	Ohio Wesleyan	2
7	Case	6
0	Illinois	37
6	Wisconsin	7
13	Indiana	3
39	Oberlin	0
27	Northwestern	0

Won 5, Lost 2

1915

19	Ohio Wesleyan	6
14	Case	0
3	Illinois	3
0	Wisconsin	21
10	Indiana	9
25	Oberlin	0
34	Northwestern	0

Won 5, Lost 1, Tied 1

1916

12	Ohio Wesleyan	0
128	Oberlin	0
7	Illinois	6
14	Wisconsin	13
46	Indiana	7
28	Case	0
23	Northwestern	3

Won 7, Lost 0
Big Ten Champions

1917

49	Case	0
53	Ohio Wesleyan	0
40	Northwestern	0
67	Denison	0
26	Indiana	3
16	Wisconsin	3

13	Illinois	0
0	Auburn	0
28	Camp Sherman	0

Won 8, Lost 0, Tied 1
Big Ten Champions

1918

41	Ohio Wesleyan	0
34	Denison	0
0	Michigan	14
56	Case	0
0	Illinois	13
3	Wisconsin	14

Won 3, Lost 3

1919

38	Ohio Wesleyan	0
46	Cincinnati	0
49	Kentucky	0
13	Michigan	3
20	Purdue	0
3	Wisconsin	0
7	Illinois	9

Won 6, Lost 1

1920

55	Ohio Wesleyan	0
37	Oberlin	0
17	Purdue	0
13	Wisconsin	7
7	Chicago	6
14	Michigan	7
7	Illinois	0
0	*California	28

Won 7, Lost 1
Big Ten Champions
* Rose Bowl

1921

28	Ohio Wesleyan	0
6	Oberlin	7
27	Minnesota	0
14	Michigan	0
7	Chicago	0
28	Purdue	0
0	Illinois	7

Won 5, Lost 2

1922

5	Ohio Wesleyan	0
14	Oberlin	0
0	Michigan	19
0	Minnesota	9
9	Chicago	14
9	Iowa	12
6	Illinois	3

Won 3, Lost 4

1923

24	Ohio Wesleyan	7
23	Colgate	23
0	Michigan	23
0	Iowa	20
42	Denison	0
32	Purdue	0
3	Chicago	17
0	Illinois	9

Won 3, Lost 4, Tied 1

1924

7	Purdue	0
0	Iowa	0
10	Ohio Wesleyan	0
3	Chicago	3
7	Wooster	7
7	Indiana	12
6	Michigan	16
0	Illinois	7

Won 2, Lost 3, Tied 3

1925

10	Ohio Wesleyan	3
9	Columbia	0
3	Chicago	3
0	Iowa	15
17	Wooster	0
7	Indiana	0
0	Michigan	10
9	Illinois	14

Won 4, Lost 3, Tied 1

1926

40	Wittenberg	0
47	Ohio Wesleyan	0
32	Columbia	7
23	Iowa	6
18	Chicago	0
13	Wilmington	7
16	Michigan	17
7	Illinois	6

Won 7, Lost 1

1927

31	Wittenberg	0
13	Iowa	6
13	Northwestern	19
0	Michigan	21
13	Chicago	7
0	Princeton	20
61	Denison	6
0	Illinois	13

Won 4, Lost 4

1928

41	Wittenberg	0
10	Northwestern	0
19	Michigan	7
13	Indiana	0
6	Princeton	6
7	Iowa	14
39	Muskingum	0
0	Illinois	8

Won 5, Lost 2, Tied 1

1929

19	Wittenberg	0
7	Iowa	6
7	Michigan	0
0	Indiana	0
2	Pittsburgh	18
6	Northwestern	18
54	Kenyon	0
0	Illinois	27

Won 4, Lost 3, Tied 1

1930

59	Mt. Union	0
23	Indiana	0
2	Northwestern	19
0	Michigan	13
0	Wisconsin	0
27	Navy	0
16	Pittsburgh	7
12	Illinois	9

Won 5, Lost 2, Tied 1

1931

67	Cincinnati	6
21	Vanderbilt	26
20	Michigan	7
0	Northwestern	10
13	Indiana	0
20	Navy	0
6	Wisconsin	0
40	Illinois	0
7	Minnesota	19

Won 6, Lost 3

1932

34	Ohio Wesleyan	7
7	Indiana	7
0	Michigan	14
0	Pittsburgh	0
7	Wisconsin	7
20	Northwestern	6
19	Pennsylvania	0
3	Illinois	0

Won 4, Lost 1, Tied 3

1933

75	Virginia	0
20	Vanderbilt	0
0	Michigan	13
12	Northwestern	0
21	Indiana	0
20	Pennsylvania	7
6	Wisconsin	0
7	Illinois	6

Won 7, Lost 1

1934

33	Indiana	0
13	Illinois	14
10	Colgate	7
28	Northwestern	6
76	Western Reserve	0
33	Chicago	0
34	Michigan	0
40	Iowa	7

Won 7, Lost 1

1935

19	Kentucky	6
85	Drake	7
28	Northwestern	7
28	Indiana	6
13	Notre Dame	18
20	Chicago	13
6	Illinois	0
38	Michigan	0

Won 7, Lost 1

Big Ten Co-Champions

1936

60	New York University	0
0	Pittsburgh	6
13	Northwestern	14
7	Indiana	0
2	Notre Dame	7
44	Chicago	0
13	Illinois	0
21	Michigan	0

Won 5, Lost 3

1937

14	Texas Christian	0
13	Purdue	0
12	Southern California	13
7	Northwestern	0
39	Chicago	0
0	Indiana	10
19	Illinois	0
21	Michigan	0

Won 6, Lost 2

269

1938

6	Indiana	0
7	Southern California	14
0	Northwestern	0
42	Chicago	7
32	New York University	0
0	Purdue	12
32	Illinois	14
0	Michigan	18

Won 4, Lost 3, Tied 1

1939

19	Missouri	0
13	Northwestern	0
23	Minnesota	20
14	Cornell	23
24	Indiana	0
61	Chicago	0
21	Illinois	0
14	Michigan	21

Won 6, Lost 2
Big Ten Champions

1940

30	Pittsburgh	7
17	Purdue	14
3	Northwestern	6
7	Minnesota	13
7	Cornell	21
21	Indiana	6
14	Illinois	6
0	Michigan	40

Won 4, Lost 4

1941

12	Missouri	7
33	Southern California	0
16	Purdue	14
7	Northwestern	14
21	Pittsburgh	14
46	Wisconsin	34
12	Illinois	7
20	Michigan	20

Won 6, Lost 1, Tied 1

1942

59	Ft. Knox	0
32	Indiana	21
28	Southern California	12
26	Purdue	0
20	Northwestern	6
7	Wisconsin	17
59	Pittsburgh	19
44	Illinois	20
21	Michigan	7
41	Iowa Seahawks	12

Won 9, Lost 1
Big Ten Champions

1943

13	Iowa Seahawks	28
27	Missouri	6
6	Great Lakes	13
7	Purdue	30
0	Northwestern	13
14	Indiana	20
46	Pittsburgh	6
29	Illinois	26
7	Michigan	45

Won 3, Lost 6

1944

54	Missouri	0
34	Iowa	0
20	Wisconsin	7
26	Great Lakes	6
34	Minnesota	14
21	Indiana	7
54	Pittsburgh	19
26	Illinois	12
18	Michigan	14

Won 9, Lost 0
Big Ten Champions

1945

47	Missouri	6
42	Iowa	0
12	Wisconsin	0
13	Purdue	35
20	Minnesota	7
16	Northwestern	14
14	Pittsburgh	0
27	Illinois	2
3	Michigan	7

Won 7, Lost 2

1946

13	Missouri	13
21	Southern California	0
7	Wisconsin	20
14	Purdue	14
39	Minnesota	9
39	Northwestern	27
20	Pittsburgh	13
7	Illinois	16
6	Michigan	58

Won 4, Lost 3, Tied 2

1947

13	Missouri	7
20	Purdue	24
0	Southern California	32
13	Iowa	13
0	Pittsburgh	12
0	Indiana	7
7	Northwestern	6
7	Illinois	28
0	Michigan	21

Won 2, Lost 6, Tied 1

1948

21	Missouri	7
20	Southern California	0
7	Iowa	14
17	Indiana	0
34	Wisconsin	32
7	Northwestern	21
41	Pittsburgh	0
34	Illinois	7
3	Michigan	13

Won 6, Lost 3

1949

35	Missouri	34
46	Indiana	7
13	Southern California	13
0	Minnesota	27
21	Wisconsin	0
24	Northwestern	7
14	Pittsburgh	10
30	Illinois	17
7	Michigan	7
17	*California	14

Won 7, Lost 1, Tied 2
Big Ten Co-Champions
* Rose Bowl

1950

27	Southern Methodist	32
41	Pittsburgh	7
26	Indiana	14
48	Minnesota	0
83	Iowa	21
32	Northwestern	10
19	Wisconsin	14
7	Illinois	14
3	Michigan	9

Won 6, Lost 3

1951

7	Southern Methodist	0
20	Michigan State	24
6	Wisconsin	6
10	Indiana	32
47	Iowa	21
3	Northwestern	0
16	Pittsburgh	14
0	Illinois	0
0	Michigan	7

Won 4, Lost 3, Tied 2

1952

33	Indiana	13
14	Purdue	21
23	Wisconsin	14
35	Washington State	7
0	Iowa	8

24	Northwestern	21
14	Pittsburgh	21
27	Illinois	7
27	Michigan	7

Won 6, Lost 3

1953

36	Indiana	12
33	California	19
20	Illinois	41
12	Pennsylvania	6
20	Wisconsin	19
27	Northwestern	13
13	Michigan State	28
21	Purdue	6
0	Michigan	20

Won 6, Lost 3

1954

28	Indiana	0
21	California	13
40	Illinois	7
20	Iowa	14
31	Wisconsin	14
14	Northwestern	7
26	Pittsburgh	0
28	Purdue	6
21	Michigan	7
20	*Southern California	7

Won 10, Lost 0
Big Ten Champions
* Rose Bowl

1955

28	Nebraska	20
0	Stanford	6
27	Illinois	12
14	Duke	20
26	Wisconsin	16
49	Northwestern	0
20	Indiana	13
20	Iowa	10
17	Michigan	0

Won 7, Lost 2
Big Ten Champions

1956

34	Nebraska	7
32	Stanford	20
26	Illinois	6
6	Penn State	7
21	Wisconsin	0
6	Northwestern	2
35	Indiana	14
0	Iowa	6
0	Michigan	19

Won 6, Lost 3

1957

14	Texas Christian	18
35	Washington	7
21	Illinois	7
56	Indiana	0
16	Wisconsin	13
47	Northwestern	6
20	Purdue	7
17	Iowa	13
31	Michigan	14
10	*Oregon	7

Won 9, Lost 1
Big Ten Champions
* Rose Bowl

1958

23	Southern Methodist	20
12	Washington	7
19	Illinois	13
49	Indiana	8
7	Wisconsin	7
0	Northwestern	21
14	Purdue	14
38	Iowa	28
20	Michigan	14

Won 6, Lost 1, Tied 2

1959

14	Duke	13
0	Southern California	17
0	Illinois	9
15	Purdue	0
3	Wisconsin	12
30	Michigan State	24
0	Indiana	0
7	Iowa	16
14	Michigan	23

Won 3, Lost 5, Tied 1

1960

24	Southern Methodist	0
20	Southern California	0
34	Illinois	7
21	Purdue	24
34	Wisconsin	7
21	Michigan State	10
36	Indiana	7
12	Iowa	35
7	Michigan	0

Won 7, Lost 2

1961

7	Texas Christian	7
13	U.C.L.A.	3
44	Illinois	0
10	Northwestern	0
30	Wisconsin	21
29	Iowa	13

16	Indiana	7
22	Oregon	12
50	Michigan	20

Won 8, Lost 0, Tied 1
Big Ten Champions

1962

41	North Carolina	7
7	U.C.L.A.	9
51	Illinois	15
14	Northwestern	18
14	Wisconsin	7
14	Iowa	28
10	Indiana	7
26	Oregon	7
28	Michigan	0

Won 6, Lost 3

1963

17	Texas A. & M.	0
21	Indiana	0
20	Illinois	20
3	Southern California	32
13	Wisconsin	10
7	Iowa	3
7	Penn State	10
8	Northwestern	17
14	Michigan	10

Won 5, Lost 3, Tied 1

1964

27	Southern Methodist	8
17	Indiana	9
26	Illinois	0
17	Southern California	0
28	Wisconsin	3
21	Iowa	19
0	Penn State	27
10	Northwestern	0
0	Michigan	10

Won 7, Lost 2

1965

3	North Carolina	14
23	Washington	21
28	Illinois	14
7	Michigan State	32
20	Wisconsin	10
11	Minnesota	10
17	Indiana	10
38	Iowa	0
9	Michigan	7

Won 7, Lost 2

1966

14	Texas Christian	7
22	Washington	38
9	Illinois	10
8	Michigan State	11
24	Wisconsin	13
7	Minnesota	17
7	Indiana	0
14	Iowa	10
3	Michigan	17

Won 4, Lost 5

1967

7	Arizona	14
30	Oregon	0
6	Purdue	41
6	Northwestern	2
13	Illinois	17
21	Michigan State	7
17	Wisconsin	15
21	Iowa	10
24	Michigan	14

Won 6, Lost 3

1968

35	Southern Methodist	14
21	Oregon	6
13	Purdue	0
45	Northwestern	21
31	Illinois	24
25	Michigan State	20
43	Wisconsin	8
33	Iowa	27
50	Michigan	14
27	*Southern California	16

Won 10, Lost 0
Big Ten Champions
* Rose Bowl

1969

62	Texas Christian	0
41	Washington	14
54	Michigan State	21
34	Minnesota	7
41	Illinois	0
35	Northwestern	6
62	Wisconsin	7
42	Purdue	14
12	Michigan	24

Won 8, Lost 1
Big Ten Co-Champions

1970

56	Texas A. & M.	13
34	Duke	10
29	Michigan State	0
28	Minnesota	8
48	Illinois	29
24	Northwestern	10
24	Wisconsin	7
10	Purdue	7
20	Michigan	9
17	*Stanford	27

Won 9, Lost 1
Big Ten Champions
* Rose Bowl

1971

52	Iowa	21
14	Colorado	20
35	California	3
24	Illinois	10
27	Indiana	7
31	Wisconsin	6
14	Minnesota	12
10	Michigan State	17
10	Northwestern	14
7	Michigan	10

Won 6, Lost 4

1972

21	Iowa	0
29	North Carolina	14
35	California	18
26	Illinois	7
44	Indiana	7
28	Wisconsin	20
27	Minnesota	19
12	Michigan State	19
27	Northwestern	14
14	Michigan	11
17	*Southern California	42

Won 9, Lost 2
Big Ten Co-Champions
* Rose Bowl

1973

56	Minnesota	7
37	Texas Christian	3
27	Washington State	3
24	Wisconsin	0
37	Indiana	7
60	Northwestern	0
30	Illinois	0
35	Michigan State	0
55	Iowa	13
10	Michigan	10
42	*Southern California	21

Won 10, Lost 0, Tied 1
Big Ten Co-Champions
* Rose Bowl

OHIO STATE TEAM FOOTBALL RECORDS

Most Points, One Game
  Non-Conference: 128, Ohio State vs. Oberlin (0), 1916
  Conference: 83, Ohio State vs. Iowa (21), 1950
Most Points, One Season (Average per game)
  Full Season: 383, 1969 (42.5 per game)
  Conference: 307, 1973 (38.3 per game)
Most Touchdowns, One Game
  Non-Conference: 19, Ohio State vs. Oberlin, 1916
  Conference: 12, Ohio State vs. Iowa, 1950
Most Extra Points Made, One Game
  Non-Conference: 14, Ohio State vs. Oberlin, 1916
  Conference: 11, Ohio State vs. Iowa, 1950
Most First Downs, One Game: 39, vs. Drake, 1935
Most Plays, One Game: 101, 1969 vs. T.C.U. and vs. Illinois
Most Consecutive Wins without Ties
  22, 1967-1969
Most Consecutive Conference Wins: 17 (1954-1956) and
  (1967-1969)
Most Consecutive Losses
  5, 1890-1891, and 1897
Most Total Net Offense Yardage
  4,439 (2,774 rush, 1,665 pass), 1969, nine games
  4,402 (3,018 rush, 1,384 pass), 1968, ten games

RUSHING

Most Yards Rushing, One Game
  Non-Conference: 440, Ohio State vs. Ft. Knox, 1942
  Conference: 517, Ohio State vs. Illinois, 1962
Most Net Yards Rushing, One Season
  3,125, 1970 (ten games)
  2,774, 1969 (nine games)
Most Rushing Plays, One Game
  86, Ohio State vs. Illinois, 1943
Most Rushing Plays, One Season
  660, 1972 (eleven games)
  656, 1968 (ten games)
  599, 1969 (nine games)
Most First Downs Rushing
  164, 1968 (ten games)
  163, 1969 (nine games)
Most Touchdowns Rushing, One Season
  40, 1942 (ten games)
  36, 1969 (nine games)

PASSING

Most Passes Attempted, One Game
  44, Ohio State vs. Pittsburgh, 1952
Most Passes Attempted, One Season
  230, Ohio State (113 completed), 1969
Most Passes Completed, One Game
  25, Ohio State vs. Pittsburgh, 1952

Most Passes Completed, One Season
  124, Ohio State (217 attempts), 1952
Most Yards Passing, One Game
  312, Ohio State vs. Washington State, 1952
Most Yards Passing, One Season
  1,709 (124 of 217), 1952
Most First Downs Passing, One Game
  15, Ohio State vs. Pittsburgh, 1952
Most First Downs Passing, One Season
  74, 1969
Most Passes Had Intercepted, One Season
  21 (of 181 attempts), 1953
Best Passing Completion Percentage, One Game 15 or
  more passes
  .875, 18 of 21 for 375 yds. and 5 TD's, Ohio State vs.
    Washington State, 1952
Best Passing Completion Percentage, One Season
  .571, 124 of 217, 1952

PUNTING

Most Punts, One Game
  21, Ohio State vs. Michigan, 1950
Most Punts, One Season
  71, 1951
Most Yardage Punting, One Game
  685, Ohio State vs. Michigan, 1950
Most Average Yardage Punting, One Season
  42.5, 1939 (54 punts)

OHIO STATE INDIVIDUAL RECORDS

Most Points, One Season
  120, Harold Henson (20 TD's), 1972
Most Points, Career
  222, Howard Cassady (37 TD's), 1952-1955 (36 games)
  210, Jim Otis (35 TD's), 1967-1969 (27 games)
Most Touchdowns, One Season
  20, Harold Henson, 1972
Most Yards Rushing, One Game
  246, Archie Griffin (30 carries), vs. Iowa, 1973
Most Field Goals, One Game
  3, Gary Cairns, vs. Illinois, 1966
Most Field Goals, One Season
  8, Dick Van Raaphorst, 1963 (nine games)
  8, Bob Funk, 1965 (nine games)
Most Extra Points Made, One Game
  10, Vic Janowicz, vs. Iowa, 1950

275

Most Extra Points Made, One Season
    45, Blair Conway (55 attempts), 1973 (11 games)
Most Consecutive Extra Points Made
    40, Fred Schram, 1970-71
Total Net Offense, One Game
    313 yards, John Borton, vs. Washington State, 1952
Total Net Offense, One Season
    1,585, Rex Kern, 1969 (nine games)
Total Net Offense, Career
    4,158, Rex Kern (1968–1,506; 1969–1,585; 1970–1,607),
    27 games
Most Rushing Attempts, One Game
    44, Harold Henson, vs. Northwestern (153 Yds.), 1972
Most Rushing Attempts, One Season
    247, Archie Griffin, 1973 (11 games)
    225, Jim Otis, 1969 (nine games)
    261, John Brockington, 1970 (ten games)
Most Net Yards Rushing, One Season
    1,577, Archie Griffin (247 attempts), 1973 (11 games)
    1,027, Jim Otis (225 attempts), 1969 (nine games)
    1,142, John Brockington (261 attempts), 1970 (ten games)

PASSING

Most Passes Attempted, One Game
    44, John Borton (25 completions), vs. Pittsburgh, 1952
Most Passes Attempted, One Season
    196, John Borton (115 completions), 1952
Most Passes Completed, One Game
    25, John Borton (44 attempts), vs. Pittsburgh, 1952
Most Passes Completed, One Season
    115, John Borton (196 attempts), 1952
Most Consecutive Passes Completed
    12, Bill Mrukowski, vs. UCLA (9) and Illinois (3), 1961
Most Passes Had Intercepted, One Season
    12, Bill Long (192 attempts), 1966
Most Net Yards Passing, One Game
    312, John Borton, vs. Washington State, 1952
Most Net Yards Passing, One Season
    1,555, John Borton, 1952
Most Scoring Passes Completed, One Game
    5, John Borton, vs. Washington State, 1952
Most Scoring Passes Completed, One Season
    15, John Borton, 1952

PASS RECEIVING

Most Passes Caught, One Game
    12, Bob Grimes, vs. Pittsburgh, 1952
    12, Bill Anders, vs. Washington, 1966
Most Passes Caught, One Season

276

55, Bill Anders, 1966
Most Passes Caught, Career
108, Bill Anders, 1965-1967
Most Pass Receiving Yardage, One Game
187, Bob Grimes, vs. Washington State, 1952
Most Pass Receiving Yardage, One Season
671, Bill Anders, 1966
Most Pass Receiving Yardage, Career
1,298, Bill Anders, 1965-1967
Most Touchdown Passes Caught, One Game
4, Bob Grimes, vs. Washington State, 1952
Most Touchdown Passes Caught, One Season
6, Bob Grimes, 1952

PUNTING

Most Punts, One Game
21, Vic Janowicz, vs. Michigan, 1950
Most Punts, One Season
62, Vic Janowicz, 1951
Most Yardage Punts, One Game
685, Vic Janowicz, vs. Michigan, 1950
Most Yardage Punts, One Season
2,446, Vic Janowicz, 1951
Most Average Yards Per Kick, One Game
57.3, Fred Morrison, vs. Wis. (4 punts, 229 yards), 1949
Most Average Yards Per Kick, One Season
42.5, Don Scott, 1939 (54 punts)

PENALTIES

Most Yards Penalized, One Game (Ohio State)
102 yards, vs. Pittsburgh, 1952
Most Yards Penalized, Two Teams, One Game
179 yards, Northwestern (94), Ohio State (85), 1953

OHIO STATE FOOTBALL RECORDS
OHIO STATE CAREER LEADERS
RUSHING

Name	Yards	Attempts	Years
1. Jim Otis	2542	585	1967-69
2. Howard Cassady	2466	435	1952-55
3. Archie Griffin	2444	406	1972-73
4. Don Clark	2216	395	1956-58
5. Bob Ferguson	2162	423	1959-61

PASSING

Name	Yards	Comp.	Att.	TD's	Years
1. Don Unverferth	2518	220	468	12	1963-65
2. Rex Kern	2444	188	364	19	1968-70
3. John Borton	2129	170	272	19	1951-54
4. Bill Long	1768	154	308	8	1966-68
5. Tony Curcillo	1249	76	171	8	1950-51

TOTAL OFFENSE

Name	Total	Rush	Pass	Plays	Years
1. Rex Kern	4158	1714	2444	716	1968-70
2. Jim Otis	2542	2542	0	585	1967-69
3. Archie Griffin	2444	2444	0	406	1972-73
4. Howard Cassady	2530	2466	64	448	1952-55
5. Don Unverferth	2395	−123	2518	610	1963-65

SCORING

Name	Points	TD's	PAT	FG	Years
1. Howard Cassady	222	37	0	0	1952-55
2. Jim Otis	210	35	0	0	1967-69
3. Chic Harley	201	23	39	10	1916, '17, 1919
4. Bob Ferguson	158	26	1	0	1959-61
5. John Brockington	144	24	0	0	1968-70

PASS RECEIVING

Name	Caught	Yards	TD's	Years
1. Billy Anders	108	1318	5	1965-67
2. Bo Rein	77	929	4	1964-66
3. Bruce Jankowski	66	967	9	1968-70
4. Jan White	61	762	8	1968-70
5. Bob Grimes	48	698	7	1950-52

INTERCEPTIONS

Name	Number	Yards	TD's	Years
1. Mike Sensibaugh	22	248	0	1968-70
2. Fred Bruney	17	212	0	1950-52
3. Ted Provost	16	124	1	1967-69
4. Arnie Chonko	11	72	0	1962-64
5. Marts Beekley	7	65	0	1950-52

278

PUNTING

Name	Avg.	Yards	TD's	Years
1. Pete Perini	39.2	4,396	112	1947-49
2. Gary Lago	38.5	5,814	151	1970-72
3. Steve Dreffer	38.4	3,496	91	1962-64
4. Vic Janowicz	37.9	4,552	120	1949-51
5. Mike Sensibaugh	37.3	2,905	78	1968-70

PUNT RETURN YARDAGE

Name	Yards	Number	TD's	Years
1. Neal Colzie	683	43	4	1972-73
2. Tom Campana	535	50	1	1969-71
3. Larry Zelina	529	40	2	1968-70
4. Mike Polaski	395	35	1	1967-69
5. Don Clark	305	27	0	1956-58

MOST VALUABLE PLAYERS

1930, Wesley Fesler, end
1931, Robert Haubrich, tackle
1932, Lew Hinchman, fullback
1933, Michael Vuchinich, center
1934, Gomer Jones, center
1935, Gomer Jones, center
1936, Ralph Wolfe, center
1937, Ralph Wolfe, center
1938, Jim Langhurst, halfback
1939, Steve Andrako, center
1940, Claude White, center
1941, Jack Graf, fullback
1942, Charles Csuri, tackle
1943, Gordon Appleby, center
1944, Les Horvath, halfback
1945, Ollie Cline, fullback
1946, Cecil Souders, end
1947, Dave Templeton, guard
1950, Vic Janowicz, halfback
1951, Vic Janowicz, halfback
1952, Fred Bruney, halfback

1953, George Jacoby, tackle
1954, Howard Cassady, halfback
1955, Howard Cassady, halfback
1956, Jim Parker, guard
1957, Bill Jobko, guard
1958, Jim Houston, end
1959, Jim Houston, end
1960, Tom Matte, halfback
1961, Bob Ferguson, fullback
1962, Bill Armstrong, center
1963, Matt Snell, halfback
1964, Ed Orazen, tackle
1965, Doug Van Horn, guard
1966, Ray Pryor, center
1967, Dirk Worden, linebacker
1968, Mark Stier, linebacker
1969, Jim Otis, fullback
1970, Jim Stillwagon, middle guard
1971, Tom DeLeone, center
1972, George Hasenohrl, tackle
1973, Archie Griffin, halfback

279

MOST VALUABLE PLAYERS IN BIG TEN

1941, Jack Graf, fullback
1944, Les Horvath, halfback
1945, Ollie Cline, fullback

1950, Vic Janowicz, halfback
1955, Howard Cassady, halfback
1973, Archie Griffin, halfback

OHIO STATE PLAYERS IN ALL-STAR GAMES

COACHES' ALL-AMERICAN GAME
(Buffalo, Atlanta, Lubbock)

Tom Barrington, 1966, halfback
Charles Bryant, 1962, end
Mike Current, 1967, tackle
Jim Davidson, 1965, tackle
Tom DeLeone, 1972, center
Bob Ferguson, 1962, fullback
David Foley, 1969, tackle
David Francis, 1963, fullback
Rex Kern, 1971, quarterback
Tom Matte, 1961, halfback

Rufus Mayes, 1969, tackle
Jim Otis, 1970, fullback
Daryl Sanders, 1963, tackle
Matt Snell, 1964, fullback
Jim Stillwagon, 1971, middle guard
Sam Tidmore, 1962, end
Doug Van Horn, 1966, guard
Bob Vogel, 1963, tackle
Paul Warfield, 1964, halfback

Head East Coach: Woody Hayes, 1962

CHICAGO TRIBUNE CHARITIES ALL-STAR GAME
(Chicago, Illinois)

John Brockington, 1971, fullback
Fred Bruney, 1953, halfback
Charles Bryant, 1962, end
Howard Cassady, 1956, halfback
Ollie Cline, 1948, fullback
Carl Cramer, 1934, quarterback
Mike Current, 1967, tackle
James Daniell, 1942, tackle
James Davidson, 1965, tackle
Dean Dugger, 1955, end
Jack Dugger, 1944-45, end
William Dye, 1937, quarterback
Gene Fekete, 1944, fullback
Robert Ferguson, 1962, fullback
Dick Fisher, 1942, halfback
Dave Foley, 1969, tackle
Joe Gailus, 1934, guard
Sherwin Gandee, 1952, end

Sidney Gillman, 1934, end
Jack Graf, 1942, fullback
Charles Hamrick, 1937, guard
Richard Heekin, 1936, halfback
Les Horvath, 1945, halfback
Jim Houston, 1960, end
Lindell Houston, 1944-46, end
Charles Hutchison, 1970, tackle
Robert Jabbusch, 1944, guard
George Jacoby, 1954, tackle
Dan James, 1959, center
Thomas James, 1947, halfback
Vic Janowicz, 1952, halfback
Jack Jennings, 1950, tackle
William Jobko, 1958, guard
Gomer Jones, 1936, center
Michael Kabealo, 1939, fullback
James Karcher, 1936, guard

280

Dave Leggett, 1956, quarterback
Vic Marino, 1940, guard
Thomas Matte, 1961, halfback
Rufus Mayes, 1969, tackle
Donald McCafferty, 1944-45, end
James McDonald, 1938, fullback
William Michael, 1957, end
Robert Momsen, 1951, guard
Regis Monahan, 1935, guard
Fred Morrison, 1950, fullback
James Parker, 1957, guard
Stanley Pincura, 1936, quarterback
Ted Provost, 1970, halfback
Trevor Rees, 1936, end
Ted Rosequist, 1934, tackle
Daryl Sanders, 1963, tackle
Esco Sarkkinen, 1940, end
Paul Sarringhaus, 1944, halfback
Richard Schafrath, 1959, tackle

Alex Schoenbaum, 1939, tackle
Inwood Smith, 1937, guard
Matt Snell, 1964, fullback
Cecil Souders, 1947, end
Jack Stephenson, 1942, tackle
Jack Tatum, 1971, halfback
Dave Templeton, 1949, guard
James Tyrer, 1961, tackle
Richard Van Raaphorst, 1964, tackle
Robert Vogel, 1963, tackle
Michael Vuchinich, 1934, fullback
Paul Warfield, 1964, halfback
Bobby Watkins, 1955, halfback
Tad Weed, 1955, quarterback
Merle Wendt, 1937, end
Damon Wetzel, 1935, fullback
William Willis, 1944-45, tackle
Ralph Wolf, 1938, center
Gus Zarnas, 1938, guard

SENIOR BOWL
(Mobile, Alabama)

Bill Anders, 1968, end
Marts Beekley, 1953, halfback
Fred Bruney, 1953, halfback
Charles Bryant, 1962, end
Tom Campana, 1972, halfback
Mike Current, 1967, tackle
Dean Dugger, 1955, end
Sonny Gandee, 1952, end
Jerry Harkrader, 1956, halfback
George Jacoby, 1954, tackle

Dan James, 1959, center
Tom Jenkins, 1964, guard
Dave Katterhenrich, 1963, fullback
Dave Leggett, 1955, quarterback
Bill Michael, 1957, tackle
Gary Moeller, 1963, guard
Daryl Sanders, 1963, guard
Dick Schafrath, 1959, tackle
Mike Takacs, 1954, guard
Bob Thornton, 1955, center

NORTH-SOUTH SHRINE GAME
(Miami, Florida)

William Anders, 1967, end
Alan Fiers, 1960, tackle
David Francis, 1962, fullback
Richard Guy, 1956, tackle
John Hlay, 1952, fullback
Alan Jack, 1969, guard
Dan James, 1958, center
Gary Moeller, 1962, guard
Robert Momsen, 1950, tackle

Bo Rein, 1966, halfback
William Ridder, 1965, guard
Daryl Sanders, 1962, tackle
Richard Schafrath, 1958, tackle
Paul Schmidlin, 1969, tackle
Matt Snell, 1963, fullback
Don Unverferth, 1965, quarterback
Stan White, 1971, linebacker

Steven Andrako, 1940, center
William Armstrong, 1962, center
Tom Barrington, 1965, halfback
John Biltz, 1951, guard
Robert Brugge, 1945, halfback
Fred Bruney, 1953, halfback
Howard Cassady, 1955, halfback
Arnie Chonko, 1965, halfback
Don Clark, 1958, halfback
Tony Curcillo, 1953, quarterback
Mike Current, 1966, tackle
Jim Daniell, 1942, tackle
Jim Davidson, 1965, tackle
Hal Dean, 1947, guard
Bob Ferguson, 1961, fullback
Richard Fisher, 1946, halfback
Richard Flanagan, 1945, halfback
Dan Fronk, 1958, center
Joseph Gailus, 1934, guard
Sherwin Gandee, 1952, end
Sidney Gillman, 1934, end
George Guthrie, 1953, tackle
William Hackett, 1945, guard
Tom Hague, 1954, end
Charles Hamrick, 1937, tackle
Robert Haubrich, 1932, guard
Richard Heekin, 1936, halfback
Jim Herbstreit, 1960, halfback
Dick Himes, 1967, tackle
Leslie Horvath, 1943-45, halfback
Jim Houston, 1960, end
Harry Howard, 1971, halfback
Mike Ingram, 1961, center
George Jacoby, 1954, guard
Victor Janowicz, 1952, halfback
Thomas Jenkins, 1963, tackle

Gomer Jones, 1936, center
Dwight Kelley, 1965, center
Frank Kremblas, 1958, quarterback
George Lynn, 1943, quarterback
Francis Machinsky, 1953, tackle
Tom Matte, 1960, halfback
Robert McCullough, 1951, center
William Michael, 1957, tackle
Richard Michael, 1960, end
Regis Monahan, 1931, guard
William Mrukowski, 1962, quarterback
James Otis, 1969, fullback
James Parker, 1957, guard
Tom Perdue, 1961, end
Ted Provost, 1969, halfback
Leo Raskowski, 1928, tackle
James Roseboro, 1957, halfback
Sam Selby, 1930, guard
Dean Sensanbaugher, 1944, halfback
Rick Simon, 1971, tackle
Cecil Souders, 1944-47, end
William Spahr, 1965, end
Mike Takacs, 1954, guard
Dave Templeton, 1949, guard
William Trautwein, 1951, tackle
Jim Tyrer, 1960, tackle
Paul Warfield, 1963, halfback
Doug Van Horn, 1965, guard
Kenneth Vargo, 1955, center
Robert Vogel, 1962, tackle
Merle Wendt, 1937, end
Robert White, 1960, fullback
Dave Whitfield, 1969, end
Ralph Wolf, 1938, center
Gus Zarnas, 1938, guard

PLAYER HONOREES,
TOUCHDOWN CLUB OF COLUMBUS

John Brockington	1972	David Foley	1969
Howard Cassady	1956-57	Randy Gradishar	1973
Galen Cisco	1957	Archie Griffin	1972-73

John Hicks	1973	Marion Motley	1969
Vic Janowicz	1956	Jim McDonald	1969
Jack Jennings	1956	Jim Parker	1957-65
Ike Kelley	1966	Dick Schafrath	1966
Rex Kern	1970-71	Jim Stillwagon	1971
James Marshall	1970	Jack Tatum	1970-71
Fred Morrison	1956-70	Tad Weed	1956

OHIO STATE ALL-AMERICANS

1916
Charles W. Harley, halfback
Robert Karch, tackle

1917
Charles W. Harley, halfback
Charles Bolen, end

1919
Charles W. Harley, halfback

1920
Gaylord Stinchcomb, halfback
Iolas Huffman, guard

1921
Iolas Huffman, tackle

1925
Edwin Hess, guard

1926
Marty Karow, fullback
Edwin Hess, guard

1927
Leo Raskowski, tackle

1928
Wesley E. Fesler, end

1929
Wesley E. Fesler, end

1930
Wesley E. Fesler, end

1932
Joseph Gailus, guard

1934
Merle Wendt, end
Regis Monahan, guard

1935
Merle Wendt, end
Inwood Smith, guard
Gomer Jones, center

1937
Gus Zarnas, guard

1939
Esco Sarkkinen, end
Donald Scott, halfback

1942
Robert Shaw, end
Lindell Houston, guard
Charles Csuri, tackle

1944
Leslie Horvath, halfback
William Hackett, guard
William Willis, tackle
Jack Dugger, end

1945
Warren Amling, guard

1946
Warren Amling, tackle

283

1950
Robert Momsen, guard
Robert McCullough, center
Victor Janowicz, halfback

1952
Mike Takacs, guard

1954
Howard Cassady, halfback
Dean Dugger, end

1955
James Parker, guard
Howard Cassady, halfback

1956
James Parker, guard

1957
Aurelius Thomas, guard

1958
James Marshall, tackle
James Houston, end
Robert White, fullback

1959
James Houston, end

1960
Robert Ferguson, fullback

1961
Robert Ferguson, fullback

1964
Arnold Chonko, halfback
Dwight Kelley, center
James Davidson, tackle

1965
Doug Van Horn, tackle
Dwight Kelley, center

1966
Ray Pryor, center

1968
David Foley, tackle
Rufus Mayes, tackle

1969
James Stillwagon, guard
Ted Provost, halfback
James Otis, fullback
Jack Tatum, halfback

1970
Jan White, end
James Stillwagon, guard
Jack Tatum, halfback
John Brockington, fullback
Mike Sensibaugh, halfback
Tim Anderson, halfback

1971
Tom DeLeone, center

1972
John Hicks, tackle
Randy Gradishar, linebacker

1973
John Hicks, tackle
Randy Gradishar, linebacker
Van DeCree, end
Archie Griffin, halfback

OHIO STATE'S FOOTBALL CAPTAINS

1890	Jesse L. Jones (Spring) Paul M. Lincoln (Fall)	1933	Joseph T. Gailus Sidney Gillman
1891	Richard T. Ellis	1934	J. Regis Monahan
1892	Richard T. Ellis	1935	Gomer T. Jones
1893	A. P. Gillen	1936	Merle E. Wendt
1894	W. G. Nagel	1937	Ralph C. Wolf James A. McDonald
1895	Renick W. Dunlap		
1896	Edward H. French William A. Reed	1938	Michael Kabealo Carl G. Kaplanoff
1897	Harry C. Hawkins	1939	Steven F. Andrako
1898	John Segrist	1940	E. James Langhurst
1899	D. B. Sayers	1941	Jack W. Stephenson
1900	J. H. Tilton	1942	George M. Lynn
1901	J. M. Kittle	1943	John R. Dugger
1902	W. F. Coover	1944	Gordon Appleby
1903	James R. Marker	1945	William C. Hackett, D.V.M.
1904	John D. Thrower	1946	Warren Amling, D.V.M.
1905	Ralph W. Hoyer	1947	Robert O. Jabbusch
1906	James F. Lincoln	1948	David I. Templeton
1907	H. J. Schory	1949	A. Jack Wilson
1908	W. D. Barrington	1950	Henry Bill Trautwein
1909	Thomas H. Jones	1951	Robert C. Heid
1910	Leslie R. Wells	1952	Bernie G. Skvarka
1911	Frank P. Markley	1953	Robert V. Joslin George Jacoby
1912	Don B. Barricklow	1954	C. Richard Brubaker John R. Borton
1913	W. Irving Geissman		
1914	Campbell J. Graf	1955	Frank C. Machinsky Kenneth W. Vargo
1915	Ivan B. Boughton,		
1916	Frank Sorenson	1956	Franklin D. R. Ellwood P. William Michael
1917	Harold J. Courtney Howard Courtney	1957	Galen B. Cisco Leo M. Brown
1918	Clarence A. MacDonald	1958	Francis T. Kremblas Richard P. Schafrath
1919	Charles W. Harley		
1920	Iolas M. Huffman, M.D.	1959	James E. Houston
1921	Cyril E. Myers, M.D.	1960	James Tyrer James Herbstreit
1922	Lloyd A. Pixley		
1923	Boni Petcoff, M.D.	1961	Thomas Perdue Michael Ingram
1924	Francis D. Young		
1925	Harold B. Cunningham	1962	Gary Moeller Robert Vogel
1926	Marty G. Karow		
1927	Theodore R. Meyer	1963	Ormonde Ricketts Matthew Snell
1928	Leo Raskowski		
1929	Alan M. Holman	1964	James Davidson William Spahr Thomas Kiehfuss
1930	Wesley E. Fesler		
1931	Stuart K. Holcomb	1965	Dwight Kelley Gregory Lashutka
1932	Lewis G. Hinchman		

1966	John Fill, Michael Current, Ray Pryor	1970	Rex Kern, Jan White, James Stillwagon, Douglas Adams
1967	Billy Ray Anders Samuel Elliott	1971	Harry Howard Tom DeLeone
1968	David Foley Dirk Worden	1972	Richard Galbos George Hasenohrl
1969	David Whitfield Alan Jack	1973	Gregory Hare Richard Middleton

HELMS FOUNDATION HALL OF FAME

Coaches
Dr. John W. Wilce, 1913-1928
Francis A. Schmidt, 1934-1940

National Championship Teams
1954   10-0-0
1968   10-0-0

Football Player Of The Year
Howard Cassady, 1955

Hall Of Fame Players
Wesley Fesler, end, 1930
Charles Harley, halfback, 1919
Leslie Horvath, halfback, 1944
James Parker, guard, 1956

Rose Bowl Players Of The Game
1950, Fred Morrison, fullback
1955, David Leggett, quarterback
1969, Rex Kern, quarterback
1974, Cornelius Greene, quarterback

NATIONAL FOOTBALL FOUNDATION AND HALL OF FAME SCHOLAR-ATHLETES
Arnold Chonko, halfback, 1964
Willard Sander, fullback, 1965
Dave Foley, tackle, 1968

ACADEMIC ALL-AMERICANS
John Borton, quarterback, 1952
Dick Hilinski, tackle, 1954
Bob White, fullback, 1958
Tom Perdue, end, 1961
Arnie Chonko, defensive back, 1964

Bill Ridder, middle guard, 1965
Dave Foley, tackle, 1966-68
Mark Stier, linebacker, 1968
Bill Urbanik, defensive tackle, 1969
Rick Simon, offensive guard, 1971

CONFERENCE MEDAL WINNERS (FOOTBALL)
1915, Arthur S. Kiefer, guard
1918, Howard Yerges, quarterback
1921, Andrew J. Nemecek, center
1922, Iolas M. Huffman, tackle
1923, Charles N. Workman
1924, Harry D. Steel, tackle

1930, Joseph A. Ujhelyi, guard
1931, Richard C. Larkins, tackle
1937, Inwood Smith, guard
1938, Ralph C. Wolf, center
1940, Esco Sarkkinen, end
1943, Esten W. Vickroy, center

1944, George R. Hoeflinger, fullback
1945, Jack R. Dugger
1946, Donald Steinberg, tackle
1947, Warren E. Amling, guard
1948, Robert Jabbusch, guard
1951, Richard D. Widdoes, halfback

1965, Arnold Chonko, halfback
1966, Donald V. Unverferth,
quarterback
1967, Willard F. Sander, fullback
1969, David E. Foley, tackle
1972, Rick Simon, tackle

ROSE BOWL SCORES
(Since Big Ten Pact in 1947)

Year	Team	Score	Opponent	Score
1947	Illinois	45	U.C.L.A.	14
1948	Michigan	49	So. California	0
1949	Northwestern	20	California	14
1950	OHIO STATE	17	California	14
1951	Michigan	14	California	6
1952	Illinois	40	Stanford	7
1953	So. California	7	Wisconsin	0
1954	Michigan State	28	U.C.L.A.	20
1955	OHIO STATE	20	So. California	7
1956	Michigan State	17	U.C.L.A.	14
1957	Iowa	35	Oregon State	19
1958	OHIO STATE	10	Oregon	7
1959	Iowa	38	California	12
1960	Washington	44	Wisconsin	8
1961	Washington	17	Minnesota	7
1962	Minnesota	21	U.C.L.A.	3
1963	So. California	42	Wisconsin	37
1964	Illinois	17	Washington	7
1965	Michigan	34	Oregon State	7
1966	U.C.L.A.	14	Michigan State	12
1967	Purdue	14	So. California	13
1968	So. California	14	Indiana	3
1969	OHIO STATE	27	So. California	16
1970	So. California	10	Michigan	3
1971	Stanford	27	OHIO STATE	17
1972	Stanford	13	Michigan	12
1973	So. California	42	OHIO STATE	17
1974	OHIO STATE	42	So. California	21

Big Ten teams have won 18
West Coast teams have won 10

(Previously, Michigan appeared in the Rose Bowl
in 1902 and Ohio State in 1921)

BIG TEN CHAMPIONSHIPS
(Since Ohio State entered the conference in 1913)

School	Outright Titles	Shared Titles	Total
Michigan	6	13	19
OHIO STATE	12	5	18
Illinois	6	5	11
Minnesota	5	6	11
Purdue	1	6	7
Iowa	2	3	5
Wisconsin	2	2	4
Northwestern	1	3	4
Michigan State	2	1	3
Chicago	2	1	3
Indiana	1	1	2

ALL-TIME BIG TEN STANDINGS—1896-1973
(Conference Games Only)

Team	Won	Lost	Tied	Pct.
OHIO STATE (1913)	233	100	20	.700
Michigan (1896)	241	114	14	.679
Michigan State (1953)	80	55	3	.593
Minnesota (1896)	221	160	25	.580
Chicago (1896)	120	99	14	.545
Purdue (1896)	178	192	26	.481
Illinois (1896)	201	217	22	.479
Wisconsin (1896)	185	206	34	.473
Northwestern (1896)	162	243	19	.400
Iowa (1900)	129	218	20	.377
Indiana (1900)	100	246	21	.289

BIG TEN STANDINGS
SINCE "WOODY" HAYES COACHED AT OHIO STATE
(1951-1973)

Team	Won	Lost	Tied	Pct.	Titles Clear	Titles Share
OHIO STATE	117	32	7	.764	7	2
Michigan	96	58	5	.603	2	3
Purdue	89	59	7	.601	0	2
Michigan State	80	55	3	.585	2	1
Minnesota	82	71	8	.536	0	2
Wisconsin	70	83	9	.458	2	1
Illinois	65	89	6	.422	2	1
Iowa	55	92	7	.374	2	1
Northwestern	56	101	3	.357	0	0
Indiana	36	106	3	.254	0	1

TOTAL SEASON STANDINGS (1951-1973)

Team	Won	Lost	Tied	Pct.	Coaches (Years)
OHIO STATE	156	49	8	.732	Hayes (23)
Michigan State	140	74	5	.654	Munn (3)
					Daugherty (19)
					Stolz (1)
Michigan	137	76	5	.643	Oosterbaan (8)
					C. Elliott (10)
					Schembechler (5)
Purdue	121	82	13	.596	Holcomb (5)
					Mollenkopf (14)
					DeMoss (3)
					Agase (1)
Minnesota	107	100	11	.517	Fesler (3)
					Warmath (18)
					Stoll (2)
Wisconsin	100	107	12	.483	Williamson (5)
					Bruhn (11)
					Coatta (3)
					Jardine (4)
Iowa	90	116	11	.437	Evashevski (10)
					Burns (5)
					Nagel (5)
					Lauterbur (3)
Illinois	92	119	7	.436	R. Eliot (9)
					P. Elliott (7)
					Valek (4)
					Blackman (3)
Northwestern	85	127	4	.401	Voigts (4)
					Saban (1)
					Parseghian (8)
					Agase (9)
					Pont (1)
Indiana	67	147	3	.313	Smith (1)
					Crimmins (5)
					Hicks (1)
					Dickens (7)
					Pont (8)
					Corso (1)

OHIO STATE ATTENDANCE FIGURES
(Since Stadium Was Built in 1922)

Year	Home Games	Home Attendance	Game Average	Total Games	Total Attendance
1922	5	162,500	32,500	7	212,500
1923	5	148,113	29,622	8	236,113
1924	6	196,072	32,678	8	246,078
1925	6	201,445	33,574	8	276,945
1926	5	183,578	36,715	8	277,116
1927	5	188,776	37,755	8	323,776
1928	5	232,256	46,451	8	305,756
1929	6	213,941	35,657	8	354,941
1930	5	189,334	37,867	8	279,334
1931	5	163,356	32,671	9	301,278
1932	5	113,718	22,743	8	167,218
1933	5	139,065	27,813	8	264,573
1934	5	205,095	41,019	8	262,475
1935	5	252,950	50,590	8	353,314
1936	5	282,575	56,515	8	391,375
1937	5	274,432	54,886	8	399,683
1938	5	314,893	62,978	8	392,893
1939	5	250,885	50,177	8	386,362
1940	5	300,947	60,189	8	392,018
1941	5	287,715	57,543	8	486,468
1942	7	307,509	43,930	10	465,165
1943	5	150,071	30,014	9	288,580
1944	7	336,802	48,114	9	460,429
1945	6	378,327	63,054	9	544,567
1946	5	371,017	74,203	9	603,600
1947	6	428,436	71,406	9	603,591
1948	6	420,930	70,155	9	566,662
1949	5	382,146	76,429	10	743,154
1950	5	368,053	73,610	9	570,287
1951	6	455,737	75,956	9	636,484
1952	6	453,911	75,652	9	593,647
1953	5	397,890	79,578	9	630,042
1954	6	480,340	80,057	10	739,748
1955	6	490,477	81,749	9	669,375
1956	6	494,575	82,629	9	651,554
1957	6	484,118	80,686	10	770,372
1958	6	499,119	83,186	9	659,280
1959	6	495,556	82,589	9	690,681
1960	5	413,583	82,716	9	665,406
1961	5	414,712	82,942	9	623,934
1962	6	481,480	80,247	9	644,410
1963	5	416,623	83,324	9	622,545
1964	7	583,740	83,391	9	713,667
1965	5	416,232	83,244	9	687,022
1966	6	488,399	81,400	9	633,634
1967	5	383,502	76,700	9	591,693
1968	6	482,564	80,427	10	725,904

1969	5	431,175	86,235	9	687,858
1970	5	432,451	86,490	10	798,924
1971	6	506,699	84,449	10	751,463
1972	6	509,420	84,903	11	850,741
1973	6	523,369	87,228	11	925,162
Totals	286	18,180,608	67,761	459	26,974,041

OHIO STATE'S RECORD CROWDS

RECORD YEARS

FIVE HOME GAMES		SIX HOME GAMES	
Year	Attendance	Year	Attendance
1970	432,451	1973	523,369
1969	431,175	1972	506,699
1963	416,623	1971	406,699
1965	416,232	1958	499,119

SEVEN HOME GAMES	
Year	Attendance
1964	583,740

TOTAL SEASON ATTENDANCE RECORDS

Year	Games	Home	Road	Total
1973	11*	523,369	401,793	924,842
1972	11*	509,420	341,321	850,741
1970	10*	432,451	366,473	798,924
1957	10*	484,118	286,254	770,372

*Includes Rose Bowl Attendance

TEN LARGEST OHIO STADIUM CROWDS

Year	Attendance	Scores
1973	87,600*	OHIO STATE 35, Mich. State 0
1973	87,453*	OHIO STATE 60, Northwestern 0
1973	87,447*	OHIO STATE 55, Iowa 13
1973	87,439*	OHIO STATE 37, Tex. Christian 3
1973	87,425*	OHIO STATE 27, Wash. State 3
1970	87,331*	OHIO STATE 20, Michigan 9
1970	86,673*	OHIO STATE 24, Northwestern 10
1970	86,667*	OHIO STATE 28, Minnesota 8
1969	86,641*	OHIO STATE 54, Mich. State 21
1971	86,616*	Mich. State 17, OHIO STATE 10

*Standing Room Permitted

TEN LARGEST CROWDS AWAY

Year	Attendance	Place	Scores
1974	105,267	Pasadena	OHIO STATE 42, So. Calif. 21
1973	106,869	Pasadena	So. Calif. 42, OHIO STATE 17
1971	104,116	Ann Arbor	Michigan 10, OHIO STATE 7
1970	103,839	Pasadena	Stanford 27, OHIO STATE 17
1969	103,588	Ann Arbor	Michigan 24, OHIO STATE 12
1969	102,063	Pasadena	OHIO STATE 27, So. Calif. 16
1957	101,001	Ann Arbor	OHIO STATE 31, Michigan 14
1950	100,963	Pasadena	OHIO STATE 17, California 14
1958	98,202	Pasadena	OHIO STATE 10, Oregon 7
1955	97,369	Ann Arbor	OHIO STATE 17, Michigan 0

OHIO STATE FOOTBALL LETTERMEN
1890 - 1973

"A"

Abbott, Albert G., '98
Ackerman, Cornelius, '25, '26, '27
Adamle, Doug O., '68, '69, '70
Adams, J. J., '00
Adderly, Nelson W., '65
Addison, Evert, '18, '22
Adulewicz, Casimir T., '59
Alber, George H., '26, '27, '28
Aleskus, Joseph P. '37, '38
Allen, Robert M., '32
Amlin, George P., '66
Amling, Warren E., '44, '45, '46
Anders, Billy, '65, '66, '67
Anderson, Charles C., '39, '40
Anderson, Kim L., '64, '65, '66
Anderson, Richard, '51, '52
Anderson, Richard L., '64, '65
Anderson, Thomas L., '64
Anderson, William T., '68, '69, '70
Andrako, Steven F., '38, '39
Andrews, Lawrence F., '51
Andrick, Thedore K., '64, '65
Antenucci, Frank L., '34, '35, '36
Appleby, Gordon E., '42, '43, '44
Arledge, Richard, '51
Armstrong, Billy J., '60, '61, '62
Armstrong, Ralph A., '49, '50, '51
Arnold, Birtho, '57, '58, '59
Arnold, George A., '07
Aston, Daniel B., '69
Auer, John J., '53
Augenstein, Jack G., '53

"B"

Bass, James W., '65, '66
Bachman, Stanley, '08, '09, '10
Backhus, Tom A., '67, '68, '69
Bahin, Michael, '95
Bailey, Ralph, '58
Baird, Charles H., '93
Baker, Ray G., '45
Baldacci, Thomas G., '55, '56, '57
Ballmer, Paul E., '58

Barnes, Robert L., '90
Barnett, Orlando T., '63, '64, '65
Barrett, Fred W., '28, '29
Barricklow, Donald B., '10, '11, '12
Barrington, Thomas G., '63, '64, '65
Barrington, Walter D., '05, '06, '07, '08
Bartley, Thomas A., '67, '68
Bartoszek, Mike, '72, '73
Bartschy, Ross D., '37, '38, '39
Baschnagel, Brian, '72, '73
Battista, Thomas, '71
Baumgarten, Eugene H., '30, '31
Baxa, Thomas L., '72
Beam, William D., '59
Bear, C. L., '11
Beatty, Hobart, '90
Beatty, Hugh G., '09, '10
Bechtel, Earl R., '52
Beecroft, Charles, '71, '72
Beekley, Marts E., '51, '52
Beerman, Raymond O., '57
Beetham, Rupert R., '99
Belgrave, Earl, '72
Bell, Frederick J., '17, '18
Bell, Robert R., '25, '26, '27
Bell, Robin A., '26, '27
Bell, William M., '29, '30, '31
Beltz, Richard H., '34, '35
Bender, Edward A., '68
Benedict, Charles Y., '97
Benis, Joe V., '30, '31
Benis, Michael K., '60
Bettridge, John W., '34, '35, '36
Betz, Wayne O., '61, '62
Biel, William J., '45
Bilkie, Edward R., '50
Biltz, John W., '49, '50
Birdseye, Claude H., '01
Blaine, Ernest D., '10, '11
Blair, Howard H., '20, '21, '22
Blanchard, Bruce J., '25
Bledsoe, John, '71, '72
Bliss, Harry W., '19, '20
Bliss, Keith H., '37, '38
Blose, M. L., '96, '97
Bobo, Hubert L., '54
Bodenbender, David G., '64

Boesel, Richard, '15, '16, '17
Boesel, Stephen W., '09, '10
Bolen, Charles W., '15, '16, '17
Bolin, Stuart R., '95
Bolser, Harvey J., '38
Bombach, Jaren D., '67
Bompiedi, Carl J., '33
Bond, Robert J., '52, '53, '54, '55
Bonica, Charles, '70, '71, '72
Bonnie, Dale B., '47
Bonnie, David M., '46, '47
Boone, Chelsea A., '09
Booth, William, '36
Booth, William A., '53, '54, '55
Boothman, Dale M., '00, '01
Borton, John R., '51, '52, '53, '54
Boucher, Arthur F., '34, '35
Boughner, Richard J., '37, '38
Boughton, Ivan B., '13, '14, '15
Bowermaster, Russell L., '56, '57, '58
Bowers, Brian, '73
Bowman, Howard, '90
Bowsher, Gerald J., '59
Boxwell, Kenneth E., '44
Boynton, A. J., '93, '94
Bradley, Robert T., '25
Bradshaw, Morris, '71, '72, '73
Breeht, Edward L., '57
Breese, Clarence, '99, '00
Bridge, Brooklyn B., '12
Briggs, Maurice, '12, '13
Brindle, Arthur B., '05
Brockington, John S., '68, '69, '70
Bronson, A. P., '90
Brophy, James F., '97, '98
Brown, G. W., '02
Brown, Jeff, '72
Brown, Leo M., '55, '56, '57
Brown, Matthew, '43, '44, '45
Brown, Stanley, '02
Brubaker, Carl R., '53, '54
Bruckner, Edwin, '40, '41
Brudzinski, Robert, '73
Brugge, Robert S., '44, '46, '47
Bruney, Fred K., '50, '51, '52
Bruney, Robert O., '62, '63
Brungard, David A., '67, '68

Brungard, George, '35
Bryant, Charles S., '59, '60, '61
Bryce, Chalmers K., '06, 07, '08
Bugel, Thomas E., '63, '64, '65
Bulen, Elwood J., '00, '01
Bullock, William M., '38
Buonamici, Nicholas, '73
Burgett, Richard K., '41
Burgin, Asbury L., '65, '66
Burrows, Roger W., '70
Burton, Arthur F., '67, '68, '69
Busich, Sam, '34, '35
Buss, Charles, '91
Butcher, Fred E., '95, '96, '97, '00
Butts, Robert W., '60, '62
Byrne, Edward G., '03, '04

"C"

Cairns, Gary L., '66, '67
Calkins, George H., '94, '95
Cameron, George D., '24
Campana, Thomas, '69, '70, '71
Campanella, Joseph A., '50
Cannavino, Joseph P., '55, '56, '57
Cannavino, Michael L., '46, '47, '48
Cappell, Richard A., '69, '70, '71
Carlin, Earl V., '39, '40
Carlin, Oscar E., '27, '29
Carroll, Paul B., '11, '12
Carroll, William M., '30, '31, '32
Carson, Samuel K., '93, '94
Carter, David W., '28, '29
Carver, Rolly J., '04
Cassady, Craig, '73
Cassady, Howard (Hop), '52, '53, '54, '55
Case, Claude H., '02, '03
Cheney, David A., '68, '69, '70
Cheroke, George, '41
Cherry, Boyd V., '12, '13, '14
Chonko, Arnie, '62, '63, '64
Chrissinger, Warren O., '36, '37
Cisco, Galen, '55, '56, '57
Claflin, Walter N., '06, '07, '08
Claggett, Edward F., '04, '06, '07
Clair, Frank J., '38, '39, '40
Clare, Robert L., '09, '10

Clark, David B., '02, '03, '04
Clark, Donald, '56, '57, '58
Clark, James, '47, '48, '49
Clark, Lovell J., '43
Clark, Myers A., '24, '25, '26
Cleary, Thomas J., '42
Cline, Oliver M., '44, '45, '47
Cline, W. D., '95
Clotz, Dennis R., '61
Coburn, James A., '70
Cochran, Kenneth L., '31
Cochran, Terrence A., '65
Coffee, Charles B., '27, '28, '29
Cole, George N., '91
Cole, Robert, '56
Collmar, William J., '54, '55
Colzie, Neal, '72, '73
Conley, William N., '70, '71
Connor, Daniel D., '61
Conrad, Frederick B., '31, '32, '33
Conroy, James, '69
Conway, Blair, '72, '73
Cooke, Clement C., '10
Cooks, Ronald L., '55, '57
Coover, Winifred F., '00, '01, '02
Cope, Harry, '98
Cope, James, '72, '73
Cornell, Fred A., '02
Cornsweet, Harold, '39
Cory, Lincoln T., '27, '28
Cott, Richard S., '19, '20, '21
Cottrell, Ernest E., '44
Courtney, Harold J., '15, '16, '17
Courtney, Howard G., '15, '16, '17
Cowman, Randy, '72
Cox, Joseph E., '26, '27, '28
Cox, Joseph F., '09, '10, '11
Cox, Melvin B., '34
Cramer, Carl F., '31, '32, '33
Cramer, William E., '17
Crane, Jameson, '45, '46, '47
Crapser, Steven R., '69
Crawford, Albert K., '56, '57, '58
Crawford, Thomas E., '57
Crecilius, Arthur W., '94, '95
Crow, Fred W., '37
Csuri, Charles A., '41, '42, '46

Culbertson, Claude L., '97
Cumiskey, Frank S., '34, '35, '36
Cummings, John, '72
Cummings, William G., '56
Cunningham, Dan, '71
Cunningham, Harold B., '23, '24, '25
Cunningham, John F., '96
Cunningham, Leo, '43
Curcillo, Anthony, '50, '51, '52
Curren, Michael F., '04
Current, Michael, '65, '66
Curto, Patrick, '73
Cusick, Peter, '72, '73
Cutillo, Dan, '71, '72

"D"

Dale, Michael D., '70
Daniell, James L., '39, '40, '41
Dannelley, Scott, '72, '73
Darst, Lester D., '07, '11
Daugherty, Harold R., '45
Daughters, Charles G., '16
Davidson, James, '63, '64
Davies, Thomas C., '18, '19
Davis, Jeff, '72, '73
Davis, Paul J., '43
Davis, Vernon H., '98
Dawdy, Donald A., '53
Dawson, Jack S., '48
Dean, C. A., '02
Dean, Harold S., '41, '42, '46
Debevc, Mark C., '68, '69, '70
DeCree, Van, '72, '73
DeLeone, Thomas D., '69, '70, '71
Delich, Peter D., '31, '32, '33
DeLong, A. Z., '95, '96
Demmel, Robert C., '47, '50
Dendiu, Traian T., '44, '48
Denker, Irv, '52
Denman, Edgar, '94
Detrick, Roger, '59, '60
DeVoe, Keith E., '23, '24, '25
Diehl, William, '32
Dike, Ed, '04
Dill, M. R., '28, '29
Dill, Raymond, '01

Dillman, Thomas M., '54, '55, '56
Dillon, Daniel D., '66
Diltz, Charles R., '01, '02, '03, '04
DiPierro, Ramon F., '44, '46, '47, '48
Disher, Larry L., '57
Dixon, Kenneth, '70, '71
Dixon, Thornton D., '39, '40, '41, '45
Doig, Hal F., '20, '21
Doll, John, '72
Donley, Fred, '08
Donovan, Brian P., '68, '69, '70
Doolittle, Francis W., '46, '47
Dorris, Victor, '37
Dorsey, Robert S., '47, '48
Dove, Robert E., '44, '45
Doyle, Richard A., '50, '52
Drake, Phillip B., '42
Drakulich, Samuel, '33
Dreffer, Stephan D., '62, '63, '64
Drenick, Douglas J., '62, '63, '64
Dreyer, Carl A., '24
Dreyer, Virgil O., '15, '16
DuBois, Wilbur L., '00
Dugger, Dean, '52, '53, '54
Dugger, John R., '42, '43, '44
Duncan, Howard D., '46, '47
Dunlap, John H., '95, '96
Dunlap, Nelson H., '21, '22, '23
Dunlap, Renick W., '91, '92, '93, '94, '95
Dunsford, Jan H., '04, '05
Durtschi, William R., '42
Dwyer, Donald W., '65, '66, '67
Dwyer, R. E., '98
Dye, William H., '34, '35, '36

"E"

Eachus, William N., '65, '66
Eagleson, John H., '98
Early, Ellis T., '21
Eberle, John J., '08, '09
Ebinger, Elbert C., '55
Eby, Byron, '26, '27, '28
Edwards, William R., '49

Egbert, Archie D., '10
Ehrensberger, Carl H., '30
Ehrsam, Gerald R., '66, '67, '68
Ehrsam, John H., '44, '45
Elder, Walter W., '01, '02
Elgin, Edward G., '22
Elia, Bruce, '72, '73
Elliott, Samuel, '65, '66, '67
Ellis, Richard T., '90, '91, '92
Ellwood, Franklin, D., '55, '56
Ellwood, Richard P., '49, '50
Endres, George J., '50
Endres, Robert L., '51
Engensperger, Albert, '96, '97
Englebeck, Amos H., '04, '06
Ernst, L. C., '91, '92
Ervin, Terry L., '66, '67
Espy, Bennie, E., '62, '63
Ewalt, Dwight S., '13
Ewart, Kenneth L., '17, '19
Ewing, Harry E., '05
Ezzo, William, '72, '73

"F"

Facchine, Richard, '55
Faehl, Paul J., '50
Fair, Robert F., '63
Farcasin, Constantine J., '18, '19, '22
Farrell, John R., '60
Fay, Sherman, '99, '00, '01, '02
Fazio, Charles A., '45, '46, '47, '48
Fedderson, Jerold V., '43
Fekete, Eugene, '42
Feldwisch, Henry W., '11
Fender, Paul E., '67
Ferguson, Robert E., '59, '60, '61
Ferko, Richard, '70, '71
Ferrall, Junius B., '30, '31, '32
Fertig, Dwight L., '67
Fesler, Wesley E., '28, '29, '30
Fields, Jerry E., '58, '59
Fiers, Alan, '59
Fill, John M., '64, '65, '66
Fioretti, Anthony R., '22, '23
Fisch, Frank, '33, '34, '35
Fischer, Louis C., '50, '51

Fisher, Richard, '39, '40, '41, '45
Flanagan, Richard E., '44
Fletcher, Kevin, '70, '71, '72
Flowers, James T., '19
Foley, David, '66, '67, '68
Foley, W. J., '93
Fontaine, Lawton L., '29
Fontes, Arnold P., '65, '66
Fontes, Leonard J., '58, '59
Fordham, Forrest P., '37, '38
Fortney, Harrison, '63
Foss, Clarence M., '02, '03, '04, '05
Foss, Earl D., '10, '11
Foster, Rodney, '61, '62
Foster, Thomas B., '05
Fouch, George E., '27, '28
Foulk, Charles W., '90, '91, '92
Fout, James E., '45
Fox, Samuel S., '40, '41
Fox, Tim, '72, '73
France, Doug, '72, '73
Francis, David L., '60, '61, '62
Frayer, Leo A., '94
Frechtling, Arthur G., '99, '00
French, Edward H., '93, '94, '95
Fried, Lawrence L., '30
Friedman, Max, '18
Fronk, Daniel A., '57, '58
Frye, Robert H., '41, '42
Fuller, Mark A., '19
Fulton, William S., '99
Funk, Robert H., '41, '42
Funkhauser, Samuel K., '08, '12

"G"

Gaffney, Mike, '72
Gage, Ralph G., '58
Gailus, Joseph T., '31, '32, '33
Galbos, Richard, '71, '72
Gales, Charles P., '36, '37, '38
Gales, Richard, '71, '72, '73
Gandee, Charles F., '45, '49, '50
Gandee, Sherwin K., '48, '50, '51
Gaudio, Angelo R., '46
Geissman, W. I., '11, '12, '13
Gentile, Jim M., '68, '69, '70

George, August, '35
German, William, '59, '60
Gibbs, George C., '93
Gibbs, Jack G., '54
Gibson, Millard F., '06, '07, '08
Giessen, Carl, '94, '95
Gilbert, Charles R., '48, '49
Gill, Arthur G., '04
Gillam, Neal, '18
Gillard, James H., '05, '06
Gilliam, Neil, '18, '21
Gillian, Lonnie R., '67, '68, '69
Gillie, George W., '05, '06, '07
Gillis, Clarence, '01
Gillman, Sidney, '31, '32, '33
Ginn, Dwight G., '14, '15
Givens, Dan D., '71
Glasser, Chester F., '27, '28, '29
Godfrey, Ernest R., '14
Goodsell, Douglas R., '51, '52
Gorby, Herbert L., '45
Gordon, George D., '44
Gorrill, Charles V., '23, '24, '25
Gradishar, Randy, '71, '72, '73
Grady, Robert J., '29, '30, '31
Graf, Campbell J., '12, '13, '14
Graf, Campbell R., '39
Graf, Jack R., '39, '40, '41
Graf, Larry, '73
Greenberg, Jack Z., '31, '32
Greene, Cornelius, '73
Greene, Horatius A., '69
Griffin, Archie, '72, '73
Griffith, A. G., '92
Griffith, William A., '29, '30
Griffith, William N., '24
Grim, Fred, '25, '26, '27
Grimes, Robert L., '50, '51, '52
Griswold, Francis H., '27
Grundies, Arthur J., '38, '40
Guthrie, George P., '51, '52
Guy, Richard S., '54, '55, '56
Guzik, Frank A., '53

"H"

Hackett, William G., '42, '43, '44, '45

Hackett, William J., '67, '69
Haddad, George A., '37
Haer, Archie H., '67
Hague, Leslie J., '47, '48, '49
Hague, Thomas R., '52, '53
Hall, Robert H., '43
Hallabrin, John D., '39, '40, '41
Hamilton, Forrest R., '45, '46, '47
Hamilton, Ian B., '22
Hamilton, Mardo M., '44
Hamilton, Ray L., '49, '50, '51
Hamlin, Stanley A., '65
Hamrick, Charles E., '34, '35, '36
Hansley, Terence, '59
Hardman, von Allen, '61
Hare, Gregory, '71, '72, '73
Hargreaves, William B., '37
Harkins, Donald L., '62, '63, '64
Harkrader, Jerry, '53, '54, '55
Harley, Charles W., '16, '17, '19
Harman, Timothy A., '70
Harre, Gilbert A., '34, '35
Harrell, James, '73
Harris, Jimmie L., '69, '70, '71
Hart, Randall J., '67, '68, '69
Hartman, Gabriel C., '58, '59, '60
Hasenohrl, George, '70, '71, '72
Haubrich, Richard, '29, '30, '31
Hauer, Oscar A., '58, '59, '60
Haupt, Richard A., '61
Havens, William F., '14, '15
Hawkins, Harry, '97
Hayden, Leophus, '68, '69, '70
Hazel, David, '71, '72
Hecker, Robert H., '43
Hecker, Robert R., '43
Hecklinger, Ronald D., '43
Heekin, Richard J., '33, '34, '35
Hefflinger, Ronald D., '43
Heid, Robert C., '49, '50, '51
Henderson, Herbert R., '20
Henry, Joseph P., '49
Henson, Harold, '72
Herbstreit, James H., '58, '59, '60
Hermann, Harvey J., '59
Herron, Kendall, '44
Hershberger, Peter J., '40, '41

Hess, Edwin A., '24, '25, '26
Hess, William W., '60, '61, '62
Hicks, John, '70, '72, '73
Hieronymous, Ted W., '25, '27, '28
Hietikko, James L., '50, '51
Hilinski, Richard, '53, '54
Himes, Richard D., '65, '66, '67
Hinchman, Lewis G., '30, '31, '32
Hlay, John, '50, '51
Hobt, Watt A., '12, '13, '14
Hoffer, Joe R., '31
Hofmayer, Edward I., '38
Holcomb, Stuart K., '29, '30, '31
Holloway, Ralph B., '68, '69, '70
Holman, Alan M., '28, '29
Holtkamp, Ferdinand, '16, '19
Holycross, Tim, '71, '72, '73
Honaker, Frank C., '21, '22, '23
Horn, Robert L., '28, '29, '30
Horvath, Leslie, '40, '41, '42, '44
Houston, Lindell L., '41, '42
Howard, Fritz, '39, '40, '41
Howard, Harry, '69, '70, '71
Howard, Harry C., '14
Howe, Frank H., '40
Howell, Carroll, '52, '53, '54
Hoyer, Ralph, '05
Hubbard, Rudy, '65, '66, '67
Hudson, Paul, '64, '65, '66
Huff, Paul, '67, '68
Huffman, Iolas M., '18, '19, '20, '21
Hughes, John, '70, '72, '73
Hunt, William P., '24, '25, '26
Hurm, Paul W., '16
Huston, Arthur C., '28
Hutchison, Charles, '67, '68, '69

"I"

Iams, Alvin L., '31
Idle, Ralph H., '28
Ingram, Robert M., '59, '60, '61
Ireland, Kenneth D., '62
Isabel, Wilmer E., '20, '21, '22

"J"

Jabbusch, Robert O., '42, '46, '47
Jack, Alan R., '67, '68, '69
Jackson, James, '01
Jackson, Paul, '01
Jackson, Richard S., '44, '45, '46
Jackson, William F., '04
Jackson, William M., '21
Jacoby, George R., '51, '52, '53
James, Daniel A., '56, '57, '58
James, Kenneth L., '32
James, Thomas L., '42, '46
Janecko, Gene K., '44
Jankowski, Bruce D., '68, '69, '70
Janowicz, Victor F., '49, '50, '51
Jeannot, Fred G., '03
Jenkins, Joseph, '67
Jenkins, Thomas G., '61, '62, '63
Jenkins, William, '24, '25
Jennings, Jack W., '47, '48, '49
Jenttes, Charles A., '60
Jesty, James B., '70
Jobko, William K., '54, '55, '56
Johnson, Ernest Y., '20
Johnson, Kenneth E., '60, '61
Johnson, Pete, '73
Johnson, Robert T., '65, '66
Jones, David L., '35
Jones, Edward S., '33
Jones, Gomer T., '34, '35
Jones, Herbert A., '72
Jones, Herbert M., '56, '57
Jones, Thomas H., '08, '09
Jones, W. C., '03
Joslin, Robert V., '51, '52, '53
Judy, Lawrence E., '22, '23

"K"

Kabealo, John, '33, '34, '35
Kabealo, Michael, '36, '37, '38
Kain, Larry, '73
Kaplanoff, Carl G., '36, '37, '38
Karch, Robert, '15, '16, '17
Karcher, James N., '34, '35
Karow, Martin G., '24, '25, '26

Kasunic, Gerald S., '63, '64
Katterhenrich, David L., '60, '61, '62
Kay, Donald F., '44
Kaylor, Ronald L., '64
Keane, Thomas L., '44
Keefe, Thomas C., '31, '32
Keiser, Thomas L., '90
Keith, Randal T., '71, '72
Kelley, Dwight A., '63, '64, '65
Kelley, John I., '66, '67
Kellough, F. C., '02
Kelly, Bob, '72, '73
Kelsey, Ray T., '45
Kennedy, Arthur, '90, '91, '92
Kern, Carl, '72, '73
Kern, Rex W., '68, '69, '70
Kessler, Carlton G., '43, '45, '46
Kiefer, Arthur S., '12, '13, '14
Kiehfuss, Thomas C., '62, '63, '64
Kile, Robert J., '97
Kilgore, David S., '58, '59
Kimball, Philip J., '15
King, Gerald L., '70
King, Robert J., '97
Kinkade, Thomas J., '39, '40, '41
Kinsey, Marvin C., '71
Kirby, R. E., '05
Kirk, Brenton S., '47, '48
Kirk, Roy E., '63
Kittle, James M., '99, '00, '01
Klee, Ollie, '22, '23, '24
Klein, Alex W., '22, '25, '26
Klein, Robert J., '60, '61, '62
Kleinhans, John L., '36
Klevay, Walter S., '49, '50, '51
Klie, Walter, '02
Koegle, Donald W., '35
Koegle, Victor, '71, '72, '73
Knoll, Elmer P., '02
Koepnick, Robert E., '50, '51, '52
Kohut, William W., '64
Krall, Gerald, '45, '46, '48, '49
Kregel, James, '71, '72, '73
Kreglow, James J., '24, '25, '26
Kremblas, Francis T., '56, '57, '58
Krisher, Gerald, '51, '52, '53, '54
Kriss, Frederick C., '54, '55, '56

Kriss, Howard E., '27, '28
Krstolie, Raymond C., '61, '62
Krumm, R. E., '91, '92
Kruskamp, Harold W., '26, '28
Kuhn, Kenneth W., '72, '73
Kumler, Karl W., '62
Kurz, Theodore R., '68, '69
Kutler, Rudolph J., '22, '23, '24

"L"

Lacksen, Frank J., '25, '26
Lago, Gary M., '70, '71, '72
Lambert, Howard L., '61
Lamka, Donald, '69, '70, '71
Landacre, Walter A., '90
Langhurst, Earl J., '38, '39, '40
Lantry, L. L., '05
Lapp, Harry R., '16
Large, Joseph H., '90
Larkins, Charles R., '28, '29, '30
Lashutka, Gregory S., '63, '64, '65
Laskoski, Richard D., '61
Lavelli, Dante B., '42
Lawrence, Paul C., '10
Lawrence, Wilbert W., '03, '04, '05
Laybourne, Paul C., '10
LeBeau, Charles R., '56, '57, '58
Leggett, William D., '52, '53, '54
Lehman, Ernest, '43
Leonard, Judson C., '05
Leonard, W. T., '97
Lewis, Donald B., '55
Lincoln, James F., '01, '03, '05, '06
Lincoln, Paul M., '90, '91
Lindner, James E., '59, '60
Lindsey, William L., '64
Lininger, Raymond J., '46, '47, '48, '49
Lipaj, Cyril M., '42
Lippert, Elmer H., '71, '72, '73
Lister, Robert C., '61
Livingston, Brian, '65
Lloyd, Erastus G., '99, '00, '01
Logan, Richard L., '50, '51
Lohr, Wendell, '37, '38
Long, David W., '71

Long, Herbert, '10
Long, Thomas N., '22, '23
Long, William E., '66, '67, '68
Longer, Robert M., '64
Lonjak, William A., '43
Lord, John C., '58
Loveberry, Clarence, '96
Lowe, Clifton D., '09
Luckay, Raymond J., '51
Ludwig, Paul L., '52, '53, '54
Luke, Steven N., '72, '73
Lukens, William, '73
Lukz, Frank M., '32, '33
Luttner, Ken, '69, '70, '71
Lykes, Robert L., '65
Lynn, George M., '41, '42
Lyons, James D., '63

"M"

Maag, Charles, '38, '39, '40
Machinsky, Francis C., '53, '54, '55
Maciejowski, Ronald J., '68, '69, '70
Mack, Richard W., '72, '73
Mackey, Frederick C., '24, '25, '26
Mackey, J. E., '97
Madro, Joseph C., '39
Maggied, Sal, '35, '36, '37
Mahaffey, William W., '32
Maltinsky, Paul R., '43, '44, '45
Mamula, Charles, '62, '63
Mangiamelle, Richard C., '62
Mann, George T., '30
Manning, Ernest P., '07
Manyak, John N., '52
Manz, Jerry Vern, '48, '49, '50
Marek, Elmer F., '25, '26, '27
Marendt, Thomas L., '71, '72
Marino, Victor I., '37, '38, '39
Marker, James B., '01, '02, '03, '04
Markley, Frank P., '10, '11
Marquardt, William B., '02, '04
Marsh, George C., '29
Marsh, James R., '70
Marshall, Clyde, '45
Marshall, James, '57, '58
Marshall, W. D., '90

Martin, Edwin D., '90
Martin, Harold P., '52
Martin, John C., '55, '56, '57
Martin, Paul D., '59
Marts, Raymond J., '23
Martz, Valorus, '14
Mascio, Joseph, '44
Mason, Glen, '70
Matheny, Oliver S., '18
Mathers, John H., '92, '93, '94
Matte, Thomas R., '58, '59, '60
Mattey, George J., '48, '49
Mathis, Almond L., '71, '72
Matz, James F., '58, '59, '60
Maxwell, Earl P., '12
Maxwell, John B., '62
Mayer, Robert E., '44
Mayes, Rufus L., '66, '67, '68
Maynard, Lee H. P., '03
McAfee, John N., '33, '34
McCafferty, Donald W., '41, '42
McCallister, H. A., '98, '07, '08
McCarthy, Timothy J., '24, '25, '26
McCarty, L. B., '08, '09
McClain, W. B., '09, '10
McClure, Donald L., '27, '28, '29
McClure, James A., '12
McConagha, Arthur B., '05
McConnell, Art, '28, '29
McCormick, Robert W., '42
McCoy, John, '64, '65, '66
McCoy, Walter E., '11
McCune, J. H., '18
McCullough, Robert E., '48, '49, '50
McDonald, Clarence A., '16, '18, '19
McDonald, James A., '35, '36, '37
McDonald, Paul A., '05, '06
McElheny, Norman E., '44
McGinnis, Robert E., '44, '45, '46
McGuire, Timothy A., '66
McLaren, James W., '00, '01, '02
McMurry, Preston V., '58
McNeal, Laird C., '67
McQuade, Robert P., '43
McQuigg, William G., '36
Means, John W., '24
Meinerding, Wesley C., '65, '66

Merrell, James, '51
Metzger, Walter E., '16, '17
Meyers, Russell L., '17
Meyer, Theodore R., '25, '26, '27
Michael, Paul, '54, '55, '56
Michael, Richard J., '58, '59
Michaels, Alton C., '22
Middleton, Richard R., '71, '72, '73
Middleton, Robert L., '60, '61, '62
Miller, Carl J., '94, '95, '96
Miller, Charles E., '53
Miller, Gary A., '64, '65, '66
Miller, James R., '37
Miller, Luke E., '20
Miller, Robert N., '35
Miller, Walter H., '90
Miller, William G., '43
Miller, William M., '48, '49, '50
Milligan, Fred J., '27
Minshall, William E., '96, '97, '98
Mirick, Chester W., '61, '62, '63
Mitchell, H. Jordan, '25
Mobley, Benjamin A., '64
Moeller, Gary O., '60, '61, '62
Moldea, Emil, '47
Moler, William A., '27
Molls, Larry, '73
Momsen, Robert E., '50
Monahan, John Regis, '32, '33, '34
Monahan, Thomas, '37
Moorehead, Lewis S., '21, '22
Morgan, Tommy Joe, '56, '57
Morrey, Charles B., '90, '91, '92
Morrisey, Edward L., '11, '12, '13
Morrison, Fred L., '46, '47, '48, '49
Morrison, Steven A., '72, '73
Moseley, Philip H., '50
Motejzik, John J., '44
Mott, William H., '53
Mountz, Gregory L., '71
Moyer, Bruce M., '67
Mrukowski, William, '60, '61, '62
Muhlbach, John L., '66, '67, '68
Mullay, Patrick L., '93
Mummey, John, '60, '61, '62
Myers, Cyril E., '19, '20, '21
Myers, Ord, '94

Myers, Robert C., '52
Myers, Russell L., '17
Myers, Steven, '72, '73

Portsmouth, Tom, '65, '66, '67
Portz, Grover C., '09
Potter, Frank D., '93, '94, '95
Potter, L. H., '95
Potthoff, William J., '24
Powell, Charles S., '91, '92
Powell, Harold P., '08, '09, '10
Powell, J. E., '01, '03
Priday, Robin, '42, '45, '46
Provenza, Russell D., '57
Provost, Ted R., '67, '68, '69
Pryor, Ray Von, '64, '65, '66
Purdy, David B., '72, '73
Purdy, Ross C., '97

"R"

Rabb, John Peter, '37, '38, '40
Rabenstein, Howard P., '30, '31
Radtke, Michael, '67, '68, '69
Rainey, Cecil D., '09
Rane, Frank W., '90
Ranney, Arch E., '02
Raskowski, (Randall) Leo, '26, '27, '28
Rath, Thomas L., '50, '51
Raymond, Arthur W., '10, '11, '12
Ream, Charles D., '35, '36, '37
Reboulet, LaVerne B., '28
Redd, John G., '43, '44, '45
Reed, Malcolm, '26
Reed, William A., '92, '93, '96
Reed, William H., '25, '26
Reemsnyder, R. C., '04, '05
Rees, James R., '42
Rees, Trevor J., '33, '34, '35
Reese, Wayne, G., '61
Reichenbach, James, '51, '52, '53, '54
Rein, Robert E., '64, '65, '66
Renard, Barney, '73
Renner, Charles E., '44, '46, '47, '48
Rhodes, Gordon M., '16
Rich, Rocco J., '71, '72, '73
Richards, Charles J., '97
Richards, David P., '55

Richardson, Hamilton H., '90, '91, '92
Richey, Lazerne A., '96
Richley, Richard C., '65
Richt, Fred H., '94, '95, '96
Ricketts, Karl R., '01
Ricketts, Ormonde B., '61, '62, '63
Ridder, William E., '63, '64, '65
Riddle, Abner E., '01, '02
Rife, Roy E., '18
Rigby, Richard R., '09
Riggs, David R., '26
Rightmire, Robert, '98, '00, '01
Riticher, Raymond J., '52
Rittman, Walter F., '03
Roach, Woodrow, '73
Roberts, Jack C., '61
Roberts, Robert L., '52, '53
Roberts, Stanley, '11
Rodriquez, Camilo A., '01
Roe, John E., '44, '45
Roemer, Wellington F., '29
Roman, James T., '66, '67, '68
Roman, Nicholas G., '66, '67, '68
Ronemus, Thor, '50, '51
Roseboro, James A., '54, '55, '56
Rosen, Andy, '39, '40
Rosen, John, '41
Rosequist, Theodore A., '32, '33
Ross, Richard L., '60
Rosso, George A., '51, '52, '53
Rothrock, Phillip, '04, '05, '06
Roush, Ernest J., '33, '34, '35
Roush, Gary S., '68
Rowan, Everett L., '25, '26, '27
Rowland, James H., '59
Rudge, William H., '93, '94
Rudin, Walter M., '34
Ruehl, James J., '52
Ruhl, Bruce, '73
Rusnak, Kevin G., '67, '68, '69
Rutan, Hiram E., '90
Rutherford, William A., '66
Rutkay, Nicholas G., '37
Ruzich, Stephen, '50, '51
Ryan, Lee E., '12

303

Smith, Ted, '73
Smurda, John R., '72, '73
Smythe, John J., '10
Sneddon, Elvadore R., '18
Snedecker, W. A., '93, '94
Snell, Matthew, '61, '62, '63
Snyder, A. J., '96
Snyder, Charles R., '12, '13, '14
Snyder, Laurence N., '23
Snyder, Thomas L., '44, '47
Snyder, William S., '27
Sobolewski, John J., '66, '68
Sommer, Karl W., '56
Sorenson, Frank G., '14, '15, '16
Souders, Cecil B., '42, '43, '44, '46
Southern, Clarence H., '23
Spahr, William H., '62, '63, '64
Sparma, Joseph B., '61, '62
Spears, Jeremiah G., '38, '39
Spears, Thomas R., '53, '54, '55
Spencer, George E., '46, '47
Spiers, Robert H., '19, '20, '21
Springer, George E., '14
Spychalski, Ernest T., '56, '57, '58
Stackhouse, Raymond L., '43
Staker, Loren J., '42
Stanley, Bernie D., '63
Stark, Samuel, '98
Steel, Harry D., '22, '23
Steinberg, Donald, '42, '45
Steinle, Charles F., '97
Stephens, Larry P., '61
Stephenson, Jack W., '39, '40, '41
Stevens, Jacob F., '96
Stier, Mark H., '66, '67, '68
Stillwagon, James R., '68, '69, '70
Stimson, George W., '98
Stinchcomb, Gaylord R., '17,
   '19, '20
Stock, Robert H., '64
Stoeckel, Donald C., '53, '54, '55
Stolp, W. J., '05, '06
Stora, Joseph, '43
Stottlemyer, Victor R., '66, '67, '68
Stover, Byron E., '11, '12
Stowe, John H., '68
Stranges, Tony J., '44

Strausbaugh, James E., '38, '39, '40
Strickland, Philip S., '68, '69, '70
Strong, Terry, '72
Stuart, John D., '21
Stungis, John J., '43, '46
Sturtz, Karl L., '49, '50
Sullivan, John K., '16
Summers, Merl G., '08, '09, '10
Surface, Frank M., '02, '03, '04, '05
Surington, Cyril T., '27, '28
Sutherin, Donald P., '55, '56, '57
Swan, Earl G., '02, '03, '04
Swartz, Donald C., '52, '53, '54
Swartzbaugh, Charles B., '13
Swartzbaugh, John D., '43
Swinehart, Rodney E., '46, '47,
   '48, '49
Sykes, W. E., '97

"T"

Takacs, Michael J., '51, '52, '53
Tangeman, Theodore H., '99, '00,
   '01, '05
Tanski, Victor T., '40
Tarbill, John W., '99
Tatum, John D., '68, '69, '70
Taylor, Charles A., '19, '20, '21
Taylor, John L., '20
Taylor, Russell E., '28, '29
Teague, Willie M., '70, '71, '72
Teifke, Howard A., '43, '46, '47, '48
Templeton, David I. '46, '47, '48
Ternent, William A., '52
Thal, Erwin R., '57
Theis, Franklyn B., '55
Thies, Wilfred L., '33
Thom, Leonard J., '39, '40
Thomas, Aurealius, '55, '56, '57
Thomas, George B., '05
Thomas, James, '49
Thomas, John R., '43, '44, '45
Thomas, Joseph A., '33
Thomas, Richard J., '51, '52
Thomas, Will C., '65, '66
Thompson, Kenneth, '55
Thompson, R. E., '05, '07

Thompson, Rollin H., '92
Thornton, Robert F., '52, '53, '54
Thrower, John D., '00, '02, '03, '04
Thurman, A. G., '93, '95
Tidmore, Samuel E., '60, '61
Tillman, J. H., '01, '02
Tilton, Josephus H., '98, '99, '00, '01
Tingley, David R., '59, '61
Titus, Clarence H., '96
Tobik, Andy Bill, '40
Tolford, George K., '59, '60, '61
Toneff, George, '44, '48, '49
Tracy, William P., '06
Treat, W. G., '10
Trapuzzano, Robert M., '69
Trautman, George M., '11, '12, '13
Trautwein, Henry Bill, '48, '49, '50
Trivisonno, Joseph J., '55, '57
Troha, Richard J., '69
Trott, Dean W., '19, '20, '21
Tucci, Dean W., '39
Turner, E. C., '02
Turner, Irwin, '16
Tyler, Julius B., '96
Tyrer, James E., '58, '59, '60

"U"

Ujhelyi, Joseph A., '28, '29
Ullery, Jack C., '25, '27
Ulmer, Edward, '60, '61
Unverferth, Donald V., '63, '64, '65
Updegraff, Winston R., '22
Urban, Harry N., '97
Urbanik, William J., '67, '68, '69
Uridil, Leo R., '25, '26, '27

"V"

Van Blaricom, Robert P., '32
Van Buskirk, Lear H., '07, '08
Van Dyne, Kelley, '16, '17
Van Horn, Douglas C., '63, '64, '65
Van Raaphorst, Richard W., '61, '62, '63
Vanscoy, Norman J., '60
Vargo, Kenneth W., '53, '54, '55

Vargo, Thomas W., '65
Varner, Martin D., '30, '31, '32
Varner, Thomas A., '60
Vavroch, William B., '52
Vecanski, Milan, '70, '71
Verdova, Alex S., '45, '46, '47, '48
Vicic, Donald J., '54, '55, '56
Vickroy, William E., '41, '42
Vogel, Robert L., '60, '61, '62
Vogelgesang, Donald A., '60
Volzer, Donald H., '20
Von Schmidt, Walter G., '27
Von Swearingen, Fiske, '09
Vuchinich, Michael N., '31, '32, '33

"W"

Wagner, Jack W., '50, '51
Wakefield, Richard, '69, '70, '71
Walden, Robert L., '64, '65, '66
Walker, Dow R., '02, '03, '04
Walker, Gordon H., '27, '28, '29
Walker, Jack E., '60
Walker, Stephen E., '71
Wallace, Robert H., '44
Walther, Richard E., '50, '51
Wandtke, Richard A., '44
Ward, Grant P., '12
Warden, Leonard G., '94
Warfield, Paul D., '61, '62, '63
Warner, Duane A., '60
Warren, Lee G., '05
Warwick, Herbert S., '04
Wassmund, James A., '56
Wasson, Harold, '22, '23
Wasson, Robert E., '95, '96, '97
Wasson, Richard, '63
Wasylik, Nicholas, '35, '36, '37
Waters, E. C., '04
Watkins, Jene, '59
Watkins, Robert A., '52, '53, '54
Watson, Thomas G., '45, '48, '49, '50
Watts, Robert S., '22, '23, '24
Waugh, Charles A., '70
Way, Rexford D., '07
Wears, Leland H., '34
Weaver, C. Robert, '20, '21

306

Weaver, David A., '53, '54, '55
Weaver, J. Edward, '70
Weber, Fred C., '98, '99, '00
Wedebrook, Howard N.,'36,'37,'39
Weed, Thurlow, '52, '53, '54
Welbaum, Thomas A., '38, '39
Welch, John W., '47
Welever, Arthur W., '31
Wells, Leslie R., '08, '09, '10
Wendler, Harold, '23, '24, '25
Wendt, Merle E., '34, '35, '36
Wentz, Burke B., '25
Wentz, William A., '59, '60
Wersel, Timothy, '72
Wertz, George P., '48, '49
West, Edward F., '36
Westwater, James G., '96, '99,
      '00, '01
Wetzel, Charles J., '08
Wetzel, Damon H., '32, '33, '34
Wharton, Homer F., '98, '99, '00
Wheeler, T. L., '02
Whetstone, Robert E., '53, '55
Whipple, Charles A., '05, '06, '07
Whisler, Joseph G., '46, '47, '49
Whitacre, H. J., '90
White, C. C., '92
White, Claude, '38, '40
White, Jan, '68, '69, '70
White, John T., '42
White, Loren R., '57, '58, '59
White, Stanley R., '69, '70, '71
Whitehead, Stuart F., '39, '40
Whitfield, David A., '67, '68, '69
Wible, Calvin D., '45
Widdoes, Richard D., '48, '49, '50
Wieche, Robert, '17, '19, '20
Wiggins, Larry, '72
Wilder, Thurlow C., '20
Wiles, A. O., '02
Wilkins, Dwight, '72
Wilks, William C., '51
Willaman, Frank R., '17, '19, '20
Willaman, Samuel S., '11, '13
Willard, Robert, '73
Williams, Albert C., '43
Williams, David M., '53, '54

Williams, Donald W., '39
Williams, Joe J., '35, '36
Williams, Lee E., '55, '58
Williams, Robert D., '68
Williams, Shad I., '70, '71, '72
Willis, William K., '42, '43, '44
Wilson, Andrew J., '46, '47, '48, '49
Wilson, C. R., '99
Wilson, Donald A., '32, '33
Wilson, John B., '22, '23, '24
Wingert, Albert C., '30
Winters, Harold A., '15
Winters, Sam C., '45
Wiper, Donald W., '20, '21
Wiper, Harold A., '17, '18, '20
Withoft, Clarence, '91, '92
Wittman, Julius W., '49, '50, '51
Wittmer, Charles G., '59, '60, '61
Wolf, Ralph C., '36, '37
Wolfe, Russell H., '46
Wood, Charles L., '92
Woodbury, Chester, '05
Worden, Dirk J., '66, '67, '68
Workman, Harry H., '20, '22, '23
Workman, Noel, '20, '21
Wortman, Robert C., '64
Wright, David W., '70
Wright, Ernest H., '58
Wright, Ward, '45
Wright, William E., '09, '10, '11
Wuellner, Richard W., '38, '39

"Y"

Yards, Ludwig, '32, '33, '34
Yassenoff, Leo, '14, '15
Yassenoff, Sol, '13, '14
Yerges, Howard F., Sr., '15, '16, '17
Yerges, Howard S., Jr., '43
Yingling, Walter E., '28
Yonclas, Nicholas, '63, '64
Young, Donald G., '58, '59, '60
Young, Francis D., '21, '23, '24
Young, Louis C., '38
Young, Norman F., '54
Young, Richard A., '53, '54
Young, William G., '25, '26, '27

Yost, Benjamin P., '98

"Z"

Zadworney, Frank S., '37, '38, '39
Zahler, Morton S., '54
Zangara, Donald, '45
Zarnas, Gust C., '35, '36, '37
Zavis, George J., '41

Zavistoske, George (Zavis), '41
Zawacki, Charles E., '55
Zelina, Lawrence P., '68, '69, '70
Ziegler, Randall K., '63
Zima, Albert J., '62
Zimmer, Frank E., '31
Zincke, Clarence F., '29
Zinsmaster, John L., '30